SEXUAL MISCONDUCT AND THE CLERGY

LIBRARY IN A BOOK

SEXUAL MISCONDUCT AND THE CLERGY

Jeffrey Ferro

■®

Facts On File, Inc.

SEXUAL MISCONDUCT AND THE CLERGY

Facts On File, Inc.
132 West 31st Street
New York NY 10001

Library of Congress Cataloging-in-Publication Data
Ferro, Jeffrey.
    Sexual misconduct and the clergy / Jeffrey Ferro.
        p. cm.—(Library in a book)
Includes bibliographical references and index.
    ISBN 0-8160-5494-0 (hc: alk. paper)
    1. Sexual misconduct by clergy. I. Title. II. Series.
BV4392.5.F47 2005
261.8'3272–dc22

                                                          2004006806

Facts On File books are available at special discounts when purchased in bulk quantities for businesses, associations, institutions, or sales promotions. Please call our Special Sales Department in New York at (212) 967-8800 or (800) 322-8755.

You can find Facts On File on the World Wide Web at http://www.factsonfile.com

Text design by Ron Monteleone

Printed in the United States of America

MP Hermitage 10 9 8 7 6 5 4 3 2 1

This book is printed on acid-free paper.

For the victims of clergy sexual misconduct,
and for those working within and outside of religious
settings who resist the forces of conformity
to make fundamental change

CONTENTS

PART III
APPENDICES

PART I

OVERVIEW OF THE TOPIC

CHAPTER 1

INTRODUCTION TO
SEXUAL MISCONDUCT
AND THE CLERGY

On August 23, 2003, defrocked Catholic priest and convicted pedophile John Geoghan, 68, was murdered at the Souza-Baranowski Correctional Center, a medium-security prison about 30 miles outside of Boston, Massachusetts, where he was serving a 10-year sentence for the 1991 sexual molestation of a 10-year-old boy. Joseph L. Druce, an inmate at the prison, was charged with the murder of Geoghan, who in 1998 was defrocked as a priest after being implicated in the molestations of some 130 minors over three decades in the Boston archdiocese. Many of those victims, who came forward after years of silence, said they took no solace in Geoghan's death.

News of Geoghan's killing was immediately picked up by the national media, largely because Geoghan was part of a much bigger story. In 2002, during Geoghan's trial, the *Boston Globe* reported that officials in the Boston archdiocese, including former archbishop Bernard F. Law, attempted to cover up Geoghan's long history of sexual misconduct with minors by transferring Geoghan from parish to parish instead of removing him from his ministry. Additional information, gathered largely from confidential church personnel records, revealed that Geoghan was not the only sexually abusive priest handled in this way. Others included former Boston priests James R. Porter and Paul Shanley. Porter was accused of molesting or raping at least 125 children, starting from his graduation from the seminary in 1960 until his resignation from the priesthood in 1974. In 1992, he was sentenced to 20 years in prison. Shanley, known during the 1960s and 1970s as a "street priest" who ministered to runaways and teenagers questioning their sexual identity, was a longtime member of the North American Man-Boy Love Associations (NAMBLA). He was arrested in 2002 and charged with 10 counts of child rape and six counts of indecent assault and battery. In all, as many as 1,000 children were sexually abused by priests in the Boston archdiocese since 1940, according to a 2003 report issued by the attorney general of Massachusetts.[1]

The scope of the sexual misconduct scandal extended beyond Boston to other archdioceses nationwide. As a result, in April 2002, Pope John Paul II summoned U.S. cardinals to an emergency summit in the Vatican and denounced child molesters in the priesthood. In June 2002, the United States Conference of Catholic Bishops (USCCB) convened their annual meeting in Dallas, Texas, and drafted a new policy on the handling of allegations of sexual misconduct against priests. The USCCB also formed a national Office of Child and Youth Protection to monitor each U.S. diocese for compliance. Still, the fallout was far from over. By 2003, more than 300 Catholic priests had resigned or were removed from their ministries as the result of the scandal. Among them was the most senior Catholic prelate in the United States, Cardinal Bernard F. Law, who on December 13, 2002, resigned as the archbishop of Boston.

The resignation of Cardinal Law was viewed by some in the Catholic Church as a watershed event and the beginning of a process of reconciliation and recovery. Others were not as sanguine. "This issue was far bigger than Cardinal Law," observed Thomas Groome, professor of religious education at Boston College. Mitchell Garabedian, an attorney for some 100 alleged victims of clergy sexual abuse, agreed. "Just because Cardinal Bernard F. Law resigned doesn't mean everything's OK now," he said. "This will turn out to be only a cosmetic change unless substantive changes are made in church communities throughout the nation."[2]

Indeed, as Groome suggested, the issue of sexual misconduct by Catholic clergy turned out to be far bigger than Cardinal Law. The true scope of the problem became apparent on February 27, 2004, when the USCCB released the results of a long awaited study of sexual misconduct by U.S. priests, commissioned by the USCCB itself, from John Jay College of Criminal Justice in New York. The report, "The Nature and Scope of the Problem of Sexual Abuse of Minors by Catholic Priests and Deacons in the United States, 1950–2000," is discussed in more detail later in this chapter. However, among the key findings worth noting:

- Allegations of sexual misconduct were made against 4 percent of the 109,694 active priests in the United States from 1950 to 2002. Allegations peaked in 1980, when some 500 U.S. priests were implicated in nearly 800 reported cases of alleged sexual misconduct.
- Some 10,667 individuals made allegations of sexual abuse by Catholic priests from 1950 to 2002. Of those, 17.2 percent also alleged that one or more of their siblings had been sexually molested by a priest.

- Approximately two-thirds of all allegations of sexual misconduct by U.S. priests between 1950 and 2002 were reported to church or civil authorities from 1993 to 2003, as growing awareness of the prevalence of child sexual abuse in society enabled victims who had remained silent for years to come forward.
- As of February 27, 2004, some $500 million had been paid out by the U.S. Catholic Church in legal fees and settlements arising from claims of sexual misconduct by priests, and to cover the costs of providing treatment to offending priests.

The impact of such findings on victims, congregations, clergy, and the very institution of the church is as broad in scope as the findings themselves.

According to attorney Anne Underwood, ministerial misconduct is a public issue of justice because it arises from an abuse of power by the offending clergy member.[3] Similarly, according to the official policy of the United Methodist Church, sexual misconduct is considered an abuse of power rather than as an exclusively sexual issue. As such, clergy sexual misconduct is viewed as a betrayal of trust and the exploitation of those who are most vulnerable in a ministerial relationship.[4]

Sexual misconduct was also an international problem among Catholic priests. For example, in 2002, Australian priest Gerald Ridsdale was sentenced to 18 years in prison after pleading guilty to 46 charges of sexual abuse involving 21 children. In Brazil, 21 girls between the ages of 10 and 16 reported sexual contact with Fr. Sebastião Luiz Tomaz, and by July 2002 nine of those claims were substantiated with medical evidence. Canadian bishop Hubert O'Connor was sentenced to prison in November 1996 for sexually assaulting five women. In England, Father Michael Hill pleaded guilty in November 2002 to six charges of molesting boys over an 18-year period, and former priest Eric Taylor was convicted in 1998 of 18 sexual offenses against boys in a Catholic orphanage. Franziskus Eisenbach, a bishop in Mainz, Germany, resigned in April 2002 after being accused of sexually exploiting a woman during an exorcism. In Ireland, Father Donal Collins was convicted in 1999 of committing "gross indecency" on boys, and in 2001 Brother John Halpin pleaded guilty to 25 counts of sexual abuse against three children between 1975 and 1981. Sexual misconduct by priests was reported in other countries, as well, including Argentina, Belgium, Bosnia, Chile, Colombia, France, Italy, Mexico, the Philippines, South Africa, and Trinidad and Tobago.[5]

The sexual abuse of minors was only part of the overall problem that emerged in the clergy sexual abuse scandal. For example, according to writer Anne A. Simpkinson,[6] about four times as many priests were sexually active with adult women, and twice as many involved themselves with adult men. As defined by diocesan policy[7], clergy sexual misconduct includes:

- **sexual harassment:** The unwanted sexual advances, requests for sexual favors, and other verbal or physical conduct of a sexual nature by an employer, supervisor, or coworker that interferes with employment, promotion, or job performance
- **sexual exploitation:** Any kind of sexual contact between a counselor (pastoral caregiver) and a client (person he or she is counseling) regardless of whether it was initiated by the counselor or client
- **sexual abuse:** When a child or vulnerable adult is manipulated, forced, or tricked into touch or sexual contact

Although much of the media's coverage of the clergy sexual misconduct scandal was focused on Catholic priests, sexual misconduct occurred among clergy of all faiths, according to Anne Simpkinson. Among Simpkinson's findings:

- In 1990, some 10 percent of mainly Protestant pastors participating in a national survey reported that they had been sexually active with an adult parishioner.
- Six percent of Southern Baptist pastors surveyed in 1993 reported having sexual contact with a current or former church member, and some 70 percent said they "knew pastors who had sexual contact with a congregant."
- In a 1990 survey conducted by the United Methodist Church, 17 percent of lay female respondents reported that their own pastor had sexually harassed them.

Examples of the scope of clergy sexual misconduct in all religious denominations were offered by Dinah Hall of the Center for the Prevention of Sexual and Domestic Violence. Hall reported that clergy sexual misconduct occurred within every religious group in every region of the United States.[8] As evidence, Hall offered the following sampling of headlines: "Church Will Investigate Allegations Against Highland Park Presbyterian Church Minister" (*People Newspapers*, 5-8-00); "Respected Reform Leader Resigns Amid Sexual Misconduct Charges" (Jewish Telegraph Agency, 12-6-01); "Hindu Priest Gets Two Years in Rape Case" (*Houston Chronicle*, 5-30-00); "Sex Abuse Lawsuit Settled by Mormon for $3 Million" (*New York Times*, 9-05-01); "Jehovah's Witnesses Sued Regarding Alleged Abuse" (*Evansville Courier & Press*, 8-11-01); "Amish Sex Offender's Kin Help Him with Deal to Avoid Jail" (*Philadelphia Daily News*, 9-19-01).

Psychologist Gary Schoener, a nationally recognized expert on clergy sexual misconduct who has consulted on more than 2,000 cases of clergy sexual misconduct, estimated that roughly two-thirds of those cases involved Protestant clergy members. Clergy sexual misconduct "is about power and trust—not sexuality," said Schoener. "Whether it's Protestant, Jewish, Hindu, or Catholic, the more devout a person is, the more they trust their clergy—and the more vulnerable they are."[9]

HISTORICAL BACKGROUND

The concept of sexual misconduct was codified in the prohibitions against rape, sodomy, and adultery contained in the Code of Hammurabi, a body of Babylonian laws compiled around 2000 B.C. During the 13th century B.C., Moses led the Israelites out of slavery in Egypt to Sinai, where, according to Jewish history, Moses received moral instructions from God called the Decalogue. More commonly known as the Ten Commandments, these rules formed the foundation for the ethical systems of Judaism, Christianity, and Islam, and contained a prohibition against adultery. However, sexual mores during the ancient Jewish era were far different from those of today. For example, according to early biblical references in the Old Testament, incestuous relationships were permitted between brothers and sisters. All the children of Adam and Eve intermarried, and Cain took his sister as his wife. Eventually, such marriages were forbidden, and in the 10th century B.C. King David forbade cousins from entering into marriage. Also permitted during the ancient Jewish era was polygyny, the practice of having more that one wife at a time, although it was generally practiced by wealthy men and leaders. King David had multiple wives, as did King Solomon. Poorer men who could not support many wives were allowed to have concubines, women who live with men without the benefit of marriage. Concubines were sometimes given to a man by his wife, as in the case of Sarah giving her handmaid to Abraham because Sarah was unable to have children. Concubines were also purchased, as were wives. Ancient Israelite tribesmen sometimes offered their daughters for the sexual gratification of honored houseguests. If the houseguest preferred the sexual company of a boy, a father might offer one of his sons, although homosexuality per se was considered immoral. Prostitution was legal, but by the sixth century B.C., Jewish rabbis were forbidden from marrying prostitutes or divorced women.

The earliest known code of ethics addressing sexual misconduct was developed by the Greek physician Hippocrates (460–370 B.C.), whose oath for physicians, known as the Hippocratic Oath, contained one of the earliest recorded references to the issue of professional sexual misconduct: "I will abstain from all intentional wrong-doing and harm, especially from abusing the bodies of man or woman, bond or free." As later rewritten for Christian physicians, that section was more specific: "Whatever houses I may visit, I will come for the benefit of the sick, remaining free of all intentional injustice, of all mischief and in particular of sexual relations with both female and male persons, be they free or slaves." Although the oath was intended for physicians, the ethical standards advanced by Hippocrates had broader application as a code of conduct for all professionals in the healing arts, including therapists and members of the clergy in their roles as counselors, ministers to the sick, and spiritual advisers.

The Old Testament tells a cautionary tale of the sexual misconduct of the priest Eli's sons, who "lay with the women who served at the entrance to the tent of meeting" (1 Sam. 2:2). Early Christian teachings promoted the idea that human sexuality was favored by God only in the context of marriage. A Christian ethic evolved that God "set parameters for sex . . . within a proper context (marriage). . . . When practiced apart from the context of a loving marriage, the sex act . . . all too readily becomes an expression of self-gratification, infidelity or exploitation."[10] Thus, as sexual mores evolved, any sexual behavior outside the institution of marriage was deemed to be a form of sexual misconduct.

Until about the fourth century A.D., Christian priests and bishops were allowed to be married at the time of their ordination and to remain married and have children while serving as clerics. In fact, the children of Catholic bishops and popes sometimes inherited their father's title as a matter of birthright. For example Anastasius I (reigned 399–401) fathered Pope Innocent I (401–417); Hormisdas (514–523) fathered Silverius (536–537); and Sergius III (904–911) fathered John XI (931–935). Sometimes, the children of clerics advanced beyond their fathers' positions in the church, even rising to the level of pope. For example, Pope Theodore I (reigned 642–649) was the son of a bishop; Damasus I (366–384), Boniface I (418–422), Felix III (483–492), Anastasius II (496–498), Agapitus (535–536), Marinus I (882–884), and John XV (985–986) were the sons of priests; and Deusdedit (later Adeodatus I, 615–618) was the son of a subdeacon.[11]

As noted by former priest and psychotherapist A.W. Richard Sipe, "a sense of reality of sexuality . . . pervaded the Church for centuries," when priests and members of the church's hierarchy had sex within marriage, in accordance with their christian code of moral behavior. However, from the inception of the church, the sense of sexual reality that Sipe spoke of was at odds with a pre-Christian view that all sexual desire was evil, even between husband and wife. In ancient Babylonia, men and women bathed and burned incense in atonement for the sin of sexual intercourse. In some ancient Jewish sects, a husband and wife were considered unclean until the evening of the day following sexual intercourse. Pre-Christian cultures excluded women from religious rituals because they were seen as the embodiment of sexual desire, and their mere presence could distract the workings of the gods.

8

Introduction

The view that sexual desire was evil, even between husband and wife, was not embodied in Islam, founded circa 610 by the prophet Muhammad when he received the first of a series of revelations from Allah. Muslims, or those who practice Islam, believe that Muhammad was the last in a line of prophets that began with Adam. Unlike Christianity, which presumes that everyone is born with original sin, the Islamic view is that people are born innocent. Thus, human desire, in and of itself, was not necessarily equated with sinfulness under Islamic tradition, and procreation was not viewed as the sole purpose for sexual relations within marriage. Although procreation served as the primary purpose of marriage, Islam encouraged companionship and enjoyment of spouses with each other, partly as a way of avoiding sinful relationships, such as adultery, outside of marriage. One example of the difference between Islamic and Judeo-Christian views of sexuality within marriage was the story in the Qur'an (Koran) of a husband and wife who had sexual relations well into their old age, past the time of the wife's menopause, making procreation impossible. In the Qur'an, the sacred book in Islam, the story was told from a positive viewpoint that sex between a husband and wife, at any age, was healthy. By contrast, in the Old Testament, Zakaria was made mute for three days and nights for having sexual relations with his menopausal wife as a sign of God's disfavor, because in the ancient Judeo-Christian view, sex within marriage was improper except for the purpose of having children. As in the Judeo-Christian tradition, Islam condemned sexual activity outside of marriage. Polygyny, initially practiced among ancient Israelites but later abandoned for monogamy, continued to be permissible in the Islamic tradition, even into the modern era.

CELIBACY

Clerical celibacy is the promise, or religious vow, to remain unmarried. Therefore, because sexual relations outside of marriage is prohibited in Judaism, Christianity, and Islam, celibacy implies a life of sexual abstinence. Among ancient Israelites in the second century B.C., celibacy was practiced by the Essenes, a small religious sect of adult males who believed in strict cleanliness and wore only white garments. Celibacy was common among religious ascetics, those who reject bodily pleasures and practice self-denial as a means of strengthening their spiritual character. Asceticism was practiced throughout history among many of the major religions, including Buddhism, Hinduism, Islam, Judaism, and Christianity, and it continued to be part of those religious traditions into the modern era.

By the third century A.D., pre-Christian attitudes about sex as unclean and non-virgin women as the embodiments of temptation began to take hold in the fledgling Catholic Church. In Spain, the Synod of Elvira (305) prohibited priests from marrying. According to A. W. Richard Sipe, if a priest was already married, he was ordered to stop having sexual intercourse, and he faced excommunication if he fathered any children.[12] Although the Council of Nicaea in 325 refused to apply the Elvira ruling to priests outside of Spain, there was a consensus that priests would no longer be allowed to marry after ordination. Essentially, the definition of sexual misconduct was broadened to include any sexual behavior by priests, within or outside the sacrament of marriage.

In 401, Augustine (354–430), bishop of Hippo Regis in the Roman province Numidia (now Algeria), wrote the treatise *On the Good of Marriage*, which set forth the basic principle that sexual relations within the sacrament of marriage was proper only for procreation and was improper and unlawful for any other reason.[13] A century later, Augustine's punitive views on sexual expression influenced church leaders, who were increasingly concerned with consolidating power and property, and unwilling to allow the wives and children of priests to inherit either. As a result, Pope Agapitus (535–536) prohibited popes from choosing their successor, which had been a common practice until then, and Pope Pelagius I (556–561) made priests with wives and children sign a document forbidding their children from inheriting church property. Eventually, Gregory the Great, pope from 590 to 604, declared as illegitimate the children of priests.[14]

According to the late Timothy Reuter, professor of medieval history at the University of Southampton, the practical rationale for prohibiting priests from marrying was because the accumulation of church property was threatened by children who stood to inherit property from their priest-fathers. In essence, clerical marriage threatened to dissipate the physical infrastructure and assets of the church. As a result, rules were adopted by a succession of church councils in an attempt to further restrict the sexual behavior of priests. The Council of Rome (743) approved legislation prohibiting a bishop from even living in the same house as a woman, regardless of their relationship—unless the woman was the bishop's mother or a close relative. In 853, the Council of Rome took the prohibition a step further and condemned any priest who had sexual relations with a woman.[15]

As celibacy laws became more serious, the "sense of reality of sexuality" within the church gave way to a sexual unreality in which sexual expression by members of the clergy was driven underground, in some cases literally. Some monasteries were connected to nunneries through underground tunnels, allowing the monks and nuns to travel freely back and forth, without public detection.[16] According to psychologist Gary Schoener, in the Middle Ages sexual relations between clergy and their parishioners occurred but it was not generally reported, and Renaissance history contains evidence that church officials were aware of the problem but did little or nothing to stop the practice. Essentially, the church went into something akin to institutional denial about the sexual behaviors of its priests, despite the fact that sexual activity was rampant within the church's clergy, even at the highest levels of authority. With marriages forbidden, illicit sexual encounters occurred with greater frequency among priests and bishops. One glaring example was the antipope[17] John XXIII (reigned 1410–15), who was rumored to have seduced 200 women during his five-year reign. Also, although neither Pope Pius II (1458–64) nor Pope Innocent VIII (1484–92) married, both had many illegitimate children.[18]

During the Protestant Reformation in the 16th and 17th centuries, reformers abandoned the requirement of clerical celibacy. On October 31, 1517, Martin Luther (1483–1546), a former Catholic monk, posted his vociferous criticism of the Catholic Church, called the 95 Theses, on the door of a Catholic church in Wittenberg, Germany, an act for which he was excommunicated four years later. Among Luther's criticisms of the Catholic Church was his rejection of the subordination of marriage to celibacy. Luther taught that it was impossible to be unmarried and remain free of sin, because human sexual desire required some form of legitimate expression. Thus, marriage was perceived as a protection against sin, not a cause of sin. Lutheran reformers rejected the right of any church to impose celibacy upon its clergy, declaring that the option of celibacy must be left to each individual. Mandatory celibacy was viewed as a cause of immoral behavior. Lutheran reformers also taught that clergy were not to be viewed as superior to the laity. They rejected the idea that clergy served as an intermediary between God's grace and the laity. In Luther's view, clergy did not require a separate set of sexual ethics or rules to set them apart from those they served. Luther taught that clergy should perform civic duties and pay taxes like anyone else, and they should also be allowed to marry and have a family life. According to Luther, church, state, and marriage comprised the three natural estates of God's earthly kingdom, and the marital household was designed to embody all Christian values and morals. Thus, married clergy were considered as role models, and the marital estate was an indispensable component of Christian redemption and social order, not simply a creation of civil law.

Luther's rejection of clerical celibacy was echoed by Swiss theologian Huldreich Zwingli (1484–1531), the leader of the early Protestant Reformation movement in Switzerland who released all priests and monks from their vows of celibacy. John Calvin (1509–64), the French theologian who fled religious persecution in France and settled in Geneva, Switzerland, rejected mandatory clerical celibacy even while advocating strict moral discipline among the laity and clergy. In 1534, the Church of England parted with the Catholic Church in Rome because of Pope Clement VII's refusal to allow King Henry VIII to divorce his wife, Catherine of Aragon. As a result, the

English monarch, not the pope, became the head of the Church of England. With the adoption of the Thirty-Nine Articles of 1563, the Church of England, which evolved into what is generally referred to as the Anglican Church in England and the Episcopal Church in the United States, merged aspects of the Catholic faith, such as sacraments, with Lutheran teachings, including the right of clergy to marry and have children. The marriage of clerics had long been permitted in Judaism and Islam. As a result, the Roman Catholic Church became the only major religion in the world that required its clergy and religious members such as nuns and monks to take vows of celibacy.

The culture of celibacy in the Catholic Church cannot be blamed, per se, for the sexual misconduct of priests. However, the repression of sexual expression combined with the marginalization of women and children that occurred as the result of forced celibacy have caused some in the Catholic Church to argue for an end to celibacy in the priesthood, including Catholic priests themselves. On September 4, 2003, the Association of Pittsburgh (Pennsylvania) Priests announced plans to gather 5,000 signatures on a petition to support clerical celibacy as an option, not a requirement. In August 2003, about one-third of priests from Milwaukee, Wisconsin, sent a letter to U.S. Catholic bishops blaming the celibacy requirement for the priest shortage. According to the letter, as of June 2003, nearly 3,040 of 19,081 Catholic parishes in the United States were without resident pastors due to the shortage. However, Bishop Wilton D. Gregory, president of the United States Conference of Catholic Bishops (USCCB), responded to the letter by saying that other strategies apart from the lifting of celibacy would have to be identified in order to deal with the shortage of Catholic priests. Milwaukee archbishop Timothy M. Dolan echoed Bishop Gregory's views and stated that the commitment to celibacy was unrelated to clergy sexual misconduct involving minors. Nonetheless, priests in New York City, Boston, Massachusetts, Chicago, Illinois, and Charleston, North Carolina, were in the process of drafting statements advocating that married men be allowed to become priests, according to the National Federation of Priests' Councils. According to research by sociologist Dean R. Hoge of the Catholic University of America, celibacy appears to be a factor in the shortage of priests in the United States. Hoge reported that, by comparison, Protestant denominations that allowed ministers to marry had no shortage of clerics in many areas of the country.[19]

HOMOSEXUALITY AND PEDOPHILIA

According to Philip Jenkins, distinguished professor of history and religious studies at Pennsylvania State University, during the Middle Ages the Catholic clergy were denounced as homosexuals and pedophiles in continental Europe as well as in North America, Britain, Asia, and Africa. Jenkins reported that, although such charges were often the result of anti-Catholic bias, there was a history of clerical homosexuality and pedophilia subcultures within the Catholic Church. As proof, Jenkins cited the author John Boswell's writings on homosexual subcultures among the clergy of medieval Europe. Jenkins also noted that scholar David Greenberg has argued that the suppression of marriage by priests helped to foster a homosexual subculture among priests. As evidence of pedophilia among priests in the Middle Ages, Jenkins cited the *Book of Gomorrah* by 11th-century saint Peter Damian, which denounced clerical homosexuality and pederasty, and even listed penalties for the seduction of young boys by clerics. In addition, court records from throughout Europe provided further evidence of scandals involving priests and young boys during the Renaissance era.[20]

Pope Alexander VI (1492–1503) celebrated the victory of Catholic Spain over the Moors by throwing a party at which both prostitutes and children were offered to bishops and priests for their sexual pleasure.[21] Historian Jenkins noted that Pope Julius II (1550–56) was an active homosexual and that Julius promoted his lover, a 15-year-old boy, to the rank of cardinal.

According to journalists Frank Bruni and Elinor Burkett, 18th-century priest Johann Arbogast Gauch, a pastor in Fürstenberg, Germany, openly exploited both girls and boys. However, as Bruni and Burkett noted, such public cases were rare. Most real-life cases of priestly sexual misconduct were hidden, largely because the issue of child sexual abuse was rarely discussed publicly. Also, because the church was exempt from civil law, individual priests were not prosecuted. Instead, priests were judged in secret ecclesiastical courts. Moreover, the concept of childhood has evolved over time. For example, as late as the 18th century, sexual relations with a child over the age of 11 was not illegal in most of the Western world. Children were viewed as small adults. They worked to help support their families, they went to prison for criminal offenses, and they were considered fair game for the sexual gratification of an adult.

According to authors Bruni and Burkett, historical evidence of priests engaged in sexual misconduct with minors was most likely found in veiled references in historical texts, or in novels. For example, in the 18th-century novel *The Nun*, French philosopher Denis Diderot explored a young girl's sexual molestation by a cleric. In *Birds without Nests*, published in 1889, Peruvian novelist Clorinda Matto de Turner wrote of the sexual abuse of Indian children by Catholic clergy.

Philip Jenkins found evidence in Victorian literature that suggested that homosexual men were drawn to the Catholic priesthood. In the late 19th century, British homoerotic writers, including Montague Summers, Frederick Rolfe, and Richard Charles Jackson, "often chose ecclesiastical settings for their tales, and many either became clergy or assumed clerical *personae*," according to Jenkins, who claimed that "one authentic clerical pederast was John Francis Bloxam, author of a short story entitled 'The Priest and the Acolyte.' The story (published in 1894) was set in a traditional Catholic context, with confession, priestly vestments, and the Mass, the spiritual beauty of which reflects the loving relationship between the twenty-eight-year-old priest and the 'little acolyte' Wilfred, a 'child' of fourteen."

BLAMING THE VICTIM

In 1850, American author Nathaniel Hawthorne published his novel *The Scarlet Letter*, which told the story of the illicit affair between a minister, Arthur Dimmesdale, and a young woman, Hester Prynne, who became pregnant and was forced to wear a scarlet "A" (for adultery) as punishment for her sexual transgression. Placing the blame on women involved in extramarital affairs with members of the clergy was a common theme of romance novels in the 19th and 20th centuries. One example, noted by psychologist Gary Schoener, was the novel *A Circuit Rider's Wife* by Corra Harris, published in 1910, which included a narration by Mary, the wife of a Methodist minister, in which a minister's adulterous affair with a female congregant was blamed entirely on the woman.[22]

Sadly, the blame-the-victim attitude toward sexual misconduct by members of the clergy was prevalent in real life. As noted by authors Bruni and Burkett, following the arrest and imprisonment of German priest Johann for molesting children, his victims were also blamed and were even beaten for their sins. When preacher Henry Ward Beecher (1813–87) (father of Catherine Beecher and Harriet Beecher Stowe) was pastor of Plymouth Congregational Church in Brooklyn Heights, New York, he engaged in an adulterous affair with congregant Elizabeth Tilton, who had sought pastoral counseling from Beecher after the death of her infant daughter. After the affair was made public in 1872 by journalist Victoria Woodhull, Beecher was brought before a congregational investigative committee and acquitted, while Elizabeth Tilton was subsequently excommunicated in 1878.

"Seductive females do lurk in the halls of the church, of course. But there are predatory pastors on the prowl as well. We acknowledge the former too easily but find it difficult to recognize the latter.... Yet we see indications that a change in attitude may be developing," according to theology professors Stanley J. Grenz and Roy D. Bell.[23] To some, that change has been slow in coming, as the tendency to blame the victims of clergy sexual abuse, especially female victims, has persisted into modern times. Jeff Anderson, a Minnesota attorney specializing in clergy sexual abuse cases, noted that often when a woman comes forward to report sexual misconduct, the first question is, "What did you do?"[24]

Introduction

Acknowledging the sexual abuse of children by members of the clergy was also slow in coming, in part because such abuse was buried beneath layers of denial and secrecy by both church officials and society. Historically, even mental health professionals often doubted the accounts of childhood victims of sexual abuse, including Sigmund Freud, according to authors Bruni and Burkett, who argued that not until the 1970s did professionals in the United States begin to understand the extent of sexual abuse of children by adults. As a result, states increasingly required health care workers and other professionals to report childhood sexual abuse to child-protection agencies or to law enforcement. As such reporting became mandatory, the number of cases began to grow—from 12,000 cases of childhood sexual abuse reported in the 1970s to more than 150,000 such cases by 1985.[25] However, despite mandatory-reporting laws, cases of clergy sexual abuse of minors continued to be handled in secret church proceedings, as part of a culture of silence within the church, according to Bruni and Burkett, who reported that during a three-year period in the 1980s, some 130 priests were evaluated for sexual behavior problems at St. Luke's Institute in Suitland, Maryland. Of those, 70 priests were found to have sexual proclivities for children. The results of the study were never reported publicly or even to church parishioners.[26]

MODERN SCANDALS

In June 1984, the Diocese of Lafayette, Louisiana, secretly paid $4.2 million to the families of nine children who had been sexually abused by Father Gilbert Gauthe, Jr. Some four months later, in October 1984, Gauthe was indicted on charges of rape and possession of child pornography, including photographs taken by Gauthe of his victims.[27] The Gauthe case was significant because the story received broad news coverage in the United States, largely due to the work of reporter Jason Berry, whose articles in the *National Catholic Reporter* prompted publications such as the *New York Times* and the *Washington Post* to pick up the Gauthe story. As a result, news organizations began to expand their coverage of the issue of clergy sexual misconduct.

In March 1987, evangelical minister Jim Bakker's adulterous affair with his former church secretary Jessica Hahn went public. Bakker, who had attempted to silence Hahn with $265,000 of his ministry's funds, was later accused of defrauding investors of some $158 million by overselling shares in his religious theme park, Heritage USA. In 1989, Bakker was convicted of 15 counts of wire fraud, as well as mail fraud and conspiracy, and was sentenced to prison. In early 1988, less than a year after the Bakker-Hahn sex scandal broke, photographs of nationally televised preacher Jimmy Swaggart in a hotel room with a prostitute were made public. Swaggart, who had been one of Bakker's harshest critics, was summoned by the elders of his church and publicly confessed to the incident. Swaggart later told reporters that he had asked the prostitute to pose naked for pornographic pictures but did not engage in sex with her. However, in an interview in *Penthouse* magazine published in March 1989, the prostitute, identified as Catherine Campen, stated that she and Swaggart had "dated" prior to the incident in the hotel room and she had performed sadomasochistic acts for Swaggart.

THE U.S. CATHOLIC SCANDAL

During the 1990s, there were more accusations of sexual misconduct by priests. Father Bruce Ritter, founder in 1969 of Covenant House, an informal street ministry for runaways, was accused of molesting a youth. Although Ritter denied the allegation, he ultimately resigned from Covenant House in 1990. In 1997, a Dallas, Texas, jury awarded damages of $120 million (later lowered to $30 million) to 11 victims based on charges that ex-priest Rudy Kos had sexually abused them.

Notably, there were also admissions of sexual impropriety among members of the U.S. Catholic hierarchy:

- In 1990, Archbishop Eugene Marino of Atlanta, Georgia, resigned admitting that he had engaged in an intimate relationship with a 27-year-old female parishioner.
- In 1993, Santa Fe, New Mexico, archbishop Robert Sanchez resigned after he admitted to his sexual involvement with five women.
- In 1998, Bishop J. Keith Symons of Palm Beach, Florida, resigned after he admitted molesting five teenage boys at three Florida parishes earlier in his career. Four years later, his successor, Bishop Anthony O'Connell, stepped down after admitting that he had sexually abused a teenage boy at a Missouri seminary during the 1970s. O'Connell's victim had received a $125,000 settlement from the Diocese of Jefferson City, Missouri, in 1996.
- In 1999, Bishop G. Patrick Ziemann of Santa Rosa, California, resigned after a priest said he was coerced into sexual acts by Ziemann, who later acknowledged the sexual relationship but claimed it was consensual.

Because incidents of clergy sexual misconduct were historically dealt with by the Catholic Church and other denominations through confidential internal proceedings, the scope of the problem was often difficult to measure. However, according to the results of a survey by the *New York Times*, incidents of sexual misconduct by Catholic priests occurred in almost every American diocese and involved more than 1,200 priests and some 4,000 victims over the last six decades.[28] The survey, which documented cases of sex-

Introduction

ual abuse by U.S. priests through December 31, 2002, found that sexual abuse by priests occurred in every region of the United States, with 206 accused priests in the West, 246 in the South, 335 in the Midwest, and 434 in the Northeast, although some offending priests who abused in more than one region were counted twice. In addition, documented cases of sexual misconduct by priests occurred in both large metropolitan centers such as Boston, Massachusetts, and Los Angeles, California, as well as smaller regions like Louisville, Kentucky, and St. Cloud, Minnesota.

Vatican officials such as Cardinal Joseph Ratzinger have suggested that fewer than 1 percent of U.S. priests abused minors. However, according to the *New York Times* survey, U.S. dioceses reported, either voluntarily or under court order, significantly higher percentages of sexually abusive priests. For example, the survey estimated that in Manchester, New Hampshire, some 7.7 percent of priests ordained since 1950 were reported for sexual misconduct with minors, 6.2 percent of priests in Baltimore, Maryland, and 5.3 percent in Boston, Massachusetts.

Among other findings reported by the *New York Times* survey:

- Half of the U.S. priests reported for sexual misconduct were accused of molesting more than one minor, and 16 percent were accused of molesting five or more victims.

- Some 80 percent of priests reported for the sexual abuse of minors were accused of molesting boys. By contrast, nearly 80 percent of child sex offenders in the general population molested girls.

- Among sexually abusive priests identified in the survey, 43 percent were accused of molesting children 12 years of age or younger.

- Ninety-four priests in the Boston archdiocese were accused of sexual misconduct with minors during 2002, the highest number nationwide. However, a dozen dioceses had a higher percentage of offending priests in 2002.

In addition, a comparison of recent historical trends found that from 1960 to 1969, some 256 U.S. priests were reported for abusing minors. During the 1970s, that number more than doubled to 537 priests and remained almost unchanged during the 1980s, when 510 U.S. priests were reported for molesting minors. From 1990 to 1999, the overall number of U.S. priests accused of molesting minors declined by more than one-half, to 211. Since 2000, some 36 U.S. priests were reported for sexually abusing minors.

THE BOSTON ARCHDIOCESE

Boston, Massachusetts, became the epicenter of the widening clergy sexual abuse scandal in the Catholic Church. In 2002, of the 3.8 million residents

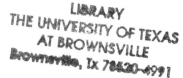

of the metropolitan Boston area, 2 million were Catholic, making the Boston archdiocese the only major archdiocese in the United States where Catholics accounted for more than half of the region's population. Accordingly, the impact of the scandal was felt deeply among Bostonians.[29]

By January 2003, some 130 priests and six Catholic brothers from the Boston archdiocese were accused of sexually molesting minors. Most of the accusations arose from incidents that allegedly occurred from 1960 through 1990, according to the *Boston Globe*.[30] In addition, eight bishops, including Cardinal Bernard F. Law, were identified for their failure to remove sexually abusive priests from parishes and, in many cases, for allowing the priests to continue their sexual abuse by transferring them to new, unsuspecting parishes throughout Massachusetts.

The first truly egregious case of clergy sexual misconduct in the Boston archdiocese that came to light was that of former Catholic priest James R. Porter. In 1993, Porter was sentenced to 18 to 20 years in prison after pleading guilty to sexually assaulting 28 minors at three parishes in southeastern Massachusetts, where he served during the 1960s. While studying for the priesthood at St. Mary's Seminary in Baltimore, Maryland, Porter, along with other seminarians, worked during the summer of 1956 at Freetown Cathedral Camp, a Catholic summer camp in Massachusetts. Porter was put in charge of the camp dormitory, where he allegedly sexually molested a 12-year-old boy camper. The victim, who recounted the molestations in 1992, reported Porter to the camp's supervisor, the Rev. William McMahon, who responded that he would "take care of it."[31] The victim said he was never bothered by Porter again. However, Porter was allowed to return to the seminary and, in 1960, he was ordained as a priest.

Following his ordination, Porter was assigned to St. Mary's Church in North Attleboro, Massachusetts. After three years, and amid complaints from parents that Porter inappropriately touched their children, Porter was transferred to Sacred Heart Parish in Fall River, Massachusetts. Again, there were complaints about Porter's inappropriate conduct with children, and again, he was reassigned. After two years at St. James Parish in New Bedford, Massachusetts, and amid more complaints of sexual misconduct, Porter entered the sex treatment program at Villa Louis Martin in Jemez Springs, New Mexico, operated by the Order of the Servants of the Paraclete, and he received additional counseling at a church-run halfway house in Nevis, Minnesota. In 1969, after two years in treatment, Porter was assigned to St. Philip's Catholic Church in Bemidji, Minnesota. Amid new allegations of sexual impropriety with minors, Porter was dismissed from St. Philip's in 1970 and, the following year, he decided to leave the priesthood. In 1974, James R. Porter was officially terminated as a Roman Catholic priest. By then, he had sexually abused as many as 100 children.

Years later, one of those children proved instrumental in bringing James R. Porter to justice. In 1989, while in therapy, Frank Fitzpatrick, a 39-year-old private investigator and insurance adjuster in Cranston, Rhode Island, said that memories of "encounters" with Porter began to surface. Fitzpatrick, who in 1960 served as an altar boy for the newly ordained Father Porter, recalled being taken to Porter's home and raped by Porter. Fitzpatrick wrote a letter describing his sexual abuse by Porter to then monsignor John Oliviera of the Fall River Diocese. According to Fitzpatrick, Msgr. Oliviera responded to the allegations by telephone and advised Fitzpatrick to leave the matter in the hands of God.[32]

Over the next five months, using Porter's birth certificate and voter registration information, Fitzpatrick tracked Porter to Akdale, Minnesota. By then, Porter was married and a stay-at-home father of four children. According to Fitzpatrick, it took him another five months to summon the courage to call Porter. Fitzpatrick, along with other victims of Porter, began assisting prosecutors in Bristol County, Massachusetts. In September 1992, Porter was indicted by a grand jury for sexually assaulting some 28 minors from August 1961 to September 1967, when he served as a priest at three parishes in Massachusetts. The indictment alleged that Porter had sexually attacked minors in the basement of a rectory, at a church day camp, in a church sacristy, in an altar-boy room, and at private homes, as well as other locations. According to Renee Dupuis, then assistant district attorney for Bristol County, school and church records corroborated the allegations of the victims and showed that church officials were aware of Porter's misconduct, and that at least one parent whose son was molested had personally confronted Porter about the abuse.[33]

A separate civil action was brought against the diocese of Fall River, Massachusetts, by 68 plaintiffs who alleged that they were sexually abused by Porter while he was a priest in the diocese. The case was settled in December 1992 for an undisclosed amount, although the settlement was estimated to be "at least $5 million."[34]

On October 4, 1993, James R. Porter pled guilty to each of the 41 counts contained in the criminal indictment against him. Victim impact testimony contained accounts of depression, broken marriages, and substance abuse. Some of Porter's victims denounced the Catholic Church for failing to act after church officials knew of Porter's sexual misconduct with minors. For his part, Porter apologized to his victims and admitted that he needed treatment. Subsequently, Porter's oldest son reported that he was sexually abused as a child by Porter. On April 2, 1999, Porter was denied parole. However, as reported by the *Boston Globe*, Porter was the first Massachusetts priest imprisoned for sexual misconduct with minors, and he was the first eligible for release in 2004.[35]

Sexual Misconduct and the Clergy

In 1992, amid extensive news coverage of the James R. Porter sexual abuse scandal, Cardinal Bernard F. Law, then the archbishop of the Boston archdiocese, assured Catholics that Porter's sexual misconduct with minors were the acts of one depraved man, and that they were not indicative of a larger problem within the Catholic priesthood. However, when the *Boston Globe* broke the John Geoghan story in 2001, it became apparent that Cardinal Law and other officials in the Boston archdiocese had long been aware that other priests were engaged in similar misconduct with minors—and that officials had done nothing to stop it.

More than 130 victims claimed they were sexually molested by Geoghan, most when they were boys enrolled in various Boston-area parish schools The sexual assaults began shortly after Geoghan's ordination in 1962. During Geoghan's first assignment at Blessed Sacrament in Saugus, Massachusetts, a fellow priest advised church officials that Geoghan was seen bringing boys to his bedroom. Although the priest, the Rev. Anthony Benzevich, later denied making the report, in 1994 Geoghan admitted that he molested four boys during his assignment at Blessed Sacrament. During Geoghan's next assignment at St. Paul's in Hingham, Massachusetts, from 1967 to 1974, he sexually abused more boys, including the nephew of a man who complained to Geoghan's superiors at St. Paul's. Despite the complaint, in 1974 Geoghan was moved to another unsuspecting parish, St. Andrew's in the Forest Hills section of Jamaica Plains, Massachusetts, where he served until 1980. While assigned there, Geoghan befriended Maryetta Dussourd, a single mother raising three sons and a daughter, as well as four nephews. Geoghan visited Dussourd's apartment almost every evening for nearly two years, ostensibly to help Dussourd. However, Geoghan was regularly molesting the seven boys in their bedrooms.[36] After Dussourd discovered what was happening, she told her sister, Margaret Gallant, and reported Geoghan's abuse of her children to the Rev. John E. Thomas, the pastor at nearby St. Thomas Aquinas parish. According to church documents, Geoghan admitted to Thomas that the allegations were true. Thomas, in turn, notified the office of the Boston archdiocese.

Geoghan was placed on sick leave and ordered to undergo therapy and psychoanalysis. It was not the first time. In 1968, Geoghan received treatment at the Seton Institute in Baltimore, Maryland, as the result of his sexual misconduct with young boys. By February 1981, the archdiocese deemed Geoghan "fit" to resume parish duties. Geoghan was assigned to St. Brendan's in Dorchester, Maryland. However, the archdiocese said nothing to St. Brendan's pastor about Geoghan's history.[37] Geoghan began befriending boys, even taking some to his family's summer home in Scituate, where, as parents later discovered, he sexually abused the youths. In August 1982, Margaret Gallant, the aunt of Geoghan's seven victims in Jamaica

Plains, Massachusetts, wrote to Cardinal Humberto Medeiros, Archbishop Law's predecessor. In her letter, Gallant expressed disbelief that Geoghan was returned to active duty at another parish. Gallant followed up with a second letter to Archbishop Medeiros asking why nothing was being done to keep Geoghan away from minors.[38]

In July 2001, Cardinal Bernard F. Law disclosed that he knew of Geoghan's history in 1984 at the time he approved Geoghan's transfer to yet another parish—St. Julia's in Weston, where Geoghan was put in charge of three youth groups, including altar boys.[39] In 1989, Geoghan was forced to go on sick leave once again amid more complaints of sexual abuse, and he spent two months in two institutions that treated sexually abusive priests. Nonetheless, the archdiocese returned him to St. Julia's, where Geoghan continued to abuse children for another three years.

In 1993, Cardinal Law removed Geoghan from parish duty. By then, Geoghan's damage was done. For some 30 years, Geoghan sexually abused children at six parishes, and for most of that time his superiors in the Archdiocese of Boston knew it. After being removed from parish duty, Geoghan lived at the Regina Coeli residence for retired priests until 1996, where he continued to seek out and molest minors, according to the multiple civil suits and criminal charges later filed against Geoghan.[40] Finally, in 1998, John Geoghan was removed from the priesthood. In 2002, he was convicted of indecent assault on a 10-year-old boy. While serving a nine-year prison sentence, on August 23, 2003, Geoghan was strangled and beaten to death, allegedly by a fellow prison inmate. On September 17, 2003, the Massachusetts Appeals Court vacated Geoghan's conviction and dismissed the original indictment against him, due to a state law allowing convictions that are on appeal to be voided upon the death of the convict. As noted by A.W. Richard Sipe, "In Geoghan's case, the church defied its own most basic values of protecting the young and fostering celibacy."[41]

In the wake of revelations about John Geoghan during 2001, the *Boston Globe* broke the story of another priest whose profile was eerily similar. Like Geoghan, the Rev. Joseph E. Birmingham compulsively molested as many as 200 minors at six parishes during his 29-year career. As in Geoghan's case, Birmingham continued to sexually abuse children despite complaints to his superiors.

Like Geoghan, Birmingham's sexual abuse of boys began soon after his ordination. In 1963, officials in the Boston archdiocese met with two parents who reported that their sons were molested by Birmingham at Our Lady of Fatima parish in Sudbury, Massachusetts. The parents were advised that Birmingham would be removed from his parish assignment and receive psychiatric treatment. However, as reported by the *Boston Globe*,

Birmingham was instead transferred from the Sudbury parish to St. James Church in Salem, Massachusetts, without receiving any type of treatment or counseling.[42] At St. James Church, Birmingham once again engaged in sexual misconduct with minors—and, once again, he was transferred, this time to St. Michael's Church in Lowell, Massachusetts, where he served from 1970 to 1977.[43] While there, Birmingham was questioned in a rape case by police in nearby Chelmsford, Massachusetts. During the police interrogation, Birmingham admitted that he had never received treatment for his sexual misconduct with minors, and that the pastor at St. Michael's Church did not know of Birmingham's history of molestation.[44] From Lowell, Birmingham was transferred to St. Columbkille's Church in Brighton, Massachusetts, where he established a youth drop-in center. Birmingham was then promoted to pastor and assigned to St. Ann's Church in Gloucester, Massachusetts.

As reported in the *Boston Globe*, Boston archdiocese personnel files contained proof that Cardinal Bernard F. Law and several of his top deputies knew of Birmingham's history of sexual misconduct with minors.[45] In 1987, Birmingham was sent to the Institute of Living for treatment. Two years later, at age 55, Birmingham died. However, complaints about Birmingham continued to be received by the Boston archdiocese.[46]

In the aftermath of the Geoghan and Birmingham revelations, Cardinal Bernard F. Law and other officials in the Boston archdiocese faced mounting criticism for their mishandling of both former priests. At the same time, there were more revelations of Boston priests with long histories of sexual misconduct with minors, including Ronald H. Paquin and Paul Shanley. As in the cases of Geoghan and Birmingham, officials in the Boston archdiocese allowed Paquin and Shanley to continue in their ministries for years despite documented evidence that both were unfit.

Ronald H. Paquin sexually abused young boys for years while serving as a parish priest in the Boston archdiocese. Paquin's case was somewhat unique in that he eventually acknowledged his history of sexually abusive behavior, and he agreed to testify against the Boston archdiocese in other sexual abuse cases involving priests. In December 2002, Paquin pleaded guilty and was sentenced to 12–15 years in state prison for raping a boy. The rapes occurred at St. John the Baptist Church in Haverhill, Massachusetts, where Paquin was assigned from 1981 until 1990, when the archdiocese removed him from active ministry as the result of his history of sexual misconduct. Paquin came to Haverhill amid allegations he was sexually abusing boys at St. Monica's Church in Methuen, Massachusetts, where he began his career after his ordination in 1973.

Paquin claimed that he was the victim of sexual abuse when, at age 11, he was raped by three older boys. Two years later, Paquin's father died.

Paquin claimed that after the death of his father, he was sexually abused for years by a priest in Salem, Massachusetts, but Paquin refused to identify the priest.[47]

Some 28 civil lawsuits were brought against Paquin by the victims of his alleged sexual misconduct. In addition, a wrongful-death lawsuit alleged that Paquin caused a car accident that killed James M. Francis of Haverhill, Massachusetts, on Thanksgiving weekend, 1981. As reported in the *Boston Globe*, Paquin drove Francis, then 16, and three younger boys to a chalet in Bethlehem, New Hampshire.[48] He gave the boys liquor, and at least one of the boys witnessed Paquin get into a sleeping bag with Francis. On the return trip to Massachusetts, Paquin claimed he lost control of his car due to icy road conditions. However, according to one of the boys in the car, Paquin had been drinking heavily and had fallen asleep at the wheel. As a result, Paquin's car rolled over, pinning Francis underneath, where he died of asphyxiation. Paquin denied that he was intoxicated at the time of the car crash.

The Boston archdiocese's knowledge of Paul Shanley's history of sexual misconduct with boys was called "astonishing" by attorney Roderick MacLeish, Jr.[49] On April 8, 2002, at a news conference in Boston, Massachusetts, MacLeish made public hundreds of pages of church records and documents obtained under court order on behalf of his client, Gregory Ford, who alleged he was sexually molested by former priest Paul Shanley from 1983 to 1989.

For his part, Paul Shanley was consistently outspoken on the issue of sex between men and boys. In 1977, Shanley delivered a speech in Rochester, New York, stating that he could think of no sexual act that caused psychological damage to children, including incest and bestiality. Further, in Shanley's opinion, the child was often the seducer in man-boy sexual relationships.[50] Church files revealed that, early on in Shanley's priesthood, officials in the Boston archdiocese had reason to suspect there might be more to Shanley's remarks about man-boy love than just words. In the late 1960s, a priest reported that Shanley routinely brought teenage boys to a cabin on weekends, and provided their names, addresses, and telephone numbers. However, according to church files, those allegations were never investigated.

By the time of Shanley's speech in 1977, Shanley had created an unconventional ministry for disenfranchised youth, some struggling with their sexual identity, and he frequently challenged official church teachings on the issue of homosexuality. However, in 1979, Cardinal Medeiros acknowledged that Shanley was a "troubled" priest when Vatican officials expressed concern to Medeiros about Shanley's public advocacy of homosexuality. Weeks later, Medeiros was made aware of an interview of Shanley that appeared in the publication *Gaysweek*, in which Shanley again spoke openly about man-boy love.[51] Despite this, Medeiros approved Shanley's transfer to St. John the Evangelist Church in Newton, a prosperous suburb west of Boston, although Shanley was ordered by the archbishop to comply with the church's teachings on sexual ethics.[52]

In 1985, Shanley was promoted to pastor of St. John the Evangelist Church by Cardinal Bernard F. Law. Four months later, the chancery was notified that Shanley gave another speech in Rochester, New York, again endorsing sexual relations between men and boys. A chancery official wrote to Shanley and requested an explanation. According to church files, there was no evidence that Shanley ever responded to the request.[53]

In December 1989, Shanley resigned as pastor of St. John the Evangelist and traveled to California. He later surfaced at St. Anne's parish in San Bernardino, California, where his arrival was preceded by a letter from Bishop Robert J. Banks, then a top aide of Cardinal Law's advising that Shanley was a priest in good standing.[54] According to a report in the *Boston Globe*, Cardinal Law and his aides appeared to be so concerned that Shanley might return to Boston that they were willing to say anything to keep Shanley as far away as possible.[55] Shanley worked on weekends at St. Anne's and spent his weekdays running a clothing-optional gay motel near Palm Springs, California, with John J. White, another Boston priest who was also on sick leave. In 1993, Shanley left St. Anne's after officials from the Boston archdiocese disclosed aspects of his past. Shanley received counseling and therapy and admitted that he had molested "several" boys. From California, Shanley moved to New York City, where he served as acting director of Leo House, a church-run hostel. However, Leo House began receiving phone calls from alleged victims of Shanley.[56]

Shanley returned to California and settled in the San Diego area. However, he could not outrun his past, made public by a mounting chorus of alleged victims who accused Shanley of sexually abusing them as children. In May 2002, Paul Shanley was arrested in San Diego, California, and returned to Massachusetts, where he was charged with 10 counts of child rape and six counts of indecent assault and battery. The victims all attended St. John the Evangelist Church in Newton, Massachusetts, during the 1980s, when Shanley was a priest and pastor there.

Both Catholics and non-Catholics demanded accountability for the mounting numbers of priests who had engaged in sexual misconduct over a period of years, often with the knowledge of their superiors in the Boston archdiocese. Largely as a result of the public's outcry, on December 13, 2002, Pope John Paul II accepted Cardinal Bernard F. Law's resignation as archbishop of Boston. A year of scandal had taken its toll on Law, who had once been rumored as likely to become the first American pope.[57]

Law, the son of an air force colonel, was ordained a priest in 1961. In 1984, he succeeded Cardinal Humberto Medeiros as archbishop of Boston. During his tenure as the leader of the Boston archdiocese, Cardinal Law was active in the anti-abortion movement and on fostering interfaith relations between Catholics, Protestants, and Jews.[58]

Despite Cardinal Law's popularity among Vatican officials, he could not escape his mishandling of sexually abusive priests under his authority as archbishop of Boston.[59] According to the *Boston Globe*, the Boston scandal's "short-term impact can be seen in reduced attendance at Mass, reduced contributions to collections, and reduced influence of bishops generally. The long-term impact will unfold over years, but the scandal has forced to the fore a variety of difficult issues—authority, gender, sexuality—that the church has in the past tried to avoid discussing." Sadly for Cardinal Law, his legacy "will probably be forever tarred as the man who chose repeatedly to keep in ministry priests who had sexually molested children and adolescents, priests who had traded drugs for sex, fathered children, and abused women."[60]

On July 30, 2003, Cardinal Law was succeeded by the Rev. Sean P. O'Malley, a Capuchin friar, who was installed as the archbishop of Boston. At his homily delivered at the installation ceremony, Archbishop O'Malley spoke of the shame brought upon the Catholic community and the pain suffered by victims as the result of sexual misconduct by priests. Responding to public criticism that Cardinal Law and other officials in the Boston archdiocese protected sexually abusive priests, O'Malley promised to avoid the mistakes of the past. Challenges facing the incoming archbishop included a decline in the number of priests, from more than 1,000 in 1983 to 550 in 2003, as well as a reduction in the level of donations by Catholic parishioners in the archdiocese, partly as the result of the sex abuse scandal. Some 40 protestors demonstrated outside the ceremony with signs reading "Criminals in Robes" and "Different Robes, Same Secret." Former archbishop Bernard F. Law was invited to O'Malley's installation ceremony but was not in attendance.[61]

On February 26, 2004, the day before the United States Conference of Catholic Bishops (USCCB) released the John Jay College of Criminal Justice's research study on sexual misconduct by Catholic clergy, the Boston archdiocese reported the results of its internal audit on clergy sexual misconduct. The major finding was that allegations of sexual abuse of minors were made against 7 percent of priests serving in the Boston archdiocese from 1950 to 2002. That was approximately 3 percent higher than the national average of allegations of sexual misconduct against priests, as reported in the USCCB research study. Of the 2,324 diocesan priests serving in the Boston archdiocese between 1950 and 2002, some 162 were accused of sexual misconduct with 815 minors. In addition, 150 allegations of sexual misconduct were made against deacons and priests of religious orders serving in the Boston archdiocese during the same time period. More troubling, seven serial predator priests, including John Geoghan, Joseph Birmingham, and Paul Shanley, were responsible for the victimization of 417 individuals. Geoghan, Birmingham, and Shanley were among those priests who were allowed to continue in ministries despite knowledge of their sexual misconduct by officials in the Boston archdiocese.

FALSELY ACCUSED

Criminal charges and civil actions for sexual misconduct have been dismissed against some priests and ministers for a variety of reasons, often because the statutes of limitations ran out. However, in the Boston archdiocese, three Catholic priests suspended from their ministerial duties were subsequently vindicated of all allegations that they engaged in sexual misconduct.

On June 26, 2002, the Rev. Ronald L. Bourgault was suspended from his ministerial duties at Saint Zepherin Church in Wayland, Massachusetts, after the archdiocese received an allegation that Rev. Bourgault had sexually abused a minor some 30 years earlier. On February 24, 2003, Rev. Bourgault was reinstated by the archdiocese after the alleged victim stated that he misidentified the priest as his abuser. Rev. Bourgault was subsequently returned to active ministry at his parish.

Monsignor Michael Smith Foster, the chief canon lawyer for the Boston archdiocese, was accused of sexual misconduct in a lawsuit filed on August 14, 2002, by Paul R. Edwards, who claimed the abuse occurred in the early 1980s. Two days later, Edwards's attorney admitted that the dates provided by Edwards for when the abuse occurred were incorrect. On August 22, a report in the *Boston Globe* raised questions as to Edwards's veracity.[62] Subsequently, the judge assigned to the case, Constance M. Sweeney, ordered Edwards to appear in her courtroom to answer questions regarding the credibility of his accusations against Msgr. Foster. On September 3, 2002, Edwards's lawsuit was dismissed with prejudice, effectively barring Edwards from ever refiling the case. Meanwhile, prosecutors for Suffolk County began a criminal investigation to determine if Edwards intentionally filed false charge. Msgr. Foster was reinstated to active duty on September 10, 2002, by then archbishop Bernard F. Law, who invited Msgr. Foster to celebrate Mass with him the following Sunday. However, three days later, Msgr. Foster was again suspended by the archdiocese after Edwards publicly renewed his allegations against him. On October 30, Msgr. Foster was once again cleared of all allegations by Edwards, and the archdiocese announced Msgr. Foster's reinstatement.

The Boston archdiocese on May 25, 2002, removed the Rev. Edward McDonagh from his ministerial duties at St. Ann's Church in West Bridgewater, Massachusetts, as the result of an allegation of sexual abuse of a minor 40 years earlier made against Rev. McDonagh. Parishioners began holding weekly candlelight vigils for Rev. McDonagh and expressed the suspicion that his suspension was motivated by the priest's outspoken criticism of Cardinal Bernard F. Law on the issue of sexual misconduct by priests. After archdiocese officials were unable to substantiate the claim against Rev. McDonagh, he was returned to active ministry on February 13, 2003. Rev. McDonagh received a standing ovation from parishioners when he celebrated his first Mass at St. Ann's Church after his reinstatement.

In these and other cases, priests publicly accused of sexual misconduct were often presumed guilty in the public mind. In response, Justice for Priests and Deacons was formed in San Diego, California, with a mission to educate Catholic clergy on their right of due process when facing an allegation of sexual misconduct. The following information was culled from their web site at http://www.justiceforpriests.org.

When an allegation of sexual misconduct is made, the following procedures, based on principles of canon law, are recommended to Catholic clergy:

- The allegation should be in writing and signed by the accuser in the presence of a notary public.
- The cleric's bishop must determine if the allegation has merit. If so, the accused may be provided with the written accusation and all information relied upon by the bishop in finding merit to the allegation.
- Both the accuser and the accused have a right to privacy and confidentiality.
- The accused is presumed innocent until proved guilty.
- The accused has the right to a defense presented at a trial or in an administrative forum.
- During the judicial process, the accused is entitled to receive his salary and sustenance provided by the church prior to the allegation, including room and board.
- The accused must be provided referrals for qualified canon lawyers and civil attorneys, and the diocese must bear the expense of the legal fees incurred in the case.

According to Catholic Canon 220, "No one is permitted to damage unlawfully the good reputation which another person enjoys nor violate the right of another person to protect his or her own privacy." The issue of privacy is particularly critical as it relates to diocesan record-keeping and confidential communications between a bishop and priest. In cases of clergy sexual misconduct that result in civil actions or criminal proceedings, even protected information may be open to discovery. However, in diocesan proceedings, the disclosure of records and privileged communications, including information presented in previous administrative hearings, may prejudice the right of the accused to a fair hearing. This is particularly relevant in cases where the accused was involved in a past incident of sexual misconduct, received treatment and counseling, and has been free of any further accusations for a period of years. To safeguard the right of the accused to due process when revealing information contained in diocesan records, Justice for Priests and Deacons prepared the following set of recommendations:

- Ambiguous notations that may lead to false interpretations by other bishops should be clarified or eliminated.
- Unsigned letters should not be retained as part of a personnel file.
- Unsubstantiated allegations should be eliminated.
- A priest should never release to a bishop his full psychological or medical reports, but instead should release a summary of such reports. Information in a full report may be misinterpreted and may also be protected by the client-professional privilege.
- Bishops and chancery officials should not make psychological judgments about clergy. A description of the offending behavior should be specific, not cloaked in professional terminology.
- Bishops and chancery officials should be apprised by legal counsel on current state laws on record-keeping, and segregate general information in personnel files, such as assignments and education, from confidential communications between a priest and bishop.
- Bishops should be advised by legal counsel on the legality of periodic shredding or destruction of diocesan files, and should comply with what state law permits.
- Bishops should publicly disclose the diocese's policy for the destruction of records in accordance with state law. Clergy should be free to inspect their files and to respond verbally or in writing to any information contained therein.

Despite these safeguards, media coverage may unwittingly foster a presumption of guilt through the use of anonymous sources, unnamed accusers, and sensational allegations that have yet to be substantiated.

SEXUAL MISCONDUCT IN OTHER CATHOLIC DIOCESES

In June 2003, on the eve of the USCCB's annual meeting, held in St. Louis, Missouri, Survivors First, an advocacy group for victims of clergy sexual abuse, released a report on U.S. priests with criminal convictions or pending allegations of sexual misconduct from 2002 to mid-2003.[63] The Survivors First report largely corroborated the findings of a *New York Times* survey, released in January 2003, that there was evidence of sexual misconduct by Catholic priests in nearly every diocese in the United States. The following is a review of six states where the extent of the sex abuse scandal was the most widespread.

Arizona

On June 2, 2003, Bishop Tomas J. O'Brien of the Phoenix diocese agreed to relinquish a substantial portion of his authority in exchange for immunity from prosecution on charges of failing to report priests accused of sexual misconduct with minors and transferring those priests to other parishes without disclosure of the sexual abuse allegations against them. The deal was offered by Maricopa County attorney Rick Romley after investigators gathered enough evidence to indict O'Brien. According to the terms of the agreement, O'Brien relinquished his authority to investigate claims of sexual misconduct to an independent special advocate, with oversight the Maricopa County Attorney's Office. In addition, O'Brien apologized to victims of sexual abuse by Phoenix priests and created a $300,000 victims' compensation fund, as well as a $300,000 victims' counseling fund. The diocese also agreed to reimburse prosecutors for the costs of the investigation. Ten priests in the Phoenix diocese were convicted on a variety of sex-related charges, including rape and sexual abuse of minors. In addition, settlements were paid out as the result of allegations of sexual misconduct by two Phoenix priests, and at least six others were being investigated.

On June 18, 2003, the Vatican accepted O'Brien's resignation following the filing of criminal charges against O'Brien for leaving the scene of a fatal accident and failing to report the incident to police. The victim, Jim Reed, was a pedestrian who was struck by a hit-and-run driver on June 16, 2003. Police traced a license plate number provided by a witness to O'Brien's car. O'Brien was subsequently convicted and, on April 1, 2004, he was sentenced to four years of supervised probation and 1,000 hours of community service. O'Brien could have been sentenced to as much as 45 months in prison and a $150,000 fine.

On January 29, 2002, the Diocese of Tucson paid $15 million to settle 11 civil lawsuits against four Diocesan priests who allegedly sexually abused minors. The settlement was paid out to plaintiffs, most of whom were allegedly victimized between 1967 and 1976. In addition, Bishops Manuel D. Moreno and Gerald F. Kicanas apologized to the victims and their families.

Sexual Misconduct and the Clergy

California

Statewide, priests were convicted, sued, or under investigation for alleged acts of sexual misconduct in the archdioceses of Los Angeles and San Francisco, and the dioceses of Fresno, Monterey, Oakland, Orange, Sacramento, San Bernardino, San Diego, San Francisco, San Jose, Santa Rosa, and Stockton. Some 30 priests from around the state were removed from their ministries as the result of allegations of sexual abuse or misconduct.

On June 23, 2003, the U.S. Supreme Court ruled as unconstitutional a 1994 California law that enabled prosecutors to charge sex offenders long after the expiration of the statute of limitations for the offense (see *Stogner v. California* in Chapter 2). As a result, some 800 individuals convicted under the 1994 California law were eligible to have charges against them dropped, including Catholic priests. By July 2003, only one month after the Supreme Court's ruling, some 24 convicted sex offenders in California were already released. Among them was an evangelical minister convicted of molesting his two daughters.

As of August 2002, in the Los Angeles archdiocese, some 33 priests were identified by the *Los Angeles Times* for alleged sexual misconduct since 1985, when Cardinal Roger Mahony was named archbishop of Los Angeles.[64] According to Survivors First, by mid-2003 that number rose to 54 Los Angeles priests who were facing such allegations. Seven priests were removed from office, six priests fled, and two priests and one deacon were convicted.

Frank Keating, former head of the USCCB National Lay Review Board, criticized Cardinal Roger Mahony for resisting requests by law enforcement authorities to turn over the names of priests suspected of sex crimes.[65] However, according to Mark Chopko, general counsel for the USCCB, Mahony was the only bishop willing to speak with victims of priest sex abuse who were protesting outside the 1992 annual meeting of the U.S. bishops in Washington, D.C. In 1998, Mahony was a key witness in the civil lawsuit brought by two brothers against Oliver O'Grady, a priest in the Stockton diocese where Mahony served as bishop before coming to Los Angeles. At the trial, Mahony testified that, despite O'Grady's admission of being a molester, Mahony reassigned him to another parish, where O'Grady sexually abused more victims. The jury awarded a judgment of $30 million, later reduced to $7 million.[66]

On February 17, 2004, Cardinal Roger Mahony reported that, from 1931 to 2003, some 244 priests, deacons, and seminarians in the Los Angeles archdiocese were accused of sexual misconduct with 656 minors. Although some of the allegations were subsequently discredited, Cardinal Mahony and other officials from the Los Angeles archdiocese acknowledged that the number of false accusations was likely outweighed by unreported cases of clergy sexual misconduct. The report concluded that sexual abuse by Catholic clergy was "a matter of tragic but isolated incidents." However, a subsequent report completed in May 2004 by Father Thomas P. Doyle and former priests Richard Sipe and Patrick Wile contended that ancient Vatican records and Latin texts showed that the problem of sexual abuse by Catholic priests was recognized by the church for some 1,700 years. "The contention that the present scandal is isolated to this era is completely debunked by the Roman Catholic Church's own documents," according to the authors of the report, entitled "Canonical History of Clerical Sexual Abuse."

Since May 2000, the Los Angeles archdiocese paid out $9.2 million in settlements for lawsuits brought by victims of clergy sexual abuse. On June 17, 2003, Los Angeles superior court judge Marvin M. Lager, Jr., was appointed to preside over all civil actions brought by victims of sexual abuse against priests who served in the Los Angeles archdiocese and the dioceses of Orange and San Diego. The litigation could involve as many as 200 individual cases, according to the *Los Angeles Times*.[67] However, in a setback for victims of clergy sexual abuse, pending criminal charges against some 20 priests statewide were likely to be dismissed as the result of the U.S. Supreme Court's ruling on June 26, 2003, that California's 1993 extension of the statutes of limitations for criminal sex offenses was unconstitutional (see *Stogner v. California* in Chapter 2).

Elsewhere in California, the Diocese of Sacramento paid $350,000 to settle a civil action brought against priest Vincent Brady for the alleged sexual abuse of a female, beginning when she was 11 years old. In the Archdiocese of San Francisco, priest James Aylward admitted during a deposition in a civil lawsuit in 2000 that he had a history of molesting boys. Aylward was placed on leave, and the diocese later settled with the victim for $750,000. The Diocese of Santa Rosa paid $1.6 million to settle a civil lawsuit arising out of priest Donald Kimball's alleged sexual abuse of girls during counseling sessions. In July 1999, G. Patrick Ziemann resigned as bishop of the Santa Rosa diocese after Ziemann admitted having sexual relations with another priest, Jorge Hume Salas, who alleged that Ziemann used his power as a bishop to extort sexual favors from Salas.

Illinois

In the Diocese of Joliet, two hospital chaplains were removed from their ministries as the result of allegations of sexual misconduct dating back two decades. Also, two priests accused of sexual misconduct while serving in the Joliet diocese who then were transferred to out-of-state dioceses were removed from their ministerial duties. In the Peoria diocese, six priests were removed from their ministerial duties in 2002 as the result of allegations of sexual misconduct.

Sexual Misconduct and the Clergy

A report issued in February 2003 by the Archdiocese of Chicago identified 55 credible allegations of sexual misconduct against 36 priests; however, all the alleged incidents occurred before 1991. Of the 36 priests implicated, all of them either resigned, retired, or were deceased. Since 1993, the Chicago archdiocese paid some $16.8 million on costs related to clergy sexual abuse, including settlements, assistance to victims, and treatment of offending priests, as well as legal costs. That amount included $1.3 million for the legal defense of a priest and a school principal who were acquitted of all charges.

Kentucky

The Archdiocese of Louisville paid $25.7 million to settle lawsuits brought by 243 alleged victims of sexual abuse by priests and church employees. At the announcement of the settlement, Archbishop Thomas Kelly apologized to victims, including the 29 victims of Louisville priest Louis Miller, who pleaded guilty to 50 criminal counts of sexual abuse and was sentenced to 20 years in state prison.

New Hampshire

The Diocese of Manchester turned over to prosecutors the names of 14 priests accused of sexual abuse, seven of whom were already suspended from ministerial duties. The diocese also disclosed that from 1943 to 2002, some 55 priests were named in internal complaints of sexual abuse, according to diocesan records. One of them, Francis A. Talbot, was later convicted of sexual abuse. A settlement of $6.5 million was awarded to 61 alleged victims of sexual abuse by New Hampshire priests. Bishop John B. McCormack, the director of ministerial personnel under Cardinal Law in the Boston archdiocese from 1984 to 1994, resigned as chairman of a national committee formed by the National Conference of Catholic Bishops to study the sex abuse scandal.

New York

Church officials turned over to law enforcement authorities information regarding allegations of sexual misconduct against a number of priests statewide. As a result, convictions for sexual abuse were handed down against Morgan Kuhl of the New York archdiocese, Francis X. Nelson of the Brooklyn diocese, William Heim of the Albany diocese, and Michael R. Hands of the Rockville Centre diocese. Suffolk County district attorney Thomas Spota announced the formation of a special grand jury to investigate cases of sexual misconduct involving priests. The grand jury's report, issued in March 2003, found that the Diocese of Rockville Centre protected priests accused of sexual abuse by transferring them to other parishes, where in some cases they were allowed to minister to children. Cardinal Edward Egan, archbishop of

New York, released a letter in which he apologized if he made any mistakes in the handling of priests under his authority. Cardinal Egan, also implicated in sheltering sexually abusive priests while he was bishop of Bridgeport, Connecticut, refused to disclose the results of an internal investigation conducted by the New York archdiocese of priests accused of sexually abusing minors.

THE CATHOLIC CHURCH'S RESPONSE

In 1984, in the wake of national news coverage of the sexual misconduct of former priest Gilbert Gauthe of Lafayette, Louisiana, several states amended their child-abuse reporting laws to include members of the clergy as mandatory reporters (see Chapter 2 for a discussion of mandatory reporting laws). As a result, the USCCB, known as the National Conference of Catholic Bishops (NCCB) until July 1, 2001, began to formulate a diocesan policy on the handling of cases of sexual misconduct and set forth the following five basic guidelines:

- Remove the alleged offender from ministerial duties.
- Refer the alleged offender for psychiatric evaluation.
- Provide solace and support to the victim.
- Keep the claim of sexual misconduct confidential.
- Notify civil authorities, as mandated by state laws.

In 1985, the USCCB was presented with the resource paper "The Problem of Sexual Molestation by Roman Catholic Clergy: Meeting the Problem in a Comprehensive and Responsible Manner," drafted by the Rev. Thomas Doyle, a canon lawyer; Raymond Mouton, an attorney who represented Gilbert Gauthe; and the Rev. Michael Peterson. Included in the resource paper was an assessment of the potential size of the problem of sexual misconduct within the Catholic clergy, as well as suggestions on how to deal with offending priests. However, the resource paper was not well received by the USCCB. Instead of adopting a uniform churchwide policy on sexual misconduct with an independent review board, as recommended by the authors of the paper, the USCCB decided that cases of sexual misconduct would continue to be handled be each individual diocese, without uniform guidelines.

Beginning in 1988, the church was faced with a new problem. Instead of dealing with isolated cases of sexual misconduct, as they occurred, an increasing number of victims were coming forward with allegations of sexual abuse that occurred years earlier, often when the victims were children. In 1993, the USCCB established a Committee on Sexual Abuse. The committee's mandates included formulating ways of dealing with sexually abusive priests, examining how to deal with victims, addressing the issue of morale among non-offending clergy, and proposing methods to screen candidates for the priesthood. In 1994, the USCCB Committee on Sexual Abuse issued its report "Restoring Trust, Volume 1," which included a review of 157 separate diocesan policies on sexual misconduct, a description of 10 treatment centers for priest offenders, and articles on topics such as pedophilia. The committee updated its report in 1995 and again in 1996, and issued six mandates on the handling of incidents of sexual misconduct by priests.

By 2002, as the sexual abuse scandal within the Catholic Church widened in scope, it became clear to church officials that existing church policies needed review. Pope John Paul II summoned 12 U.S. cardinals to the Vatican for a meeting on the crisis, which took place April 23–24, 2002. In his opening remarks to the assembly, Pope John Paul II stressed that "there is no place in the priesthood and religious life for those who would harm the young." The pope urged U.S. bishops to respond to the ongoing crisis "with pastoral charity for the victims, as well as for the priests and the entire Catholic Community in your country."[68]

By the end of the two-day meeting, U.S. cardinals reaffirmed a set of basic principles, including a condemnation of sexual abuse of children and the need to provide assistance to victims and their families. The cardinals also recommended that, absent a causal link between celibacy and pedophilia, celibacy should remain a requirement of all Catholic priests. In addition, the 12 U.S. cardinals made several proposals for the USCCB to implement formally, including:

- A set of national standards for dealing with the sexual abuse of minors.
- A special process for the dismissal of an offending priest.
- Rigorous screening of applicants to the priesthood.

On June 14, 2002, at its annual meeting in Dallas, Texas, the USCCB voted 239 to 13 to approve a new churchwide policy on sexual misconduct that required bishops to report all allegations of sexual abuse of minors to civil authorities. However, in November 2002, that provision was weakened by the Vatican to require that bishops report allegations of sexual misconduct with minors to civil authorities only as required by law. In other words, in states where members of the clergy were not included as mandatory reporters of child abuse, there was no duty for bishops to report incidents of sexual misconduct with minors.

On November 13, 2002, the USCCB voted 246 to 7 to approve the policy on sexual misconduct, as revised by the Vatican. The new procedures required bishops to conduct a preliminary investigation of any allegation of sexual misconduct and, if evidence exists, to notify the Vatican and temporarily remove the priest from ministry pending an investigation of the allegations. Even in cases where the allegations proved to be true, the policy stopped short of mandatory defrocking and, instead, left it up to the offending priest or the priest's bishop to request defrocking from the Vatican.

The new policy also mandated background checks of all diocesan and parish personnel who have contact with children, and full disclosure of a priest's background by his bishop when the priest is transferred. The policy banned legal confidentiality agreements with victims, except in certain cases when the victim requests confidentiality, and required local diocesan review boards of predominately lay people to review all allegations of sexual misconduct made against priests. However, the revised policy clarified that lay review boards were advisory in nature. As such, their recommendations were not binding on church officials.

The USCCB established a national Office for Child and Youth Protection (OCYP) with the mandate to assist dioceses in implementing programs to ensure the safety of all minors at church facilities. In December 2002, Kathleen McChesney, then the third highest ranking official of the FBI and the bureau's highest ranking female, was named executive director of the OCYP.

The USCCB also established a National Review Board (NRB) comprised of laity to study the church's handling of sexual misconduct by priests. Former Oklahoma governor Frank Keating was named chairman of the NRB but resigned in 2003 as the result of a dispute in which Keating alleged that certain U.S. bishops, such as Los Angeles archbishop Roger Mahony, were not cooperating in a nationwide study on sexual misconduct in U.S. dioceses.

On July 29, 2003, slightly more than one year after it was established, the NRB released a status report on the board's six major goals. Among them, the NRB reported that the OCYP was auditing all 195 U.S. Catholic dioceses for compliance with the policies adopted by the USCCB in June 2002. In addition, the OCYP was implementing training programs on Safe Environment Standards for children in all Catholic institutions. The NRB announced an ongoing national statistical survey on clergy sexual misconduct commissioned by the NRB and conducted by the John Jay College of Criminal Justice. (See Chapter 2 for a full discussion of church policies on sexual misconduct.)

Results of the National Survey

"The Nature and Scope of the Problem of Sexual Abuse of Minors by Catholic Priests and Deacons in the United States, 1950–2000" was released by the USCCB on February 27, 2004. It was designed as a research study to present empirical data on the incidence of sexual misconduct by U.S. Catholic clergy over a period of 50 years. As such, the study was never intended to provide any historical or social perspective on the issue of clergy sexual misconduct. However, the research study was jointly released with a report by the USCCB's NRB. The NRB's report interpreted the data in the research study and examined the causes and social context of the problem of sexual misconduct by Catholic priests. The NRB's report was written by its 12 members, who included Catholic lawyers, judges, and other lay professionals.

The research study by the John Jay College of Criminal Justice was compiled using data from three surveys distributed to some 195 U.S. Catholic dioceses. Each of the surveys elicited different types of information. The first survey dealt with the characteristics of each diocese, including its size, as well as the total number of allegations of sexual misconduct reported in the diocese, and the diocese's total expenditures as the result of those allegations, including legal settlements, attorneys' fees, and the costs of treatment for offending clerics. The second survey examined personnel and other church records for priests accused of sexual misconduct. In the third survey, church records relating to victims of clergy sexual misconduct were reviewed in order to further illuminate the extent and nature of the misconduct.

Data from the three surveys revealed that allegations of sexual misconduct were made against 4 percent of the 109,694 priests serving in the United States between 1950 and 2002. That amounted to a total of 4,392 individual priests, after accounting for priests with multiple allegations from different parishes or dioceses. The percentage of accused priests rose slightly, to 4.3 percent, when measured against data provided by the Center for Applied Research in the Apostolate (CARA), which reported a total of 94,607 active U.S. priests between 1960 and 1996. Just over one-third of allegations of sexual misconduct that occurred during the 50-year period examined by the study were reported between 1970 and 1979. In 2002, some 36 percent of all victims who reported sexual misconduct by a priest claimed that the misconduct occurred from 1970 to 1979, and another 30 percent claimed that the misconduct occurred from 1960 to 1969. Factors including shame, repressed memory, and fear of publicity by victims accounted for their reluctance to report allegations any sooner.

Significantly, of the 10,667 individuals cited in the research study who made allegations of sexual misconduct against Catholic clergy between 1950 and 2002, all the allegations involved the sexual abuse of minors. By comparison, from 2 to 3 percent of Protestant clergy have sexually abused minors, according to data presented by the Catholic League for Religious and Civil Rights.

Slightly more than half the victims of sexual abuse by Catholic clergy were between the ages of 11 and 14 at the time of the alleged misconduct, while 27.3 percent were from 15 to 17 years of age, according to the research study. Sixteen percent of victims cited in the research study were between the ages of eight and 10 at the time of the allegations, and 6 percent were seven years of age or younger. Males accounted for more than 40 percent of alleged victims between the ages of 11 and 14, while females were more often victimized at younger ages.

In just over 38 percent of cases, the alleged sexual misconduct by a priest occurred within a single year. With regard to allegations of ongoing sexual misconduct by a priest with the same victim, in 21.8 percent of such cases the sexual abuse lasted for a period of one to two years, and in 28 percent of cases the sexual misconduct was ongoing for a period of two to four years. Slightly more than 11 percent of cases of alleged sexual abuse were ongoing between a priest and a victim for five years or longer.

About 56 percent of priests allegedly abused a single victim, according to the research study. Some 149 priests had more than 10 allegations each of sexual misconduct, involving a total of 2,960 victims. Such serial predators accounted for 27 percent of all allegations of sexual abuse by priests. Serial predators were much more adept at avoiding discovery by law enforcement than were priests facing fewer allegations. For example, police contact was reported for only 4 percent of serial predators, compared to 14 percent of priests with fewer allegations of sexual misconduct. Also, only 3 percent of serial predator priests were ever charged with a crime—the same percentage as priests with fewer allegations of sexual misconduct. In all, only 3 percent of priests with allegations of sexual misconduct were convicted of a crime for their actions, and about 2 percent were sentenced to prison as a result.

As for the church's handling of priests with substantiated allegations of sexual misconduct, about one-third were referred for some type of evaluation, and about one-fourth were placed on administrative leave. However, the data was unclear as to how many of those priests were eventually either returned to their ministries or transferred to other ministries. Six percent of priests with substantiated allegations of sexual misconduct were reprimanded and returned to their ministries. In 10 percent of cases, no action at all was taken by church officials against priests with substantiated allegations of sexual misconduct.

The personnel files of clergy reviewed in the research study indicated that 7 percent of priests with allegations of sexual misconduct had, themselves, been childhood victims of physical, sexual, or emotional abuse. Nearly 20 percent also experienced alcohol or substance abuse problems.

In "A Report on the Crisis in the Catholic Church in the United States," released on February 27, 2004, the NRB attempted to explain the causes and context of the sexual abuse scandal in the U.S. Catholic Church. Some 85 Catholic bishops and cardinals were interviewed for the NRB's report, as were Vatican officials, experts in the field of sexual abuse, and a small number of victims of clergy sexual misconduct by priests. Everyone interviewed was guaranteed anonymity in order to foster a more forthright dialogue with board members.

Sexual Misconduct and the Clergy

The NRB defined the crisis in the Catholic Church as a twofold problem of the sexual abuse of minors by clergy, and the failure of many in the church's hierarchy to appropriately respond to allegations of sexual misconduct by priests.

As to why so many priests were involved in the sexual abuse of minors, the NRB's report identified a failure by dioceses and religious orders to properly screen candidates for the priesthood, resulting in the admission of some priests who were sexually aberrant or who demonstrated a high degree of emotional or sexual immaturity. The NRB also faulted Catholic seminaries for their inadequate preparation of seminarians to live chaste and celibate lives successfully, as required of them upon ordination. The NRB's report noted that neither celibacy nor the homosexual inclination of some priests could be blamed, per se, for the sexual misconduct of priests.

In discussing the failure of many church leaders to respond to allegations of sexual misconduct by priests, the NRB's report listed the following factors:

- Bishops either failed to understand the nature of the problem of sexual misconduct or responded to allegations of sexual misconduct in a sporadic manner.
- The fear of scandal prevented some bishops from taking action against offending clerics.
- The threat of litigation caused some bishops to become adversarial with victims of sexual misconduct, instead of ministering to victims.
- Some bishops failed to comprehend the extent of harm suffered by victims of sexual abuse by priests.
- Bishops tended to rely too heavily on managing the crisis through legal strategies or on the advice of mental health professionals who claimed to provide effective treatment for offending clergy, instead of approaching the problem of clergy sexual misconduct as a moral issue.
- Bishops did not utilize the resources of other priests to help monitor offending clergy who were returned to their ministries.
- By placing the interests of accused priests above those of victims, some bishops engaged in a form of denial that the misconduct took place.
- Although limited by canon law on removing priests from their ministries, some bishops failed to utilize the canonical authority they had to take administrative actions against offending priests.

In addition, the NRB's report singled out several church officials for their mishandling of priests accused of sexual misconduct. Among those criticized by name were Cardinal Bernard F. Law, the former archbishop of the

38

Introduction

Boston archdiocese, and Cardinal Edward M. Egan, the archbishop of New York and former bishop of the Diocese of Bridgeport, Connecticut, for their failure to take action against sexually abusive priests under their authority. Also criticized was Cardinal Roger Mahony, archbishop of Los Angeles, for resisting grand jury subpoenas for personnel records and other church documents relating to priests accused of sexual misconduct. The resignation of Frank Keating in 2002 as chairman of the NRB was, in part, the result of his public displeasure with Cardinal Mahony's lack of cooperation in turning over personnel files of accused priests to civil authorities and to investigators conducting the research study for John Jay College of Criminal Justice.

The NRB's report concluded with the following series of recommendations:

- Further study and analysis of the problem of sexual misconduct by priests.
- Better screening and supervision of candidates for the priesthood.
- Increased sensitivity to victims of clergy sexual misconduct in responding to allegations of clergy sexual misconduct.
- Holding bishops and other church leaders directly accountable for their decisions regarding offending clerics.
- Better cooperation between church leaders and civil authorities, such as law enforcement agencies or social service agencies, that are investigating allegations of sexual misconduct or sexual abuse.

Both the research study by the John Jay College of Criminal Justice and the NRB's report are freely available online at http://www.catholic-reviewboard.com, or by writing the USCCB in Washington, D.C.

THE FINANCIAL COST TO THE CATHOLIC CHURCH

On July 6, 2004, the Roman Catholic Archdiocese of Portland, Oregon, became the first of the 195 Catholic dioceses in the United States to file for bankruptcy in order to limit its financial exposure in pending lawsuits over clergy sexual misconduct. In the Roman Catholic Church, each diocese functions as a separate legal entity. After filing for protection under Chapter 11 of the federal bankruptcy laws, the Portland archdiocese continued to operate while its debts were reorganized in bankruptcy court, which can prioritize which debtors will be paid first, including plaintiffs who are awarded legal damages from the archdiocese. As a result of the Chapter 11 filing, the bankruptcy court began the process of taking over from the archbishop the management of the archdiocese's financial affairs, causing the operations of the archdiocese to be placed under the scrutiny of the court. In a letter to members of the archdiocese, Portland's archbishop John G. Vlazny stated that the bankruptcy filing was not an attempt by the archdiocese to avoid compensating victims of clergy sexual misconduct. Rather, Archbishop Vlazny characterized the decision as a way of assuring fairness in the distribution of the archdiocese's available funds. However, David Clohessy, the national director of the Survivors Network of those Abused by Priests (SNAP), expressed skepticism about Archbishop Vlazny's statement and claimed that Vlazny had failed to demonstrate that the archdiocese lacked sufficient assets to settle pending lawsuits. Under church law, the archbishop is prohibited from seizing the property of local parishes in the archdiocese or using assets held in charitable trusts in order to pay creditors. Since 2000, the Portland archdiocese paid some $53 million to settle over 130 claims of clergy sexual misconduct, about half of which was covered by insurance carried by the archdiocese. At the time of the bankruptcy filing, an additional 25 lawsuits were pending. In only two of those cases, plaintiffs were seeking $155 million in damages arising from sexual misconduct by priests.

On September 9, 2003, the Boston archdiocese agreed to pay $85 million to settle lawsuits brought by more than 552 plaintiffs who claimed they were victims of sexual abuse by priests over several decades. The settlement, which was $30 million more than the $55 million originally offered by the archdiocese, marked the largest single pay-out to settle claims of sexual misconduct in the history of the church. Under the agreement, most of the plaintiffs would be paid between $80,000 and $300,000 each, depending upon the nature and extent of their victimization. In addition to monetary compensation, the agreement also included provisions to include victims on lay review boards to monitor clergy sexual misconduct and to provide victims with counseling and treatment.

Including this settlement, the Boston archdiocese paid out a total of $110 million to settle civil actions brought by victims of clergy sexual abuse since 1990. From 1997 to early 2002, the Archdiocese of Boston settled some 50 civil actions brought by victims of John Geoghan alone for an estimated $10 million. In September 2002, the Boston archdiocese settled with an additional 84 plaintiffs for an estimated $10 million, bringing their total cost to $20 million in settlements arising from the sexual misconduct of just one priest.

In order to pay the settlements, the Boston archdiocese planned to mortgage churches and other buildings owned by the archdiocese. As a further cost-saving measure, the archdiocese planned to consolidate between 15 and 20 parishes. Although insurers of the Boston archdiocese refused to pay any of the $85 million settlement announced on September 9, 2003, Archbishop O'Malley was considering suing at least two insurance companies to help pay for the cost of the settlement. However, both state and federal courts have upheld an insurer's right to refuse claims arising from harm that was the result of the policyholder's reckless behavior. In 2002, Archbishop O'Malley's predecessor, Cardinal Bernard F. Law, threatened to put the archdiocese in Chapter 11 bankruptcy as the result of financial problems caused by the clergy sexual misconduct scandal. Instead, the archdiocese borrowed some $38 million from the Knights of Columbus, a Catholic service organization.

Millions more were paid out in settlements in other dioceses nationwide. Estimates for the total costs of settlements, legal defense, and treatment for sexually abusive priests was put as high as $1 billion. Mark Chopko, general counsel for the USCCB, stated that the total expenditures were $250 million.[69] However, that figure was increased to $500 million by the USCCB on February 27, 2004, as reported in the research study "The Nature and Scope of the Problem of Sexual Abuse of Minors by Catholic Priests and Deacons in the United States, 1950–2002," conducted by the John Jay College of Criminal Justice.

In 1998, the Diocese of Lafayette, Louisiana, paid some $18 million to settle claims of sexual abuse made against former priest Gilbert Gauthe. Also in 1998, the Diocese of Dallas, Texas, paid $31 million to settle claims of sexual misconduct brought by the victims of former priest Rudy Kos. Of that $31 million, the diocese raised some $11 million by mortgaging or selling church properties.

In 1999, the Diocese of Stockton, California, paid $13 million to two brothers who were sexually abused by former priest Oliver Francis O'Grady. In California, the Archdiocese of Los Angeles and the Diocese of Orange collectively paid $5.2 million in damages in 2001 to the victim of sexual abuse by former Monsignor Michael Harris. Also in 2001, the Diocese of Bridgeport, Connecticut, settled 27 clergy-abuse lawsuits filed since 1993 for $15 million.

In 2002, the Diocese of Tucson, Arizona, paid an estimated $15 million to settle 11 lawsuits brought by victims of sexually abusive priests. In Rhode Island, the Diocese of Providence settled with 36 alleged sexual abuse victims in 2002 for a total of $13.5 million, part of which was raised by the sale of the bishop's summer residence. On June 10, 2003, the Archdiocese of Louisville, Kentucky, announced a settlement of $25.7 million to some 243 alleged victims of sexual misconduct by priests.

The Diocese of Santa Rosa, California, sold property and took loans and donations from other dioceses to offset a $16 million debt incurred as the result of sexual misconduct by priests. The Archdiocese of Sante Fe, New Mexico, considered filing for bankruptcy protection as the result of paying $50 million to settle 40 sexual abuse cases.

On October 16, 2003, the Diocese of Bridgeport, Connecticut, announced a settlement of $21 million with 40 victims of sexual misconduct by 16 priests. The alleged incidents occurred beginning in the 1960s and continued until the 1990s, when New York archbishop Edward Egan was bishop of Bridgeport. Previously, the Bridgeport diocese paid out $16.7 million to settle 47 claims of sexual misconduct by priests.

The total cost of sexual misconduct to the U.S. Catholic Church as the result of court judgments and legal settlements has been estimated as high as $1 billion. As of October 2003, financial settlements with victims of clergy sexual misconduct by priests in 23 dioceses had reached $292.8 million, according to appeals court justice Anne Burke, the acting chairperson of the USCCB NRB. That figure was expected to grow as hundreds of lawsuits worked their way through courts nationwide.

In addition, the sexual abuse scandal threatened to erode future financial contributions to U.S. Catholic dioceses and Catholic charities. According to results of a Gallup Poll conducted in November 2002, some 55 percent of church-going Catholics expressed fear that the cost of settlements from the priest sex abuse scandal would negatively impact Catholic programs that assist the homeless and poor. Nearly half the respondents said they were considering contributing to alternative nondiocesan charities instead of to their parish or local Catholic charity, and about 25 percent said they would reduce their current level of giving if their contributions were used to pay for legal settlements and judgments arising from sexual misconduct by priests.

CLERGY SEXUAL MISCONDUCT IN OTHER DENOMINATIONS

Beginning with the case of former Louisiana priest Gilbert Gauthe, national news coverage of clergy sexual misconduct was primarily focused on the U.S. Catholic Church. That focus intensified in 2002 in response to the sexual abuse scandal in the Boston archdiocese and nationwide. Although the coverage was justified, even notable in the case of the *Boston Globe*, which won a Pulitzer Prize in 2002, incidents of sexual misconduct among other religious faiths were not as widely reported. For example, at the height of the U.S. Catholic scandal in 2002, Baptist minister Lawrence French resigned as pastor of First Baptist Church of Winchester, Massachusetts, after he was found guilty by a church review panel of sexually abusing three boys between 1960 and 1982. In June 2002, two Episcopalian priests in St. Petersburg, Florida, resigned as the result of allegations of sexual misconduct, prompting the Episcopal diocese of Southwest Florida to review some 700 clergy personnel files dating back to 1969, when the diocese was founded. In December 2002, Episcopal priest Andrew Barasda resigned as pastor of

Introduction

St. Mary's Episcopal Church in Provincetown, Massachusetts, after admitting to sexual misconduct with a male teenager in 1966.

Also in 2002, Rabbi Baruch Lanner was convicted and sentenced to seven years in state prison for sexually abusing minors at an Orthodox youth group in New York over a period of three decades, and Rabbi Richard Marcovitz pleaded guilty and was sentenced to 20 years in state prison for sexual misconduct involving two female employees at a religious school and two minors who attended classes at the school. Lutheran minister Gerald P. Thomas, Jr., former pastor of Good Shepherd Lutheran Church in Marshall, Texas, pleaded guilty to possession of child pornography, prompting the filing of a civil action in 2002 against him by nine plaintiffs who alleged that Thomas sexually abused them as children, between the ages of seven and 16. In October 2002, Michael Skoor, former pastor of Cavalry Lutheran Church in Solana Beach, California, was sentenced to 29 years in prison for the sexual abuse of an 11-year-old boy and the attempted sexual abuse of the boy's younger brother. In February 2002, the family of Deborah Yardley was awarded $10 million in damages arising from the sexual misconduct of Methodist minister Steven Colliflower in Columbus, Ohio. Yardley, deceased, had sought counseling for alcoholism and emotional problems from Colliflower. In December 2002, a former Presbyterian pastor in Mount Kisco, New York, was charged by church officials of sexual misconduct with eight minors over a period of years. In June 2002, a civil action was filed against the Church of Jesus Christ of Latter-day Saints in Salt Lake City, Utah, alleging that Mormon Church officials sheltered religion instructor Mitchell Blake Young, who in 1988 pleaded guilty to criminal charges of sexual misconduct at a Salt Lake City youth center. The lawsuit alleged that the church knew of Young's previous history of sexually abusing minors during the six years when Young abused the plaintiffs, beginning in 1987 when the plaintiff was six years old. In 1993, Young was convicted in criminal court of sexually abusing the plaintiff and was sentenced to 15 years in a Utah state prison.

An annual survey conducted by the Christian Ministry Resources (CMR) of about 1,000 churches nationwide found that, since 1993, there were an average of 70 allegations of child abuse per week made against clergy, staff, or church volunteers in U.S. churches.[70] The survey data showed that there were slightly more than an average of 70 such allegations per week from 1993 to 1997, and slightly less since then, suggesting the effectiveness of preventative steps taken by churches, such as implementing policies on the reporting of sexual misconduct. Since 1993, about 1 percent of churches surveyed by CMR reported sexual misconduct allegations. Of the 350,000 churches in the United States, 19,500, or about 5 percent, are Roman Catholic. By extrapolation, most allegations of sexual misconduct since 1993 occurred in non-Catholic denominations.

Sexual Misconduct and the Clergy

More recently, on April 22, 2004, a Texas court awarded $37 million to nine victims of sexual misconduct by former Evangelical Lutheran Church in America minister Gerald Patrick Thomas, Jr. When combined with previous settlements of $32 million, a total of $69 million in damages was awarded to victims of Thomas's sexual misconduct. The plaintiffs, who were minors at the time of the alleged sexual abuse by Thomas, contended that Thomas's superiors in the church, including former bishop Mark Herbener, ignored warnings about Thomas's inappropriate behavior with minors. In those respects, the case was similar to many brought by victims of clergy sexual misconduct by Catholic priests. In 2003, Thomas was sentenced in criminal court to 397 years in state prison for sexually molesting minors while serving as minister from 1997 to 2001 at the Good Shepherd Lutheran Church in Marshall, Texas.

Among other findings in the CMR annual survey of churches:

- Most cases of sexual misconduct involving a child is limited to one victim, not to multiple victims, as occurred in the Boston archdiocese, for example.
- Some 21 percent of allegations resulted in lawsuits or out-of-court settlements.
- The most likely group of offenders were church volunteers in cases of sexual misconduct with minors. Clergy accounted for about 25 percent of such incidents nationwide.

The misperception that sexual misconduct is a Catholic problem may be due, in part, to the Catholic Church's slow response to the issue, and to the lack of a binding national policy on clergy sexual misconduct until June 2002, when U.S. bishops adopted such a policy at their meeting in Dallas, Texas. By contrast, since the early 1990s, many mainline Protestant denominations, which are more centrally organized than the Catholic diocesan system, have instituted national policies on clergy sexual misconduct and taken other measures to curb its occurrence within their congregations, according to Minnesota psychologist Gary Schoener.[71] Heightened awareness of the issue among many Protestant churches came in the aftermath of the 1991 Colorado case in which a woman was awarded $1.2 million in civil damages from her Episcopal diocese and the presiding bishop of Colorado for covering up the sexual misconduct of her priest. The case demonstrated that church officials, not just the offending clergy member, could be held accountable in cases of sexual misconduct. Unlike the hierarchy in the Catholic Church, where priests receive parish assignments by a bishop, many Protestant congregations hire their own pastors. Prior to the Colorado case, higher church officials argued that they were not liable for bad hiring decisions and blamed individual congregations, which often lacked the financial resources for large settlements, therefore discouraging litigation. After the Colorado case, U.S. Episcopal Church officials were advised by their insurers to develop policies on misconduct and implement training programs aimed at prevention within two years or risk losing their coverage. The Episcopal Church did so, offering mandatory churchwide training of clergy and staff, including volunteer lay workers, that included video presentations and discussions on such topics as identifying offenders and maintaining and respecting personal boundaries. In effect, as a result of the 1991 lawsuit, the Episcopal Church established what was considered by other denominations as the gold standard of sexual misconduct policies.

National policies were subsequently adopted by other mainline Protestant denominations, including the Methodists, Presbyterians, and Lutherans. The Central Conference of American Rabbis (CCAR) also addressed the issue in a 1998 conference by offering detailed guidelines on how to report, respond to, investigate, and adjudicate allegations of sexual misconduct. Under the CCAR guidelines, suspension or expulsion of rabbis must be publicly reported in the conference newsletter, and offenders are barred from using the rabbinical placement service to look for new appointments. Policies on clergy sexual misconduct were also adopted by Conservative and Orthodox Jewish rabbinates.

According to a 1993 survey by the *Journal of Pastoral Care*, some 14 percent of Southern Baptist ministers surveyed said they had engaged in inappropriate sexual behavior with congregants, 70 percent said they knew a minister who had done so, and 80 percent reported that they lacked written guidelines on clergy sexual misconduct. As a result, training on sexual misconduct was instituted at Southern Baptist seminaries.

In 1999, the Hartford Institute for Religion Research interviewed 76 clergy members, most of them Protestants, who had served more than 500 congregations during their careers. They reported 122 cases involving clergy sexual misconduct, most involving illicit affairs between adults. Although the study was anecdotal, it provided a window on the prevalence of clergy sexual misconduct in non-Catholic congregations.

THE IMPACT ON VICTIMS

At the United States Conference of Catholic Bishops' (USCCB's) meeting in June 2002, four victims of sexual misconduct by priests spoke to the assembly about the effects of sexual abuse, including feelings of shame, substance abuse, mental illness, sexual promiscuity, and even suicide. While there are a lack of clinical studies on the specific effects of clergy sexual abuse, there is a significant body of information on childhood sexual abuse, which is a problem in the United States among individuals of all racial and socioeconomic backgrounds. The most commonly experienced short-term effect of childhood sexual abuse is posttraumatic stress disorder (PTSD), which is a clinical syndrome with symptoms that include the mental reenactment of the traumatic event, emotional withdrawal and avoidance of cues associated with the traumatic event, and physiological hyperreactivity in certain situations that may trigger a memory of the traumatic event. Victims with PTSD often experience nightmares and flashbacks in which the traumatic event is reexperienced, sleep disorders, and feelings of detachment.

The psychological symptoms of PTSD are exacerbated by depression, substance abuse, and memory impairment, which can produce negative social ramifications such as job instability, family discord, and divorce. Victims of sexual abuse develop psychiatric disorders at four times the rate of nonabused individuals and are three times more likely to abuse alcohol and drugs.[72] Without intervention through counseling or psychotherapy, PTSD may become a chronic problem that continues throughout the victim's childhood and into adulthood.

Another short-term effect of childhood sexual abuse is the development of sexualized behavior. In other words, children who are sexually abused are statistically more likely to engage in sexualized behavior than nonvictims, including children with other types of mental health issues. In addition, childhood victims of sexual abuse tend to experience more depression and anxiety than nonvictims. Promiscuity, poor self-esteem, and disruptive behavior disorders are also more common among childhood victims of sexual abuse.

Some childhood victims of sexual abuse appear asymptomatic following the traumatic event. In some cases, there may simply be a delay in the appearance of symptoms. Also, certain mitigating factors may reduce the impact of the sexual abuse some child victims experience. Mitigating factors include the characteristics of the traumatic event. For example, traumatic events that involve violence or sexual penetration, or multiple traumatic events, are more likely to elicit symptoms in child victims than traumatic events that are isolated or do not involve sexual penetration. Childhood victims of sexual assault by a parent are more likely to exhibit symptoms than children who are victimized by an adult stranger or an older child. The age, developmental level, and psychological condition of a child at the time of a sexual assault are also factors that may increase the likelihood of the appearance of symptoms. For example, children with low self-esteem experience more distress as the result of the traumatic event, and they are more likely to be symptomatic. Children who cope with stress by avoidance prior to the traumatic event are more likely to develop symptoms after the event.

Introduction

The reaction of the adult in whom the child confides about sexual abuse can bear significantly on the child's adjustment and recovery. Childhood victims of sexual abuse fare better when the adults they tell are respectful and caring and give credibility to the child's experience. By contrast, a response involving panic, shock, or disbelief can have a negative impact on the child's recovery. Because child victims sometimes blame themselves for the sexual abuse, they fare better when the adults they tell emphasize that the abuse was not the child's fault and that disclosing the information was the right thing to do.

If criminal charges are filed after the reporting of the incident, the ensuing legal process is often intimidating and frightening for child victims, as well as for adult victims who come forward after years of silence about their sexual abuse. During the lengthy process of being interviewed by authorities or providing testimony in court, victims are at risk of being retraumatized by repeatedly recalling the traumatic event. Child victims may also be fearful of retaliation by their adult offender.

The potential long-term effects of childhood sexual abuse may continue well into a victim's adulthood. They include depression, anxiety, PTSD, sexual dysfunction, substance abuse, and suicidal ideation. Adults who were sexually abused as children are more likely to develop a psychiatric disorder than their nonabused counterparts. About two-thirds of female victims of childhood sexual abuse that involved sexual penetration develop PTSD at some point in their lifetime.

TREATMENT

There are several types of psychological treatments that are effective for reducing the short-term and long-term effects of childhood sexual abuse by helping victims to develop coping strategies for symptoms of depression, anxiety, and PTSD. Trauma-focused play therapy is sometimes used in the treatment of children who are victims of sexual abuse. Group-based psychotherapy is effective in allowing sexual abuse victims to interact and thereby reduce feelings of isolation. Group counseling of the victim and the victim's family is focused on strengthening the parent-child relationship in order to better process the trauma and improve family dynamics. Therapists may include a social worker, psychologist, or psychiatrist and should have specific training and experience in working with childhood victims of sexual abuse.

Incest, considered one of the most damaging forms of molestation because of the close, trusting relationship between the victim and the abuser, is often likened to clergy sexual abuse of minors because of the trusting role of the cleric in relation to the victim. Among incest victims, children who promptly reported the molestation and received immediate treatment tended to experience a higher degree of recovery. By contrast, incest victims who carried their secret for years, either because they did not report the molestation or because they tried to but were not believed, tended to fare worse. In addition, less permanent injury occurs in victims of abuse that is infrequent and not physically invasive and that occurs either before or after adolescence.[73] One of the primary goals in treatment is to dispel the idea commonly held by victims that the abuse was their fault, which in later life can lead to self-destructive behaviors such as alcoholism, substance abuse, and eating disorders. Psychotropic medications are sometimes utilized to alleviate depression and anxiety.

Support groups have also proved to be an effective component in the treatment of victims of sexual abuse, including abuse by clergy. In addition to allowing victims to talk openly about their abuse, support groups also show that the victim is not alone and need not suffer in isolation. One such group is the Survivors Network of those Abused by Priests (SNAP). Founded in 1988, SNAP grew from nine local chapters in 2002 to a membership of more than 4,500 people in 44 chapters nationwide by February 2003. "Our self-help groups provide a safe, confidential and independent place for hurting men and women to recover from this traumatic childhood pain," according to Terrie Light, a San Francisco social worker and founding member of the organization. "Through our support groups, individual survivors learn they are no longer alone. They learn coping and recovery strategies and become empowered to break their silence, report their abuse to the proper authorities, and protect others at risk."[73] SNAP founding member Barbara A. Blaine, a Chicago lawyer and social worker, cited a study by the University of Chicago that identified as many as 100,000 possible victims of clergy sexual misconduct in the United States.[74] For such victims, Blaine compiled "Survivors Wisdom," a document that provides a step-by-step guide for victims of clergy sexual misconduct. The guide encourages victims to:

1. Acknowledge their courage
2. Know that they are not alone
3. Avoid confronting church officials before seeking legal advice
4. Avoid meeting alone with church officials
5. Seek alternative help
6. Learn their legal rights

In addition, the guide offers advice on seeking treatment for behaviors that arose as the result of the sexual misconduct, such as alcoholism, drug addiction, and eating disorders, and it emphasizes that victims remember that the abuse was not their fault. The full text of "Survivors Wisdom," as well as myriad information for victims of clergy sexual misconduct, is available at SNAP's web site, at www.snapnetwork.org.

The Interfaith Sexual Trauma Institute (ISTI) at St. John's Abbey and University in Collegeville, Minnesota, provides a web page (http://www.csbsju.edu/isti/Victims%20Affiliations.html) with an extensive listing of groups that provides assistance to victims of sexual abuse. ISTI, established in 1994, is composed of an advisory board with members from various denominations with the goal of preventing clergy sexual abuse and misconduct through research, education, and publications.

Treatment is also available to sexual abuse offenders, although there is some debate whether the proclivity to sexually abuse children can ever be overcome. Thus, the primary goal of treating sexual offenders is to minimize the likelihood that the individual will reoffend and to rely on an appropriate aftercare setting that eliminates any contact between children and the sexual offender. Treatment of the sexual offender is designed to modify the emotional and psychological factors that support the offender's desire to offend. Successful treatment of the sexual offender focuses on educating the offender about his or her individual pattern of offending, including an awareness of the cues that lead to the pattern of behavior. In other words, the goal is to teach sexual offenders how to identify circumstances that place them at greater risk for reoffending and how to avoid placing themselves in those circumstances. Other components of sexual offender treatment include accepting responsibility for sexually offending, developing empathy for victims, and changing thinking patterns that allow sexual offenders to rationalize their behavior.

PREVENTION

Prevention of childhood sexual abuse includes the use of public awareness campaigns to address the issue and raise awareness of the warning signs of victimization. Symptoms that indicate possible sexual abuse in children and adolescents include attempts to touch the genitals of others, sexualized play, detailed knowledge of sexual activity that is age-inappropriate, reluctance to undress, avoidance of touch, being easily startled, bed-wetting, and excessive fatigue. Emotional symptoms in children and adolescents can include regression to a younger age, withdrawal, irritability, excessive guilt, feelings of helplessness, excessive crying, self-mutilation, and suicidal thoughts.

Prevention also involves offering services to specific groups considered to be at high risk of victimization. For example, prevention programs include school-based safety education and assault prevention classes for children. The goal of such programs is to increase awareness among children on the issue of sexual abuse and how best to respond to a suspected incident of sexual abuse.

Sexual Misconduct and the Clergy

To help prevent clergy sexual abuse and misconduct, ISTI developed the following recommendations for clergy in all religious denominations:

- Examine how abuse of power through the sexual misconduct of clerics is reinforced by the documents and traditions of their faith.
- Eliminate entitlement, which is defined as appropriating for oneself privileges of position for personal advantage at the expense of others, to reduce the likelihood of the abuse of a privileged position.
- Establish regular forums within faith communities to foster a closer relationship between clergy and congregants in an atmosphere of equality.
- Foster an awareness among clergy that their power is rooted in the community of the faithful and in the service of their congregation's spiritual growth.
- Eliminate the appearance of secrecy and implement a policy of complete disclosure concerning incidents of suspected clergy sexual misconduct in the interest of providing justice to victims and a sense of truthfulness within the congregation.
- Promote gender equality, including an awareness that many of the religious symbols and the language of texts that have historically condescended toward women may have fostered a dependence that made women vulnerable to clergy sexual misconduct.
- Require courses on human sexuality in seminaries and training programs for clergy.
- Develop meaningful programs to offer consolation, assistance, and treatment to victims of clergy sexual misconduct and their families.
- Establish training programs for clergy on recognizing and respecting personal boundaries.
- Recognize how some theologies and religious teachings may have contributed to unhealthy attitudes about sexuality and thereby increased vulnerability to being both sexually abusive and abused.
- Educate congregations about clergy sexual misconduct and church procedures on how to deal with incidents of suspected misconduct.
- Cooperate with researchers attempting to compile empirical data on the incidence and causes of clergy sexual misconduct and rely on empirical data when establishing and refining policies to prevent clergy sexual misconduct.

Prevention may also be facilitated through programs that offer services to victims of childhood sexual abuse with the goal of minimizing the risk of victims becoming offenders. Many sexual abuse offenders claimed that they were sexually abused as children.

IMPACT ON CONGREGATIONS

Incidents of clergy sexual misconduct have a severely negative impact on the church where the offending cleric served, according to psychologist and former priest Stephen Rossetti. One measure of congregational response to clergy sexual misconduct is financial. According to results of a Gallup Poll released in December 2002, 40 percent of Catholics said they were less likely to contribute money to the church because of the sexual abuse of young people by priests.

In the Boston archdiocese, a fund-raising campaign launched in June 2001 with the goal of raising $300 million by the end of 2002 had raised only $190 million during that time period. In addition, the 2002 annual appeal drive to raise funds for diocesan operations collected less than half its $17 million target. Nationally, foundations that contribute to Catholic dioceses reported that contributors were sometimes demanding assurances that their money would not be used to fund sex abuse settlements or creditors in the event of a diocesan bankruptcy.[76]

The public's perception of the clergy has suffered as the result of clergy sexual misconduct, particularly the Roman Catholic sexual abuse scandal. According to a 2003 Gallup Poll, when asked to rate the honesty and ethics of 21 professions, only 52 percent of Americans gave high ratings to clergy, down from 64 percent in 2002, and a peak of 67 percent in 1985. Catholics who were surveyed were particularly critical of their clergy, with only 50 percent of Catholic respondents giving high ratings to their clergy, compared with 57 percent of Protestants.[77]

According to the poll, clergy ranked fourth in honesty and ethics overall, behind nurses (79 percent), military officers (65 percent), and high school teachers (64 percent). Business executives fared worse than clergy, with a 17 percent approval rating, possibly as the result of recent business scandals involving companies such as Enron and WorldCom. Car salesmen and telemarketing representatives received the worst ratings at six and five percent, respectively.

HOMOSEXUALITY AS A RISK FACTOR FOR PEDOPHILIA

Homosexuality was identified as a risk factor in the sexual abuse of adolescent males but not the cause of such abuse, according to information presented at a private Vatican symposium in April 2003, attended by officials charged with managing the sexual abuse crisis in the Catholic Church.[78] Among the presenters was Dr. Martin P. Kafka of the Harvard Medical School. Kafka, a specialist in sexual impulsivity disorders, emphasized that while it was a risk factor, it was not the cause of sexual abuse by priests. Kafka noted that other risk factors included stress and recent ordination, since most priests who abused minors did so within seven years after ordination. Presenters at the symposium urged church leaders to foster open discussions on sexuality among newly ordained priests and to improve the supervision of priests.

However, according to professor of psychology Michael R. Stevenson, a review of scientific research literature strongly suggested that adult males who sexually molest young boys are not likely to be homosexual. Writing in the September 2002, edition of *Angles*, the policy journal of the Institute for Gay and Lesbian Strategic Studies, Stevenson stressed the need for leaders of the Catholic Church and other denominations to foster healthy sexual development among seminarians and candidates for the ministry, regardless of their sexual orientation. Stevenson differentiated sexual orientation, which refers to feelings of emotional or romantic attraction and sexual interest, from sexual behavior, including the aberrant behavior of child sexual abuse, and cautioned against equating same-sex behavior with homosexual orientation. In other words, according to Stevenson's research, deviant sexual behavior, including same-sex behavior, was not a reliable indicator of an individual's sexual orientation, be it homosexual or heterosexual.

Pedophilia is defined as the act or fantasy of engaging in sexual activity with prepubescent children as the preferred or exclusive method of achieving sexual excitement. Pedophiles often delude themselves into believing that their sexual contact with a victim is beneficial to the child. Offenders are usually known to the children they molest, and are often friends or family members. While the exact causes of pedophilia are not known, certain risk factors have been identified, one of which is a history of childhood sexual abuse. Methods of treatment for pedophilia include aversive conditioning, in which negative stimuli are used to discourage the offending behavior, such as a foul odor at the time of arousal. Aversive behavioral conditioning that uses shame as the negative stimulus is sometimes known as shame therapy. Positive conditioning, such as social skills training, are also sometimes utilized. In empathy training, the offender takes the perspective of his victim in order to understand the harm caused by the offender. Thus far, the effectiveness of treating pedophilia has been uneven. For example, men who prefer boys are twice as likely to re-offend as those who prefer girls, and the use of alcohol increases the likelihood of relapse.[79]

Pedophilia, the sexual attraction to prepubescent children, is distinguished from ephebophilia, which is the sexual attraction to children or adolescents around the time of puberty, often teenagers. However, the term pedophilia is commonly used to refer to the sexual attraction to a minor of any age.

MOVING FORWARD

On February 28, 2004, a day after the United States Conference of Catholic Bishops (USCCB) released the John Jay College of Criminal Justice's research study on the nature and scope of the problem of sexual misconduct by U.S. Catholic priests between 1950 and 2002, USCCB president Bishop Wilton D. Gregory declared that the sexual abuse scandal was history, saying it was time for the Catholic Church to move forward. At the same time, victims' advocacy groups, including Survivors Network of those Abused by Priests (SNAP), issued statements that many issues were yet to be addressed by the USCCB, including the possible removal of bishops who allowed sexually abusive priests to continue in ministries with young people. Other questions lingered as well, such as whether the Catholic Church should abandon its requirement of priestly celibacy, or if the historical culture of secrecy within the Catholic clergy will hinder the enforcement of reforms on sexual misconduct implemented by the USCCB.

Clergy of other faiths face similar challenges. There are roughly 500,000 Protestant clergy in the United States. Surveys vary as to the prevalence of sexual misconduct among Protestant clergy, but it is generally estimated in the range of 1 to 3 percent. By extrapolation, that would amount to between 5,000 and 15,000 clergy—a significant number. Buddhism, Judaism, Islam, and other major religions have also grappled with incidents of sexual misconduct.

Instituting serious reforms, as done by the Catholic Church and other denominations, represents a beginning. However, the success of such reforms depends on the willingness of the traditionally closed cultures of clergy and religious hierarchy to open themselves to review and monitoring by secular authorities.

---

[1] Butterfield, Fox, "789 Children Abused by Priests since 1940, Massachusetts Says," *New York Times*, July 24, 2003, p. 1A.

[2] Both quotes from Getlin, Josh, and Geraldine Baum, "Cardinal Law Steps Down, Apologizes for 'Mistakes.'" *Los Angeles Times*, December 14, 2002, p. A1.

[3] Underwood, Anne. "Abuse of Power as a Justice Issue." *Paper, Voice of the Faithful*, 2002, p. 2.

[4] United Methodist Church. "Definition of Sexual Misconduct." *The 2000 Book of Resolutions*, 2000, p. 136.

[5] Catholics for a Free Choice. "Sexual Abuse and Misconduct in the Catholic Church: Selected Cases from Media Reports Through 2002." *Sex Abuse Chart*, 2003, p. 1.

Example

[6] Simpkinson, Anne A. "Soul Betrayal." *Paper*, Beliefnet, Inc., 2001, p. 1.

[7] Diocese of San Jose. "Some Definitions from Diocesan Policy on Sexual Misconduct." *The Valley Catholic: The Official Good News of the Diocese of San Jose Since 1982*, vol. 20, May 21, 2002, p. 5.

[8] Hall, Dinah. "It's Not Just Happening in Boston." *Working Together to Prevent Sexual and Domestic Violence*, vol. 22, Spring 2002, p. 1.

[9] Von Sternberg, Bob, "Sexual Misconduct by Clergy Is Found among All Faiths," *Star Tribune*, April 23, 2002, p. A1.

[10] Grenz, Stanley J., and Roy D. Bell. *Betrayal of Trust: Confronting and Preventing Clergy Sexual Misconduct, Second Edition*. Grand Rapids, Mich.: Baker Books, 2001, p. 55.

[11] Sipe, A. W. Richard. *A Secret World: Sexuality and the Search for Celibacy*. New York: Brunner/Mazel, Inc., 1990, p. 32.

[12] Sipe, *A Secret World*, p. 33.

[13] De Rose, Peter. *Vicars of Christ: The Dark Side of the Papacy*. New York: Crown Publishers, Inc., 1988, p. 111.

[14] Sipe, *A Secret World*, p. 36.

[15] Hehl, E. D., ed. *Die Konzilien Deutschlands und Reichsitaliens, Vol 6*. Hannover: Hahn, 1987, translated by Professor Timothy Reuter, p. 33.

[16] Sipe, *A Secret World*, p. 36.

[17] The term *antipope* refers to a pontiff elected in accordance with canon law who sat in opposition to the actual pope and whose claim to the papacy has since been declared invalid.

[18] Sipe, *A Secret World*, p. 37.

[19] Goodstein, Laurie, "Celibacy Issue Flares Again within Ranks of U.S. Priesthood," *New York Times*, September 5, 2003, p. A5.

[20] Jenkins, Philip. *Pedophiles and Priests: Anatomy of a Contemporary Crisis*. New York: Oxford University Press, 1996, p. 94.

[21] Bruni, Frank, and Elinor Burkett. *A Gospel of Shame: Children, Sexual Abuse, and the Catholic Church*. New York: HarperCollins Publishers, Inc., 2002, p. 35.

[22] Gary R. Schoener. From a presentation at the Second International Conference of Sexual Exploitation by Professionals, Minneapolis, Minn., 1992, p. 5.

[23] Grenz, Stanley J., and Roy D. Bell. *Betrayal of Trust*, p. 34.

[24] Lampman, Jane, "A Wider Circle of Clergy Abuse," *Christian Science Monitor*, June 14, 2002, p. 31.

[25] Bruni, *A Gospel of Shame*, p. 39.

[26] Bruni, *A Gospel of Shame*, p. 37.

[27] Investigative staff of the *Boston Globe*, *Betrayal: The Crisis in the Catholic Church*. New York: Little, Brown and Company, 2003, p. 29.

[28] Goodstein, Laurie, Anthony Zirilli, and the research staff of the *New York Times*. "Decades of Damage: Trail of Pain in Church Crisis Leads to Nearly Every Diocese." *New York Times*, January 12, 2003, p. 1–1.

[29] Investigative staff of the *Boston Globe*, *Betrayal*, p. 7.

[30] Rezendes, Michael, and Matt Carroll, "16 Priests Named for First Time in Sexual Abuse Lawsuits," *Boston Globe*, January 30, 2003, p. B6.

Introduction

31 Matchan, Linda, and Stephen Kurkjian, "Man Says Charge Made Before Porter Was Priest," *Boston Globe*, October 23, 1992, p. A1.
32 Arnold, David, "Questions Are Catching Up to Ex-Priest in Abuse Case," *Boston Globe*, May 20, 1992, p. A1.
33 Franklin, James L., and Linda Matchan, "Porter Gets 18–20 Years," *Boston Globe*, December 7, 1993, p. A1.
34 Kurkjian, Stephen, "68 Victims Settle Porter Case with Catholic Church," *Boston Globe*, December 4, 1992, p. A1.
35 Matchan, Linda, and Stephen Kurkjian, "Despite Past, Jailed Ex-Priest Seeks 'Just One Chance,'" *Boston Globe*, July 14, 2002, p. A1.
36 Carroll, Matt, et al., "Church Allowed Abuse by Priest for Years," *Boston Globe*, January 6, 2002, p. A1.
37 Carrol, "Church Allowed Abuse by Priest for Years," p. A1.
38 Margaret Gallant, quoted in Carroll, "Church Allowed Abuse by Priest for Years," p. A1.
39 Carroll, "Church Allowed Abuse by Priest for Years," p. A1.
40 Carroll, "Church Allowed Abuse by Priest for Years," p. A1.
41 A. W. Richard Sipe, quoted in Carroll, "Church Allowed Abuse by Priest for Years," p. A1.
42 Pfeiffer, Sacha, "Dozens More Allege Abuse by Late Priest," *Boston Globe*, April 4, 2002, p. A1.
43 Pfeiffer, Sacha, "Memos Reveal Trail of Charges," *Boston Globe*, June 5, 2002, p. A16.
44 Investigative staff of the *Boston Globe*, *Betrayal*, p. 59.
45 Pfeiffer, "Memos Reveal Trail of Charges," p. A16.
46 Pfeiffer, "Memos Reveal Trail of Charges," p. A16.
47 Pfeiffer, Sacha, and Steve Kurkjian, "Priest Says He, Too, Molested Boys," *Boston Globe*, January 26, 2002, p. A1.
48 Kurkjian, Stephen, and Walter V. Robinson, "Suit Ties Boy's Death to Abuse by Priest," *Boston Globe*, April 11, 2002, p. A1.
49 Roderick MacLeish, Jr., quoted in Robinson, Walter V., and Thomas Farragher, "Shanley's Record Long Ignored," *Boston Globe*, April 9, 2002, p. A1.
50 Investigative staff of the *Boston Globe*, *Betrayal*, p. 67.
51 Investigative staff of the *Boston Globe*, *Betrayal*, p. 67.
52 Cardinal Humberto S. Medeiros, quoted in Investigative staff of the *Boston Globe*, *Betrayal*, p. 68.
53 Investigative staff of the *Boston Globe*, *Betrayal*, p. 68.
54 Bishop Robert J. Banks, quoted in Investigative staff of the *Boston Globe*, *Betrayal*, p. 70.
55 Rezendes, Michael, and Sacha Pfeiffer, "Church Steps on Shanley Detailed," *Boston Globe*, January 28, 2003, p. B1.
56 Robertson, Tasha, "Shanley Couldn't Outrun Past," *Boston Globe*, April 19, 2002, p. A1.
57 Investigative staff of the *Boston Globe*, *Betrayal*, p. 205.
58 Paulson, Michael, "Scandal Eclipses a Far-Reaching Record," *Boston Globe*, December 14, 2002, p. A1.

[59] Paulson, Michael, "Scandal Eclipses a Far-Reaching Record," p. A1.

[60] Paulson, Michael, "Scandal Eclipses a Far-Reaching Record," p. A1.

[61] Butterfield, Fox, "Catholic Church Installs New Boston Archbishop," *New York Times*, July 31, 2003, p. A1.

[62] Robinson, Walter V., and Stephen Kurkjian, "Allegations against Two Priests Draw Scrutiny," *Boston Globe*, August 22, 2002, p. A1.

[63] Survivors First, Inc., *Interim Report of Number of Allegedly Abusive Priests in the United States*, June 18, 2003, p. 7.

[64] Bunting, Glenn F., Ralph Frammolino, and Richard Winton, "Archdiocese for Years Kept Claims of Abuse from Police," *Los Angeles Times*, August 18, 2002, p. A1.

[65] Stammer, Larry B., "Mahony Resisted Abuse Inquiry, Panelist Says," *Los Angeles Times*, June 12, 2003, p. A1.

[66] Jones, Arthur, "Church in Crisis: A Chronology of Sex Abuse in Southern California," *National Catholic Reporter*, January 31, 2003, p. 14.

[67] Guccione, Jean, "L.A. Judge to Oversee Sex Abuse Civil Suits." *Los Angeles Times*, June 18, 2003, p. B1.

[68] Pope John Paul II, quoted in "A Sin and a Crime." CBS News, April 19, 2002, p. 1. Available online. URL: http://www.cbsnews.com/stories/2002/04/19/national/main506674.shtml.

[69] Staff and wire reports, "Dioceses Across U.S. Sell Land, Borrow Money," *Cleveland Plain Dealer*, March 11, 2002, p. A1.

[70] Clayton, Mark, "Sex Abuse Spans Spectrum of Churches," *Christian Science Monitor*, April 5, 2002, p. A1.

[71] Watanabe, Teresa, "A Crisis of Many Faiths," *Los Angeles Times*, March 3, 2002, p. A1.

[72] Boodman, Sandra G., "How Deep the Scars of Abuse?" *Washington Post*, July 29, 2002, p. A1.

[73] Terrie Light as quoted in Survivors Network of those Abused by Priests, "Press Release." February 6, 2003, p. 1. Available online. URL: http://www.snapnetwork.org/snap_press_releases/35_new_chapters.htm.

[74] Blaine, Barbara A. "Survivors Wisdom" Survivors Network of those Abused by Priests, 2002, p. 1. Available online. URL: http://snapnetwork.org/survivors_wisdom/Survivors_wisdom_1.htm.

[75] Dominguez, Renee Z., et al. *Encyclopedia of Crime and Punishment, 2001*. Great Barrington, Mass.: Berkshire Publishing Company, 2001, p. 144.

[76] Paulson, Michael, "Refocused Church Seeking Donations," *Boston Globe*, December 22, 2002, p. A1.

[77] Religion News Service, "Clergy Ratings at Lowest Point Ever." *Christianity Today*. February 2003, p. 21.

[78] Allen, John L., Jr., "Homosexuality a Risk Factor, Vatican Told," *National Catholic Reporter*, April 18, 2003, p. 14.

[79] Nathan, P. E., et al. *Treating Mental Disorders: A Guide to What Works*. New York: Oxford University Press, 1999, p. 117.

CHAPTER 2

THE LAW OF CLERGY
SEXUAL MISCONDUCT

Clergy sexual misconduct occurs in a variety of settings and victimizes both children and adults. Federal remedy for sexual harassment under Title VII of the U.S. Civil Rights Act of 1964 has historically been unavailable to victims of clergy sexual misconduct due to the ministerial exception, which is codified under Title 42 of the U.S. Code, Section 2000e-1(a): "This subchapter shall not apply . . . to a religious corporation, association, educational institution, or society with respect to the employment of individuals of a particular religion to perform work connected with the carrying on by such corporation, association, educational institution, or society of its activities." However, in the case of *Bollard v. California Province of the Society of Jesus* (1999), the U.S. Court of Appeals, Ninth Circuit, ruled that the ministerial exception did not apply to a man who alleged that he was sexually harassed while attending a Catholic seminary. The case is discussed later in this chapter.

Offending clergy members have been successfully prosecuted under criminal law in state courts nationwide. Some states have modified their mandatory reporting laws to include clergy members among those who are duty-bound to report incidents of sexual abuse to law enforcement or child welfare agencies. In addition, victims of clergy sexual misconduct have filed hundreds of lawsuits in state civil courts. In 2002, the United States Conference of Catholic Bishops (USCCB) estimated that settlements in actions brought against the Catholic Church had already reached $250 million. At the same time, many states made it easier for victims to sue by extending statutes of limitations, thereby allowing victims to seek redress for offenses committed decades ago. To defend against allegations of clergy sexual misconduct, the Roman Catholic Church and other denominations have raised First Amendment issues, arguing that the U.S. Constitution's separation of church and state precludes state governments and the federal government from prosecuting or suing churches and church officials in cases of clergy sexual misconduct.

Clergy sexual misconduct is also governed by a growing body of policies by religious denominations. These policies put clergy members of all faiths on notice that they will be investigated and may be removed from their ministries at even the allegation of sexual misconduct. Church policies usually set forth procedures for the handling of allegations of sexual misconduct, such as establishing church committees to investigate the allegations and developing protocols for reporting the allegations to law enforcement authorities.

FEDERAL LAW

Just as each of the 50 states has statutes governing sexual assault, the U.S. government has laws against the sexual abuse of adults and minors that apply to residents of U.S. territories and federal prisoners who might otherwise fall outside the legal jurisdiction of a state. These laws are found in the U.S. Code, Title 18, Part I, Chapter 109A, sections 2241 through 2245, which deal with aggravated sexual abuse, sexual abuse, sexual abuse of a minor or ward, abusive sexual contact, and sexual abuse resulting in death, respectively.

SEXUAL HARASSMENT

Under U.S. law, sexual harassment is considered a form of sexual discrimination. Victims of sexual harassment that occurred in any of the 50 states may seek remedy in federal court, under Title VII of the Civil Rights Act of 1964. However, due to the ministerial exception contained in Title VII, victims of sexual harassment have historically been barred from bringing such actions against a church or religious organization. The ministerial exception was implemented so that Title VII would not be in conflict with the freedom of religion guarantees contained in the First Amendment of the U.S. Constitution.

In 1980, the U.S. Equal Employment Opportunity Commission (EEOC) issued guidelines on the identification and elimination of sexual harassment as an illegal form of sex discrimination in workplaces. Under the EEOC guidelines, sexual harassment was defined as

unwelcome sexual advances, requests for sexual favors, and other verbal or physical conduct of a sexual nature when: 1) submission to the conduct is made either explicitly or implicitly a term or condition of an individual's employment, or 2) submission to or rejection of the conduct by an individual is used as a basis for employment decisions affecting such individual, or 3) the conduct has the purpose or effect of unreasonably interfering with an individual's work performance or creating an intimidating, hostile, or offensive working environment.

The 1986 decision by the U.S. Supreme Court in *Meritor v. Vinson* clarified and strengthened the concept of "unwanted conduct," named sexual harassment as a form of illegal sex discrimination, and found that companies may be held liable for the misbehavior of an employee against another. In 1992, in *Franklin v. Gwinnett County Public Schools*, the U.S. Supreme Court expanded protection from sexual harassment to students in school classrooms, on playgrounds, on college or university campuses, and in the vocational training programs. The Court held that sexual harassment occurs whenever a student is demeaned or intimidated on the basis of gender, and the intimidation interferes with that student's education. Following up on *Franklin*, in 1999 the Supreme Court ruled in *Davis v. Monroe* that schools may be held liable for the sexual harassment of students if school officials knew about the harassment and did not take action to stop the harassment. In 1999, in *Bollard v. The California Province of the Society of Jesus*, the U.S. Court of Appeals, Ninth Circuit, effectively allowed a challenge to the ministerial exception under Title VII for actions arising out of allegations of sexual harassment. All the cases referenced are presented later in this chapter.

FIRST AMENDMENT ISSUES

Under the First Amendment to the U.S. Constitution, "Congress shall make no law respecting an establishment of religion, or prohibiting the free exercise thereof; or abridging the freedom of speech, or of the press; or the right of the people peaceably to assemble, and to petition the Government for a redress of grievances." Accordingly, some religious organizations faced with legal actions as the result of sexual misconduct by their clergy have attempted to shield themselves from litigation or criminal prosecution, arguing that because churches are entitled to complete autonomy under the First Amendment, they do not have to defend their handling of clergy in courts of law.

This rationale, known as the church autonomy doctrine, was unsuccessfully used in the 1990 U.S. Supreme Court case *Employment Division v. Smith*, in which the Court held that a defense of religious freedom under the First Amendment cannot be used under generally applicable criminal law. The issue in *Smith* was whether the religious use of peyote by certain Native American tribes was exempt from antidrug laws. The Court ruled that there is no religious exemption from criminal laws when those laws apply to all citizens. The *Smith* case is discussed later in this chapter.

In *Smith*, the church autonomy doctrine was unsuccessfully applied in a criminal prosecution. In 2003, the Boston archdiocese attempted to use the church autonomy doctrine in the civil arena to avoid being sued in some 500 separate lawsuits arising out of sexual misconduct by priests. Boston superior court judge Constance M. Sweeney rejected the archdiocese's argument that church officials were immune from civil actions based upon the First Amendment's guarantee of freedom of religion. Judge Sweeney ruled that it was unfair for church representatives to enjoy all the rights afforded by secular law yet bear none of the responsibilities imposed by the law to protect society. Because the civil lawsuits did not involve internal church disputes, plaintiffs were not barred from seeking redress from church officials for their allegedly negligent supervision of priests who were engaging in sexual misconduct with minors. However, in her ruling Judge Sweeney made two exceptions: She granted the archdiocese's motion to dismiss claims made in several lawsuits that church officials were negligent for allowing certain offending priests to be ordained and then not removing them from the priesthood. Judge Sweeney held that ordination and defrocking were purely ecclesiastical matters and, as such, were protected by the First Amendment. Judge Sweeney also dismissed the idea raised in several lawsuits that because a priest may function in his official capacity 24 hours a day, seven days a week, church officials must be held accountable for everything a priest does. Holding church officials to that standard would interfere with the separation of church and state, according to Judge Sweeney's ruling. The Boston archdiocese appealed the ruling, in part to satisfy its insurance carriers that the archdiocese was exhausting all legal avenues to defend itself. However, on April 1, 2003, a Massachusetts appeals court refused to hear arguments on the matter by the Boston archdiocese, effectively affirming the superior court ruling.

First Amendment protections have also been invoked by church officials to keep court documents under seal in order to avoid public disclosure of their contents. However, in a number of rulings, courts nationwide have either unsealed or refused to seal documents in sexual misconduct lawsuits, thereby making them available for public dissemination. In 2001, Boston Superior Court judge Constance Sweeney unsealed records from some 86 lawsuits brought by victims of former priest John Geoghan on the grounds that the public had a clear interest in the lawsuits. In May 2002, Connecticut Superior Court judge Robert F. McWeeney ordered the release of thousands of documents in 23 lawsuits against priests accused of sexual misconduct with minors, ruling that not releasing the documents would essentially make the court a party to a coverup. In 2002, newspapers in Tennessee, Kentucky, Ohio, Illinois, and Wisconsin successfully persuaded courts in their respective states to unseal court documents relating to clergy sexual abuse lawsuits. In January 2003, the *Arizona Republic* newspaper prevailed on motions before the Arizona Court of Appeals to release more than

2,000 documents relating to a grand jury investigation of the Phoenix diocese. In each ruling, courts placed the public interest over churches' claims of a right to confidentiality under the First Amendment's guarantee of freedom of religion. Although not binding as legal precedent, the rulings were expected to hold some sway on courts in other states in matters of public disclosure of church documents relating to clergy sexual misconduct.

STATE LAW

Most sex offenders are criminally prosecuted or sued in civil court under state law, and cases of clergy sexual misconduct and abuse are no exception. States also have what are known as mandatory reporting laws, which require certain professionals, such as doctors or teachers, to report suspected incidents of child sexual abuse to authorities. Increasingly, states are including members of the clergy as mandatory reporters.

STATUTES OF LIMITATION

Under both state and federal laws, sex offenses must be prosecuted within a certain period of time. These time limits are known as statutes of limitations. Although they vary from state to state, statutes of limitations for sex offenses usually run several years and customarily begin when the incident occurred. There are also statutes of limitations for civil causes of action, which allow victims of clergy sexual misconduct to sue in civil court for monetary damages. After the statute of limitations has expired, the crime or action can no longer be redressed under the law. A state-by-state listing of applicable statutes of limitations is provided in Appendix A.

Beginning in January 2003, California extended its statute of limitations for civil lawsuits brought by victims of clergy sexual misconduct. In addition to California, measures to extend the statutes of limitations for civil lawsuits were introduced in Arizona, Florida, Illinois, Maryland, Minnesota, New Hampshire, New York, Ohio, Pennsylvania, Wisconsin, and Washington.

In 1993, California enacted a new statute of limitations for sex-related crimes against minors that extended the time for the criminal prosecution of such offenses. Under the new law, a sex crime against a child could be prosecuted within one year after the crime was reported to police, no matter how long ago the crime was committed. On June 26, 2003, the U.S. Supreme Court ruled in *Stogner v. California* that the California law was unconstitutional if the statute of limitations in effect at the time of a sex crime against a minor had run out prior to the enactment of the new law. In other words, if the previous statute of limitations for a crime expired before the

1993 law took effect, that crime could not be prosecuted in criminal court. The decision in *Stogner* is presented later in this chapter.

MANDATORY REPORTERS AND PRIVILEGED COMMUNICATIONS

Each state and the District of Columbia has laws that identify mandatory reporters—persons who are duty-bound by law to report suspected incidents of child abuse, including sexual abuse. Some states require any person who suspects that a child is being physically or sexually abused to report the matter to authorities. They include Delaware, Florida, Idaho, Indiana, Kentucky, Maryland, Mississippi, Nebraska, New Hampshire, New Jersey, New Mexico, North Carolina, Oklahoma, Rhode Island, Tennessee, Texas, Utah, and Wyoming. Other states identify only certain professionals such as physicians and social workers as mandatory reporters. Members of the clergy are specifically listed as mandatory reporters in Arizona, California, Connecticut, Maine, Minnesota, Mississippi, Montana, Nevada, New Hampshire, North Dakota, Oregon, Pennsylvania, and West Virginia. However, in certain cases, mandatory reporting laws may sometimes be at odds with the issue of privileged communications, which is the legal duty of certain professionals to maintain confidentiality with their clients or patients. This can include the clergy-penitent privilege. Generally, such privileged communications are exempt from the reporting laws. However, in some states, including New Hampshire and West Virginia, the clergy-penitent privilege is denied in cases of suspected child abuse and neglect.

Appendix B contains a state-by-state listing of mandatory reporting laws and how those laws apply in cases involving privileged communications.

U.S. SUPREME COURT CASES

Sexual Harassment

MERITOR SAVINGS BANK V. VINSON, 477 U.S. 57 (1986)

Background

In 1974, Michelle Vinson was hired by Sidney Taylor, a vice president of Meritor Savings Bank in Washington, D.C., and she began working at the bank as a teller. In September 1978, Vinson notified Taylor that she was taking sick leave for an indefinite period. On November 1, 1978, the bank terminated Vinson for excessive use of that leave. Vinson then alleged that she had been sexually harassed by Taylor during her four years of employment at the bank, in violation of Title VII of the Civil Rights Act of 1964.

During an 11-day bench trial, Vinson testified that, soon after she began working at Meritor Savings Bank, Taylor invited her out to dinner and suggested that they go to a motel together. According to Vinson's testimony, at first she refused, but out of fear of losing her job she agreed. From 1974 until 1977, Vinson estimated that she had sexual intercourse with Taylor between 40 or 50 times and that Taylor fondled her in front of other employees, exposed himself to her in the women's restroom, and forcibly raped her. Taylor denied having any sexual activity with Vinson.

Legal Issues

The trial court denied Vinson's claim for monetary relief without resolving the conflicting testimony about the existence of a sexual relationship between Vinson and Taylor. Instead, the court ruled that if a sexual relationship existed, it was a voluntary relationship and, therefore, Vinson "was not the victim of sexual harassment and was not the victim of sexual discrimination" while employed at the bank. On appeal, the Court of Appeals for the District of Columbia Circuit concluded that the trial court's finding that the sexual relationship between Vinson Taylor "was a voluntary one" did not address the central issue: If "Taylor made Vinson's toleration of sexual harassment a condition of her employment," the voluntary nature of their sexual relationship "had no materiality whatsoever." The court also held that evidence of advancement in exchange for sexual favors was not the only measure of sexual harassment, and that the creation of a hostile or offensive working environment, in and of itself, constituted sexual harassment.

Decision

The Court of Appeals for the District of Columbia Circuit reversed the trial court's decision and held that an employer is liable for sexual harassment practiced by supervisory personnel, whether or not the employer knew or should have known about the misconduct. The U.S. Supreme Court unanimously affirmed the decision, holding that a claim of "hostile environment" sex discrimination is actionable under Title VII, and that "the [trial court's] findings were insufficient to dispose of [Vinson's] hostile environment claim."

Impact

The Supreme Court's ruling expanded the meaning of sexual harassment beyond advancements in exchange for sexual favors by affirming the court of appeals holding that a hostile working environment created by sexually inappropriate behavior constituted sexual harassment. Also, the Court established that the voluntary nature of a sexual relationship between an employee and a supervisor did not preclude actionable conduct under Title VII of the Civil Rights Act of 1964. The Court's ruling was later successfully applied in a religious setting in the 1999 case of *Bollard vs. the Society of Jesus* (discussed later in this chapter), in which a Catholic seminarian claimed he was sexually harassed by a superior and prevailed in his action against the superior's religious order under Title VII.

FRANKLIN V. GWINNETT COUNTY PUBLIC SCHOOLS, 503 U.S. 60 (1992)

Background

Christine Franklin was a student at North Gwinnett High School in Gwinnett County, Georgia, from September 1985 to August 1989. On December 29, 1988, Franklin filed a complaint in the U.S. District Court alleging that she was subjected to continual sexual harassment beginning in the 10th grade from Andrew Hill, a coach and teacher at the high school. Franklin alleged that Hill asked about her sexual experiences with her boyfriend and inquired if she would consider having sexual relations with an older man. In addition, Franklin alleged that Hill forcibly kissed her on the mouth in the school parking lot, that he telephoned her at her home and asked if she would meet him, and that, on three occasions in her junior year, Hill coerced Franklin into having sexual intercourse with him. Franklin also alleged that the school district investigated Hill's sexual harassment of Franklin and other female students, teachers, and administrators but took no action to stop it, and that the school district discouraged Franklin from pressing charges against Hill. On April 14, 1988, Hill resigned on the condition that all matters pending against him be dropped. In response, the school district closed its investigation of him.

Legal Issues

The District Court dismissed Franklin's complaint on the ground that Title IX of the Education Amendment of 1972 did not authorize the awarding of monetary damages. As a result, Franklin's only legal remedy under Title IX was denied to her—even if she could prove that the allegations regarding Hill were true.

Decision

The Supreme Court reversed the ruling by the district court and held that monetary damages were available as a remedy for actions brought under

Title IX. In a unanimous ruling, the Court ruled that "the longstanding general rule is that, absent clear direction to the contrary by Congress, the federal courts have the power to award any appropriate relief in a cognizable cause of action brought pursuant to a federal statute."

Impact

By allowing legal remedy under Title IX of the Education Amendment of 1972, the Court expanded the rights of victims of sexual harassment, be they employees or students. Because of the religious exception, which historically barred action under Title VII against religious institutions to protect the constitutional separation of church and state, the significance of the Court's decision was not immediately felt in religious settings. However, in 1999, a Catholic seminarian successfully brought a suit against his religious order under Title VII, thereby creating the possibility of such actions in the future. (See *Bollard v. Society of Jesus* later in this chapter.)

BURLINGTON INDUSTRIES, INC. V. ELLERTH, 524 U.S. 742 (1998)

Background

Kimberly Ellerth quit her job after 15 months as a salesperson for Burlington Industries and alleged that she was subjected to constant sexual harassment by one of her supervisors, Ted Slowik, a mid-level manager who had the authority to promote employees, subject to approval by his higher-ups. In her complaint, Ellerth emphasized three incidents she construed as threats to deny her job benefits. Ellerth refused all Slowik's sexual advances, she suffered no retaliation, and was promoted once. Moreover, Ellerth never reported Slowik to his supervisors, despite her knowledge that Burlington Industries had a policy against sexual harassment. As a result, Ellerth's case was dismissed by the trial court, which granted a summary judgment to Burlington Industries.

Legal Issues

The Federal Circuit Court reversed the decision by the trial court. However, the reversal was based on eight separate opinions by the justices, without any consensus on a controlling legal rationale. One of the legal issues raised was if the standard for an employer's liability in sexual harassment cases could be based on the theory of vicarious liability or negligence. In other words, by allowing the sexual harassment to exist, even without the knowledge of higher-ups, Burlington Industries was culpable.

Decision

The Supreme Court held that, under Title VII of the Civil Rights Act of 1964, an employee who refuses the unwelcome and threatening sexual advances of a supervisor but suffers no adverse job consequences may still recover damages from the employer without showing the employer is negligent or otherwise at fault for the supervisor's actions.

Impact

In a 7 to 2 opinion, with Justices Clarence Thomas and Antonin Scalia dissenting, the Court established that, even when not carried out, threats to retaliate against an employee for not conceding to the sexual harassment of a supervisor constitute sexual discrimination by creating a hostile working environment. In other words, the Court held that a showing of severe or pervasive conduct, such as Ellerth made, constitutes proof of sexual harassment. The Court also established that an employer is negligent if the employer knew or should have known about sexual harassment in the workplace and failed to stop the offending conduct. Thus, under the ruling, an employer is vicariously liable for sexual harassment by an employee who is acting under the authority of the employing company or agency. However, in such cases, the Court ruled that an employer is entitled to present an affirmative defense that fulfills two necessary elements: (1) The employer exercised reasonable care to prevent and promptly correct the sexually harassing behavior, and (2) that the complaining employee unreasonably failed to take advantage of any preventive or corrective opportunities provided by the employer. At the time of the Court's ruling in 1998, recourse under Title VII against religious institutions was precluded under the ministerial exception, which was designed to protection the constitutional separation of church and state. However, in 1999, in the case of *Bollard v. the Society of Jesus* (presented later in this chapter), a Catholic seminarian prevailed in his challenge of the ministerial exception for sexual harassment under Title VII.

BETH ANN FARAGHER, PETITIONER V. CITY OF BOCA RATON, 524 US 775 (1998)

Background

Beth Ann Faragher was employed as a lifeguard for the city of Boca Raton, Florida. After terminating her employment, Faragher alleged that her immediate supervisors, Bill Terry and David Silverman, had created a "sexually hostile atmosphere" at work by repeatedly subjecting Faragher and other female lifeguards to "uninvited touching" and other offensive and sexually provocative conduct that constituted discrimination under Title VII of the Civil Rights Act of 1964.

Legal Issues

The trial court ruled that the city was liable for the harassment of its supervisory employees, Terry and Silverman, for the following reasons: (1) the sexual harassment was pervasive and the city should have known of the harassment, (2) Terry and Silverman were acting as the city's agents when they committed the harassing acts, and (3) a third supervisor knew of the harassment and failed to notify city officials. On appeal, the U.S. Court of Appeals, Eleventh Circuit, reversed the trial court's ruling. Relying on *Meritor v. Vinson*, the Court of Appeals held that Terry and Silverman were not acting within the scope of their employment when they engaged in the harassing conduct, and that, despite the pervasiveness of their conduct, the City of Boca Raton did not have constructive knowledge of the sexual harassment. Therefore, the city was not negligent in failing to prevent the sexual harassment of Faragher by Terry and Silverman.

Decision

In a 7 to 2 ruling, with Justices Antonin Scalia and Clarence Thomas dissenting, the U.S. Supreme Court held that "the Eleventh Circuit's judgment must be reversed." In so ruling, the Court noted that "the degree of hostility in [Faragher's] work environment rose to the actionable level and was attributable to Silverman and Terry, and it is clear that these supervisors were granted virtually unchecked authority over their subordinates." In addition, the Court found that the city of Boca Raton "entirely failed to disseminate its sexual harassment policy among the beach employees and that its officials made no attempt to keep track of the conduct of supervisors. . . . Under such circumstances, the Court holds as a matter of law that the City could not be found to have exercised reasonable care to prevent the supervisors' harassing conduct."

Impact

By applying the vicarious liability standard to employers in sexual harassment cases, the Court clarified that employers have a proactive duty to protect their employees from sexually harassing supervisors or fellow employees. In effect, the Court said that it was not sufficient for an employer to simply put forth a policy on sexual harassment without appropriate follow-up and without providing lower-level employees with access to senior supervisors in order to enforce such a policy. As in previous decisions by the U.S. Supreme Court on the issue of sexual harassment as defined under Title VII, the impact of the ruling was not immediately felt in religious settings due to the ministerial exception, designed to protect the constitutional separation of church and state. However, the 1999 case of *Bollard v. Society of Jesus* (presented later in this chapter) successfully challenged the ministerial exception and set the stage for possible future action against religious organizations for sexual harassment.

DAVIS V. MONROE COUNTY BOARD OF EDUCATION, 120 F.3D 1390 (1999)

Background

In 1992, LaShonda Davis was a fifth-grade student at Hubbard Elementary School in the public school district of Monroe County, Georgia. One of her male classmates, identified as G.F., attempted to grope LaShonda's breasts and genital area and made sexually suggestive statements to LaShonda. The conduct continued over a period of months, and LaShonda reported each incident to her mother and to two classroom teachers. LaShonda's parents also contacted the teachers, who assured them that the school principal had been informed of G.F.'s conduct. However, G.F.'s conduct toward LaShonda escalated, and LaShonda's grades began to drop because she was unable to concentrate in G.F.'s presence. In April 1993, LaShonda's father discovered a suicide note written by LaShonda, stating in part, "I don't know how much longer I can keep G.F. off me." The incidents ended in May 1993, when G.F. pleaded guilty to sexual battery arising from his actions toward LaShonda. At no time during the period of LaShonda's harassment did the principal, or the school district, take any disciplinary action against G.F., except to warn him verbally about his conduct toward LaShonda.

Legal Issues

On May 4, 1994, a suit was filed in U.S. District Court against the Monroe County School District, the school district's administrator, and the principal of Hubbard Elementary School, alleging that G.F.'s actions constituted sexual harassment against LaShonda because they interfered with LaShonda's ability to attend school and study. The lawsuit further alleged that the defendants' "deliberate indifference" to G.F.'s sexual harassment of LaShonda created an "intimidating, hostile, offensive and abusive school environment," in violation of Title IX of the Education Amendments of 1972, which prohibits a student from being subjected "to any discrimination under any education program or activity receiving Federal assistance," as was the Monroe County School District at the time of the incidents involving G. F. and LaShonda.

Decision

The district court dismissed the case, in part by concluding that there was no basis for liability under Title IX unless the school board or an employee of the school board had a role in the sexual harassment. On appeal, the U.S. Court of Appeals, Eleventh Circuit, first reversed the district court, then, in a turn-about, granted a re-hearing and affirmed the district court's dismissal of the case, ruling that while school boards are liable for employees who engage in discriminatory conduct, they are not liable from student-on-student harassment.

The U.S. Supreme Court granted review and reversed the district court, holding that under Title IX, a school board is liable for cases of student-on-student harassment where the board showed a "deliberate indifference" to the sexual harassment, and when the harassment is "so severe, pervasive, and objectively offensive that it can be said to deprive the victims of access to the education opportunities or benefits provided by the school."

Impact

By allowing action under Title IX of the Education Amendments of 1972 for sexual harassment in schools, the Court broadened the avenues of remedy for victims of sexual harassment. In addition, the Court set a new standard of liability of school boards by holding them responsible not only for the actions of their employees but also for the actions of students and others under their authority when the school board demonstrates "deliberate indifference" to sexual discrimination occurring within a school district. Although the application of the Court's ruling in religious settings was unclear due to the ministerial exception, which was designed to protect the constitutional separation of church and state, two cases of note successfully challenged the ministerial exception. In the 1999 case *Bollard v. the Society of Jesus* (presented later in this chapter), a seminarian successful sought remedy for sexual harassment from a superior under Title VII. In 2002, in the case of *McKelvey v. Pierce* (presented later in this chapter), the New Jersey Supreme Court allowed a former candidate for the Catholic priesthood who claimed he was subjected to a sexually hostile work environment to proceed with a lawsuit for wrongful termination. Because the action was not pursued under Title VII, the decision in *McKelvey* opened the door for a wider range of lawsuits arising from sexual harassment to be brought against religious organizations, including the possibility of legal action under Title IX.

The First Amendment and Freedom of Religion

EMPLOYMENT DIVISION, OREGON DEPT. OF HUMAN RESOURCES V. SMITH, 494 U.S. 872 (1990)

Background

Alfred Smith and Galen Black were members of a Native American Church in Oregon. Smith and Black engaged in the sacramental use of peyote, a hallucinogen, during the course of religious services. Oregon law prohibited the "knowing or intentional possession of a controlled substance," unless prescribed by a doctor, and classified such possession as a felony. Because Smith and Black were in violation of Oregon drug laws, they were fired from their jobs with a drug rehabilitation agency. They applied for unemployment compensation but were found to be ineligible for benefits because they were terminated for work-related "misconduct" as the result of their illegal possession of a controlled substance.

Legal Issues

Smith and Black appealed the decision by the Oregon Employment Division, arguing that the denial of unemployment benefits and the criminalization of their use of peyote violated their First Amendment rights to the free exercise of their religious beliefs. The Oregon Court of Appeals agreed with them and reversed the decision to deny unemployment benefits to Smith and Black. The Oregon Employment Division then appealed to the state supreme court, arguing that the denial of unemployment benefits was justified because, by consuming peyote, Smith and Black had engaged in criminal conduct in violation of Oregon's drug laws. The Oregon State Supreme Court upheld the lower court's decision in favor of Smith and Black. The Oregon Employment Division then appealed to the U.S. Supreme Court.

Decision

In a 6 to 3 decision delivered by Justice Antonin Scalia, the Supreme Court reversed the rulings of the Oregon courts and held that the denial of benefits to Smith and Black was justified under Oregon law and did not violate the free exercise of religion clause of the First Amendment. The Court ruled that conduct in the free exercise of an individual's religious belief does not excuse that individual from complying with valid state or federal laws that prohibit such conduct. In other words, secular laws that apply to all citizens trump an individual's right to engage in conduct in violation of those laws in the name of freedom of religion. As Justice Scalia wrote, "Because the ingestion of peyote was prohibited under Oregon law, and because that prohibition is constitutional, Oregon may, consistent with the Free Exercise Clause, deny Smith and Black's unemployment compensation when their dismissal results from use of the drug."

Impact

In *Smith*, the Court clarified that the First Amendment's guarantee of religious freedom was not intended as a blanket of immunity for individuals who engage in unlawful conduct, as long as the laws that are violated apply to all citizens. In cases of clergy sexual misconduct, courts nationwide have interpreted this ruling to mean that neither individuals nor church officials can claim First Amendment protection to avoid accountability for their illegal conduct. Courts have ruled that, although the ruling in *Smith* applied to criminal conduct, the same reasoning is valid in the civil arena. As a result, victims of clergy sexual misconduct have successfully sued monetary damages in civil court, while news organizations and others have prevailed in the unsealing of court documents in cases where church organizations have attempted to invoke the First Amendment to keep those documents secret.

Statutes of Limitations and Ex Post Facto Clauses

STOGNER V. CALIFORNIA, 123 S. CT. 2446 (2003)

Background

In 1998, Marion Stogner was indicted by a grand jury in California for child sexual abuse that occurred from 1955 to 1973, when the statute of limitations for such offenses was three years under California law. Stogner's indictment was made possible by a law enacted by the California legislature in 1993. As codified under California Penal Code section 803, the law permitted criminal prosecution for the sexual abuse of minors in cases where the statute of limitations at the time of the crime had expired, under the following conditions: "(1) A victim has reported an allegation of abuse to police; (2) There is independent evidence that clearly and convincingly corroborates the victim's allegation; and, (3) The prosecution is begun within one year of the victim's report [of sexual abuse]." Without the 1993 statute, the state of California could not have prosecuted Stogner because the three-year statute of limitations in effect at the time of Stogner's alleged crimes had expired by 1998, when charges were filed against him.

Legal Issues

Stogner moved for a dismissal of all charges on the ground that both the federal and state ex post facto clauses contained in Article I of the U.S. Constitution "forbids revival of a previously time-barred prosecution." Under the ex post facto clauses, the government cannot enact laws that apply retroactively to crimes that otherwise could not be prosecuted. Stogner argued that the California statute enacted in 1993 was just such a law and was therefore unconstitutional for permitting the retroactive prosecution of child sexual abuse crimes where the statute of limitations had already expired.

Decision

The trial court agreed with Stogner and granted his motion for dismissal. However, the California Court of Appeals reversed the decision and held that the 1993 California law did not violate the ex post facto clauses in the U.S. Constitution. Citing the California Supreme Court case of *People v. Frazer*, the court of appeal noted that "young victims often delay reporting sexual abuse because they are easily manipulated by offenders in positions of authority and trust, and because children have difficulty remembering the crime or facing the trauma it can cause." As a result, the court of appeal reasoned that the reporting of a child sexual abuse offense within the statute of limitations was sometimes precluded by the nature of the crime.

In a 5 to 4 decision, the U.S. Supreme Court reversed the California Court of Appeal and held that the 1993 California law was unconstitutional under the ex post facto clauses. In delivering the opinion of the Court, Justice Stephen Breyer, joined by Justices John Paul Stevens, Sandra Day O'Connor, David Souter, and Ruth Bader Ginsburg, held, in part, that "California's law subjects an individual such as Stogner to prosecution long after the State has, in effect, granted an amnesty. . . . [The statute] is unfairly retroactive as applied to Stogner. . . . We conclude that a law enacted after expiration of a previously applicable limitations period violates the *Ex Post Facto* Clauses when it is applied to revive a previously time-barred prosecution."

Justice Anthony M. Kennedy, joined by Chief Justice William Rehnquist and Justices Antonin Scalia and Clarence Thomas, delivered a strong dissent, noting that "the California statute does not criminalize conduct which was innocent when done; it allows the prosecutor to seek the same punishment as the law authorized at the time the offense was committed and no more; and it does not alter the government's burden to establish the elements of the crime. Any concern about stale evidence can be addressed by the judge and the jury, and by the requirement of proof beyond reasonable doubt. . . . Moreover, [the California statute] contains an additional safeguard: It conditions prosecution on a presentation of independent evidence that corroborates the victim's allegations by clear and convincing evidence. The statute does not violate petitioner's rights under the Due Process Clause. . . . The [majority of the] Court also disregards the interests of those victims of child abuse who have found the courage to face their accusers and bring them to justice."

Impact

The *Stogner* decision effectively derailed the criminal prosecutions of hundreds of cases of child sexual abuse in California, as well as in other states that enacted similar laws. In California alone, state officials estimated that pending prosecutions would be dropped in some 800 cases. "The best known cases are those involving Roman Catholic priests, more than 20 of whom have been arrested statewide [since January 2002] for allegedly abusing children," according to the *Los Angeles Times*. "Nearly all those cases will now have to be dismissed."[1] Indeed, on June 27, 2003, at 2:26 a.m., defrocked priest Lawrence Lovell was released from the Los Angeles County Jail, where he was awaiting trial on charges of sexually abusing four altar boys. Some 12 hours later, retired priest Michael Wempe was released from the same jail. Wempe was charged with the sexual abuse of five boys that occurred some 20 years ago. His bail had been set at $2 million.

Although the Supreme Court's ruling in *Stogner* did not apply to civil lawsuits brought by victims of alleged clergy sexual abuse, it may still have some impact on such cases. As reported in the *Los Angeles Times*, "Without criminal convictions, the work of lawyers representing hundreds of people who claim they are victims of childhood sexual abuse by Roman Catholic priests just got a little tougher." The ruling in *Stogner* effectively increased the burden of victims of clergy sexual misconduct "because they, not the state, are going to be the ones who will have to actually prove that the molestations occurred," according to Loyola Law School professor George Vairo. "The responsibility falls on us as the sole remaining road to justice for the survivors of clergy sexual misconduct," said Larry Drivon, a Stockton, California, attorney representing some 300 alleged victims of clergy sexual abuse.[2]

OTHER COURT CASES

John Bollard v. the California Province of the Society of Jesus, et al., U.S. Court of Appeals, Ninth Circuit 196 F.3d 940 (1999)

Background

In 1988, John Bollard began studying to become a Catholic priest in the Society of Jesus, a religious order also known as the Jesuits. Between 1990 and 1996, Bollard alleged that he was sexually harassed by his Jesuit superiors at St. Ignatius College Preparatory School in San Francisco, California, and at the Jesuit School of Theology in Berkeley, California. Bollard claimed that his superiors made unwelcome sexual advances toward him, attempted to engage him in inappropriate sexual conversations, and sent him pornography. Bollard claimed that he reported the conduct to Jesuit superiors but they took no action. According to Bollard, the sexual harassment was so severe that he was forced to leave the Jesuit order in December 1996.

Bollard filed a complaint of sexual harassment with the California Department of Fair Employment and Housing, which, in turn, cross-filed his complaint with the U.S. Equal Employment Opportunity Commission (EEOC). In January 1997, Bollard received a "right to sue" letter from the EEOC and filed a lawsuit in Federal District Court alleging that he was sexually harassed in violation of Title VII of the Civil Rights Act of 1964.

Legal Issues

The district court ruled that Bollard had no valid legal complaint due to the ministerial exception to Title VII, which "precludes civil courts from adjudicating employment discrimination suits by ministers against the church or religious institution employing them." On appeal, the U.S. Court of Appeals, Ninth Circuit, noted that the "source of the ministerial exception is the Constitution . . . [and] courts have uniformly concluded that the Free Exercise and Establishment [of religion] Clauses of the First Amendment require a narrowing construction of Title VII in order to insulate the relationship between a religious organization and its ministers from constitutionally impermissible interference by the government."

Decision

The court of appeals reversed the district court's dismissal of Ballard's claim under Title VII (although the court noted that dismissal might be warranted on other technical grounds). Significantly, the court held that the application of Title VII was constitutionally permissible because Bollard's allegations in no way interfered with the free exercise of religious beliefs, as guaranteed by the First Amendment. The court found that the "Jesuits do not offer a religious justification for the harassment Bollard alleges; indeed, they condemn it as inconsistent with their values and beliefs. There is thus no danger that, by allowing this suit to proceed, we will thrust the secular courts into the constitutionally untenable position of passing judgment on questions of religious faiths or doctrine. The Jesuits' disavowal of the harassment also reassures us that the application of Title VII in this context will have no significant impact on their religious beliefs or doctrines. Moreover . . . Bollard does not complain that the Jesuits refused to ordain him or engaged in any other adverse personnel action" that would be outside the scope of federal relief under ministerial exception of Title VII. "On the contrary . . . the Jesuit order has enthusiastically encouraged Bollard's pursuit of the priesthood. . . . [Thus], the only relevant decision that we can reasonably attribute to the Jesuits on the facts alleged here is the decision not to intervene to stop or curtail the sexual harassment Bollard reported."

Impact

The court permitted Bollard's claims to proceed under Title VII while, at the same time, acknowledging the validity of the ministerial exception that allows churches and religious organizations the freedom to choose their own clergy without being subjected to allegations of employment discrimination under Title VII. In other words, had Bollard demanded reinstatement in the Jesuit order, the court could not have allowed Bollard to proceed under a Title VII claim because that would have constituted interference in a religious organization's freedom to choose its own clergy. Because Bollard was only seeking damages, not reinstatement, the court held that Bollard's allegations had no impact on the Jesuit's selection of their priests and, therefore, Bollard was entitled to pursue his claim of sexual harassment under Title VII.

CHRISTOPHER J. MCKELVEY V. WILLIAM C. PIERCE, ET AL., 173 N.J. 26 (2002)

Background

From 1989 to 1993, Christopher J. McKelvey attended St. Charles Borromeo Seminary in Wynnewood, Pennsylvania, in preparation for becoming a Catholic priest. A student handbook in use at St. Charles during that time stated that "seminarians were expected to refrain from dating." In

Sexual Misconduct and the Clergy

1993, Bishop McHugh of the Camden, New Jersey, diocese issued a statement in response to allegations of sexual abuse made by other individuals in the diocese that "the Church vehemently opposes all sexual misconduct . . . by clergy and others in Church positions." Upon his graduation from St. Charles, McKelvey began internships at Our Lady of Lourdes in Glassboro, New Jersey, and at the Church of the Incarnation in Mantua, New Jersey. While living at a rectory, McKelvey alleged that one of the priests there repeatedly discussed his homosexual lifestyle with McKelvey and invited McKelvey to accompany him to gay bars. McKelvey alleged that the same priest attempted to draw him into conversations about "masturbation and other sexual acts." In addition, McKelvey alleged that one of his supervisors at the rectory "attempted to engage him in sexually related topics [of conversation], including homosexual acts." McKelvey also alleged that a third individual at the rectory invited him "to go dancing at gay bars." In November 1993, as a result of the unwanted sexual advances, McKelvey took a voluntary leave of absence. When he did not return, the diocese terminated his candidacy for the priesthood.

Legal Issues

After his candidacy for the priesthood was terminated, McKelvey was notified by the Diocese of Camden that he owed more than $69,000 for tuition, books, and other fees paid on McKelvey's behalf by the diocese while McKelvey was studying for the priesthood. In turn, McKelvey filed suit against the diocese of Camden for breach of implied contract and tortious interference with his vocation. In other words, McKelvey alleged that "but for" the sexual harassment he suffered while an intern in the diocese, he could have completed his internship and become a candidate for ordination. Had he done so, McKelvey would have owed the diocese nothing for his education. Notably, McKelvey did not seek remedy under Title VII of the Civil Rights Act of 1964.

Decision

The New Jersey trial court dismissed McKelvey's case. The appellate division affirmed the trial court's decision and declined to decide whether McKelvey had an implied contract with the diocese. The appellate court held that "a decision to entertain [McKelvey's] action here would require the judicial branch to delve into religious matters outside our province, such as the conditions of the plaintiff's association with the Diocese, its disciplinary and supervisory decisions; whether [McKelvey] would have otherwise been ordained into the priesthood; and the extent to which he could be made whole from loss of life of spiritual service."

On appeal, the New Jersey Supreme Court reversed both lower courts. Citing the Ninth Circuit's ruling in *Bollard*, the New Jersey Supreme Court held that the

> *First Amendment is not violated so long as resolution of a claim does not require the court to choose between competing interpretations of religious tenets or to interfere with a church's autonomy rights. Churches and their ministers are not above the law and may be held liable for tortious conduct or contractual undertakings. It is simply not correct to conclude that secular courts lack jurisdiction to hear any dispute between a ministerial-type plaintiff and his or her church. The critical factor in the application of the ministerial exception to a given cause of action must be that resolution of the claim requires an impermissible inquiry into the propriety . . . of a church's choice concerning the hiring, termination, relocation, benefits or tenure of a person whose function at the church concerns the propagation of its faith. That is not the case here. No choice regarding McKelvey's ordination or employment was exercised by the Diocese.*

Impact

In it ruling, the New Jersey Supreme Court noted that it expressed no opinion regarding the merits of McKelvey's case against the diocese. The court's finding was that McKelvey had a right to pursue remedy and that others similarly situated have the same right, so long as there is no interference by a court in the operation of a church or religious organization.

CHURCH POLICIES ON SEXUAL MISCONDUCT

Many denominations have established policies on clergy sexual misconduct, while others continue to develop and revise such standards. Some faiths, generally those that are less hierarchical in structure, like Buddhism and Hinduism, have not set forth churchwide policies on clergy sexual misconduct. Still other denominations have opted to keep their policies internal, including the Mormon Church of Jesus Christ of Latter-day Saints, whose *Church Handbook of Instructions* includes procedures for disciplining members of their clergy. For those reasons, and because of the large number of religious congregations and sects in the United States, the following summary of church policies is not comprehensive. The omission of any religious organization does not imply a failure on their part to address the issue of sexual misconduct, nor should it be construed as such by the reader. On the contrary, congregations large and small throughout the United States have grappled with the issue of clergy sexual misconduct.

The six church policies summarized in this chapter are representative of major religious faiths in the United States: the Roman Catholic Church, the Episcopal Church, the Greek Orthodox Church, Reform Judaism, the Presbyterian Church U.S.A., and the United Methodist Church. Collectively, in 2003, these denominations accounted for some 80 million members nationwide. Of those, more than 65 million were Roman Catholics.

THE ROMAN CATHOLIC CHURCH

Roman Catholic Canon Law

Canon law governs the worldwide Catholic Church in religious matters, such as the sacraments of baptism, marriage, and ordination. All policies enacted by the church must comply with this body of law, which is found in legal codes such as the 1983 *Code of Canon Law* for the Latin Catholic Church and the 1990 *Code of Canons for the Eastern Churches*. Latin refers to the official language of canon law. Most Catholics in the United States belong to the Latin church. The body of canon law codifies some 2,000 years of religious life, much as federal and state laws in the United States represent legal norms that evolved over hundreds of years from the laws of England as well as those of ancient Rome and Greece.

In 1983, Pope John Paul II introduced the following into the general law for Catholics of the Latin rite: "If a cleric has . . . committed an offense against the Sixth Commandment of the Decalogue (Ten Commandments) with force or threats or publicly or with a minor below the age of sixteen, the cleric is to be punished with just penalties including dismissal from the clerical state if the case warrants it" (Cannon 139, Section 2). Although the Sixth Commandment literally forbids adultery, its meaning has been broadened to include all sins arising out of sexual misconduct. On April 25, 1994, in a temporary change to canon law for the U.S. Catholic Church, the pope extended the age of minority from 16 to 18 in cases of sexual abuse by a priest. That change was extended for 10 years in November 1998. Three years later, on May 18, 2001, Pope John Paul II made the change permanent and extended the scope of the law to the worldwide Catholic Church.

In 1983, a judicial process to investigate and prosecute crimes of clergy sexual abuse was added to canon law. In certain cases, a church trial is required by canon law. Also known as an ecclesiastical or canonical trial, a church trial is presided over by a bishop, acting as judge and jury, who may

The Law of Clergy Sexual Misconduct

appoint other judges to assist him. The pope is the supreme judge for the Catholic Church. Some key provisions added to canon law in 1983 included:

- A bishop must undertake a preliminary investigation of criminal allegations unless it would be "entirely superfluous." After the investigation, the bishop determines guilt and, if required, imposes a penalty.
- A bishop's ability to impose a penalty is limited. For example, dismissal from the clergy requires a church trial and cannot be imposed unilaterally by the bishop. Also, there is a statute of limitations of five years, generally, in cases of sexual misconduct. However, since 1994, actions may be brought until the victim reaches 28 years of age.
- At the commencement of church trial, the bishop may restrict the scope of ministry or duties of the accused cleric.
- A priest may reveal to law enforcement or other secular authorities any information relating to criminal conduct—unless the priest learns of the criminal conduct in the sacrament of confession. All information related to the priest during confession is secret, and a priest who reveals such information is subject to punishment, including excommunication.

Canon law also provides certain protections for the alleged perpetrator and victim of sexual misconduct. For example:

- The accused has the rights to counsel and to testify at trial and may be punished only in accordance with canonical procedure. Also, an offending cleric may appeal to the Vatican any decision rendered by a bishop or a church court.
- Alleged victims have the right to be present at trial and to petition for damages. The petition for damages must be submitted at trial or it is forfeited.

In May 2001, the Vatican announced changes to canon law governing the way bishops may investigate and punish acts of clergy sexual abuse. Contained in a letter approved by Pope John Paul II, the following changes were sent to Catholic bishops worldwide with the understanding that they take precedence over other church policies or guidelines:

- All information in cases of clergy sexual misconduct is protected by pontifical secret and must be submitted to the Vatican. A pontifical secret denotes the highest level of secrecy in the Catholic Church, and a breach of pontifical secrecy is punishable under canon law. Previously, there were no provisions for secrecy, except the requirement that records of criminal cases be retained in a secret archive of the diocese for 10 years. After 10 years, a summary of each record is retained and all remaining documentation is destroyed.

- Bishops may not take action beyond a preliminary investigation without permission from the Vatican. Previously, diocesan bishops were charged with applying the law themselves in accordance with the applicable provisions of canon law.
- Laypersons are forbidden from participating in church proceedings in cases of clergy sexual abuse of minors. Previously, a layperson could participate in such proceedings, except as the notary.

Canon law provides penalties for the negligent use of power, as follows:

- "One who abuses ecclesiastical power or function is to be punished in accord with the severity of the act or the omission not excluding deprivation from office unless a penalty for such abuse has already been established by law or precept" (Canon 1389, Section 1).
- "One who through culpable negligence illegitimately places or omits an act of ecclesiastical power, ministry, or function which damages another person is to be punished with a just penalty" (Canon 1389, Section 2).
- "Anyone who unlawfully inflicts damage upon someone by a juridic act, or indeed by any other act placed with malice or culpability, is obliged to compensate for the damage inflicted" (Canon 128).

Abuses governed by these canonical laws might include the scenario in which a bishop who is aware of credible allegations of sexual misconduct by a priest but nonetheless assigns that priest to a parish (a juridic act) without notifying the parish of the allegations. Similarly, a bishop's failure to investigate or punish a priest after having received allegations of sexual abuse might be construed as negligence.

The Five Principles

In 1985, the United States Conference of Catholic Bishops (USCCB), then called the National Conference of Catholic Bishops/United States Catholic Conference (NCCB/USCC), established five general guidelines for dioceses in cases of alleged sexual misconduct by a priest. Known as the Five Principles, the guidelines called for

1. removal of a priest accused of sexual offenses from his assignment;
2. referral of the offending priest for medical/psychiatric evaluation;

3. the offering of "solace and support" to the victim of the alleged sexual abuse and the victim's family;
4. protection of the confidential nature of the claim of sexual misconduct; and,
5. compliance with applicable laws, including mandatory reporting requirements.

Also in 1985, the Rev. Michael Peterson, president of the St. Luke Institute; the Rev. Thomas Doyle, a canon lawyer; and attorney Raymond Mouton drafted the resource paper "The Problem of Sexual Molestation by Roman Catholic Clergy: Meeting the Problem in a Comprehensive and Responsible Manner." An NCCB/USCC staff review of the final report concluded that most of the issues identified by the authors had already been analyzed for the bishops by other experts. As a result, one of the report's primary recommendations—to establish a national intervention team to respond to complaints of sexual misconduct in individual dioceses—was never implemented. Guided by the Five Principles, each diocese was free to use experts and other personnel of its own choosing in evaluating allegations of sexual misconduct by priests.

In June 1992, at its general meeting, the NCCB/USCC issued a statement on clergy sexual misconduct that basically restated the Five Principles developed seven years earlier. In November, a group of bishops, led by Los Angeles archbishop Roger Mahony, met in Washington, D.C., with victims of clergy sexual abuse. The NCCB/USCC announced the formation of a subcommittee on Priestly Life and Ministry on Sexual Abuse, which in February 1993 convened a think tank in St. Louis, Missouri, on the issue of clergy sexual abuse. In June 1993, an ad hoc committee on sexual abuse was created, with the following mandate:

1. assist bishops in dealing with sexually abusive priests;
2. examine ways to assist victims of clergy sexual abuse and their families;
3. examine the issue of morale among the Catholic clergy as it deals with offending priests;
4. assist bishops in screening candidates for ministry and in the reassignment of priests found guilty of sexual misconduct;
5. recommend safeguards against sexual abuse of minors by employees and volunteers of the church; and
6. address the national problem of sexual abuse of children.

The committee's report, *Restoring Trust, Volume I*, released in November 1994, reviewed more than 150 separate diocesan policies for dealing with clergy sexual misconduct. The report also included a listing of treatment centers for sex offenders, as well as articles on pedophilia and the impact of sexual abuse on victims and their families. In November 1997, the NCCB/USCC reauthorized the committee for three years with a mandate to focus on healing the victims of clergy sexual abuse, educating the clergy on the issue of sexual abuse, and exploring options for priest sex offenders with regard to their future role in the church, if any.

Charter for the Protection of Children and Young People, Revised

In January 2002, in response to the growing scandal involving pedophile priest John Geoghan and the mismanagement of Geoghan and other offending priests in the Boston archdiocese, then archbishop Cardinal Bernard Law announced a zero-tolerance policy on abusive clergy and agreed to turn over the names of all priests accused of sexual abuse to prosecutors. However, as the scandal widened beyond Boston and became national in scope, in June 2002, the USCCB met in Dallas, Texas, and drafted a national policy on clergy sexual misconduct. Entitled *Charter for the Protection of Children and Young People*, the policy was later revised by the Vatican. In November 2002, the revised policy was formally approved by the USCCB by a vote of 246 to 7. As revised by the Vatican, the policy reinforced the strictly advisory role of lay boards in reviewing allegations against priests. In addition, the revised policy clarified the definition of sexual abuse and strengthened the rights of the accused by allowing them to have trials before church tribunals. The policy can be applied not only to diocesan priests but also to priests who belong to a religious order, which accounts for about one-third of priests in the United States. According to the policy, when a priest is accused of sexual misconduct, a bishop must conduct a preliminary investigation. If there is evidence of the misconduct, the bishop then temporarily removes the priest from ministry and notifies the Vatican. The priest is entitled to a trial before a panel of church judges. In no case can a priest or deacon found to have committed sexual misconduct be transferred to another diocese, as was done in the Boston archdiocese, for example.[3]

The sexual abuse of a minor was defined as sexual molestation or sexual exploitation of a minor "and other behavior by which an adult uses a minor as an object of sexual gratification." The charter emphasized that sexual abuse of a minor need not be a complete act of intercourse, nor does an act "need to involve force, physical contact, or a discernible harmful outcome."

U.S. bishops apologized for the pain and suffering caused to victims and their families as the result of sexual abuse of minors by Roman Catholic priests, and for the mishandling of some of those priests by church officials. An atmosphere of secrecy in the church was blamed for allowing abusive priests to continue their sexual misconduct, sometimes for many years. However, the charter called for recognition of those bishops who implemented polices to safeguard minors based upon the Five Principles introduced by the NCCB/USCC in 1992, and gave credit to those bishops who took appropriate steps to deal with priests accused of sexual misconduct with minors. The bishops acknowledged the long-lasting damage inflicted on victims of clergy sexual misconduct and denounced the sexual abuse of minors as a crime against society and a sin in the eyes of God. Included in their condemnation were quotes of verses from the New Testament, including Jesus' warning that for anyone who would lead children astray, it would be better for that person "to have a great millstone hung around his neck and to be drowned in the depths of the sea" (Matthew 18:6). U.S. bishops promised to direct their energies toward providing a safe atmosphere for minors within the church, and to "repair the breach" with victims of clergy sexual misconduct, including opening a dialogue with victims and their families in order to demonstrate to society that the U.S. Catholic Church appreciates and understands the gravity of the sexual abuse of minors. To fulfill those goals, the bishops pledged to implement the following objectives:

1. **Promote healing and reconciliation with victims of clergy sexual abuse of minors.** Dioceses were required to establish outreach programs to victims and their families, if such programs were not already in place. Each diocese's outreach program was required to include all victims of clergy sexual misconduct within that diocese, whether the alleged misconduct occurred recently or many years before, and to offer counseling, spiritual assistance, support groups, and other social services agreed upon by the victim and the diocese. The bishop of each diocese or his representative was required to personally meet with each victim. For newly reported incidents of clergy sexual misconduct, each diocese was mandated to provide immediate pastoral care to the victim of the alleged misconduct. A review board with a majority of members not employed by the diocese was required to be in place to investigate the allegations, determine if the priest is suitable to remain in his ministry, and advise the bishop of its assessment. Procedures for lodging a complaint of sexual misconduct were required to be available in a printed format. Dioceses were forbidden from entering into so-called confidentiality agreements requiring victims to remain silent about the sexual misconduct in exchange for a settlement, except in certain cases where the victim requests confidentiality.

2. **To guarantee an effective response to allegations of sexual abuse of minors.** Dioceses were required to report any allegation of sexual misconduct with a minor to the civil authorities, to comply with all

laws governing the reporting of allegations of sexual abuse of minors and to cooperate with law enforcement and social service agencies charged with investigating the incident—even in cases where the victim is no longer a minor. Consequences for the alleged offender included immediate removal from his ministry, if warranted by preliminary findings, and a recommendation to seek immediate psychological evaluation. In cases where the allegations were unfounded, the diocese was required "to take every step possible . . . to restore the good name of the priest or deacon." However, in cases where the allegations were proved credible, either by the offender's admission or as the result of an investigation, the diocese was required to remove the offending priest from his ministry, pending possible removal from the priesthood if requested by the bishop and after a church hearing conducted according to the rules of canon law. In cases where the allegations of misconduct were proved true but the priest was not defrocked, he may still be banned from celebrating the Mass publicly, administering the sacraments, and wearing the clothing of a priest.

3. **To ensure the accountability of these procedures, the USCCB authorized the creation of the Office for Child and Youth Protection (OCYP).** Under its mandate, the OCYP was charged with assisting individual dioceses in the implementing of "safe environment" programs, auditing diocesan compliance with the USCCB's sexual misconduct policy, and issuing an annual report on the implementation of the policy that names dioceses found to be out of compliance with the policy. In addition, the USCCB's National Review Board (NRB) was charged with commissioning a comprehensive study of the causes and extent of clergy sexual misconduct within the U.S. Catholic Church, including statistics on perpetrators and victims.

4. **To protect the faithful in the future, each diocese was mandated to establish a "safe environment" program.** This program would provide education and training for children, parents, and clergy on creating and maintaining a safe environment for children within all church facilities and at church functions outside church facilities. Each diocese was required to evaluate the background of all diocesan and parish personnel who have regular contact with minors, including background checks conducted by law enforcement agencies. In addition, all candidates for ordination to the priesthood were required to be evaluated to determine their fitness for ordination with respect to issues of potential sexual misconduct. Any priest or deacon found guilty of an act of sexual misconduct with a minor was forbidden from being transferred for a ministerial assignment in another diocese. In addition, prior to any transfer of a priest, even to an administrative or

other non-ministerial position, the transferring diocese was required to provide the receiving diocese with all information concerning any act of sexual abuse of a minor and any other information indicating that the priest poses a potential danger to minors.

The charter concluded with a pledge by the USCCB to:

- Work for the protection of children and youth.
- Devote to this goal the resources and personnel necessary to accomplish it.
- Ordain to the priesthood and put into positions of trust only those who share this commitment to protecting children and youth.
- Work toward healing and reconciliation for those sexually abused by clerics.

Essential Norms for Diocesan/Eparchial Policies Dealing with Allegations of Sexual Abuse of Minors by Priests or Deacons

On June 14, 2002, the USCCB approved a list of rules governing the handling and reporting of clergy sexual misconduct known as the Essential Norms for Diocesan/Eparchial Policies Dealing with Allegations of Sexual Abuse of Minors by Priests or Deacons, to accompany the *Charter for the Protection of Children and Young People*. It was finalized after Vatican review on December 8, 2002. Some of the norms were technical in nature and dealt with bureaucratic mechanisms within the church. Those norms were omitted in the following summary. The remaining norms were condensed or simplified where appropriate.

- Each diocese must have a written policy on the sexual abuse of minors by priests and other church personnel.
- Each diocese must designate an individual to coordinate immediate assistance to any person who alleges they were the victim of sexual misconduct by a priest.
- Each diocese must establish a review board to serve in an advisory capacity to the bishop on incidents of clergy sexual misconduct. The board's functions include assessing the veracity of allegations of sexual abuse of minors and determining the suitability for ministry of the priest who is accused of sexual misconduct with a minor.
- Each review board must have at least five members, the majority of whom cannot be employed by the diocese or the Catholic Church. However, "at least one member should be a priest who is an experienced and respected pastor of the diocese in question, and at least one member should have

particular expertise in the treatment of the sexual abuse of minors." Board members serve for a period of five years, and their terms may be renewed by the bishop.

- When an allegation of sexual abuse of a minor by a priest is received, the reputation of the accused priest during the preliminary investigation will be protected as much as possible. If there is sufficient evidence to indicate that the allegation is true, as a precautionary measure the bishop will remove the accused priest from the ministry or from any ecclesiastical office or function and prohibit the priest from publicly participating in the Mass or from administering the sacraments pending the final outcome of the investigation. The alleged offender may also be asked, but not required, to seek psychological evaluation.

- In cases where "even a single act of sexual abuse by a priest" is established through admission by the priest or as the result of an investigation, the offending priest or deacon will be removed permanently from the ministry and may be removed from the priesthood on the recommendation of his bishop and pending an ecclesiastical hearing.

- The diocese in which the sexual misconduct occurred must comply with all applicable laws governing the reporting of allegations of sexual abuse of minors and cooperate in the ensuing investigation conducted by a law enforcement of social service agency.

- No priest who has sexually abused a minor may be transferred for ministerial assignment to another diocese for a ministerial assignment. In transferring such priests to non-ministerial assignments, the transferring diocese must advise the receiving diocese of all information concerning any act of sexual abuse of a minor and any other information indicating that he has been or may be a danger to children or young people.

Importantly, the policy provides that, in cases of substantiated sexual misconduct by a priest, removal from ministry is required whether or not the cleric is diagnosed as a pedophile or as suffering from a related sexual disorder that requires professional treatment.

THE EPISCOPAL CHURCH IN THE UNITED STATES OF AMERICA

Guidelines and Procedures for Preventing and Responding to Sexual Misconduct

The Episcopal Church's policy framed the issue of sexual misconduct within the broader scope of human sexuality, stating that "God values sexuality as good, blessed, and purposeful," and sexual misconduct deviates from "what it means to be Christian, to be a sexual person living by the Christian faith, and to be a servant in the church." The faithful are called upon to adhere to Christian ethical principles in their sexual conduct, as well as in their exercise of power and authority. Ministers are expected to model God's trustworthiness in their relationships with others within the church and to recognize the potential for serious harm if a betrayal of trust occurs within a ministerial relationship. In addition to being a violation of trust, clergy sexual misconduct is viewed as a breach of professional ethics with the potential of alienating a victim from the church.

As defined in the Episcopal policy, clergy sexual misconduct is an inappropriate and immoral act between a pastor and another person within the pastoral relationship that occurs whenever a member of the clergy uses the ministerial position of authority for the purpose of securing sexual gratification, including sexual contact that is criminalized under applicable laws. The policy distinguishes sexual abuse, sexual harassment, and sexual exploitation as follows:

- Sexual abuse is a sexual involvement or contact by a cleric with a person who is a minor or who is legally incompetent.

- Sexual harassment includes sexually oriented humor or language, questions or comments about sexual behavior or preference, unwelcome or undesired physical contact, inappropriate comments about clothing or physical appearance, or repeated requests for social engagements in a situation where there is an employment or colleague relationship.

- Sexual exploitation is a betrayal of trust in a pastoral relationship by the development, or attempted development, of a sexual or romantic relationship between a cleric and a person with whom the cleric has a pastoral relationship, and may include sexual intercourse, oral copulation, kissing, touching of breasts or genitals, dating during the course of a counseling relationship, verbal suggestions by a cleric of sexual involvement, or sexually demeaning comments by a cleric.

The policy also distinguishes between consensual and nonconsensual clergy sexual misconduct. In consensual, misconduct occurs when a legitimate romantic relationship is undertaken with the mutual consent of the cleric and the other person but there are subtle forms of coercion or abuse of the ministerial position of authority. On the other hand, nonconsensual sexual misconduct consists of unsolicited, unwelcome, nonreciprocal sexual overtures or conduct, either physical or verbal, by a cleric toward a colleague or congregant.

Several general guidelines were set forth in the policy, including the following:

- Clergy must maintain professional relationships when in the service of the church, including a pastoral counseling.
- Clergy must maintain "the highest ethical standards" when involved in parish activities for educational or recreational purposes.
- All employees of the church, whether members of the clergy or not, must exhibit ethical behavior with their colleagues at all times.
- The local bishop should be consulted in cases of a consensual romantic relationship between a cleric and a congregant.
- Members of the clergy as well as congregants are expected to obey all applicable laws relating to sexual misconduct.

The policy also set forth a series of "Guiding Principles" for the prevention and handling of clergy sexual misconduct, including the following:

- Every allegation of sexual misconduct reported to a bishop in writing must receive a formal response.
- Clergy accused of sexual misconduct are presumed innocent until proved guilty.
- The church will cooperate fully with law enforcement and any criminal investigation that ensues as the result of the sexual misconduct.

In cases of suspected clergy sexual misconduct with an adult, allegations must be made in writing to the bishop by the alleged victim, who must be identified by name. Should the victim report the sexual misconduct to a third party, such as a cleric or a member of the church staff or congregation, it is the responsibility of the third party to report the incident to the bishop, according to church guidelines. Upon receipt of the allegation, the bishop is required to respond with written acknowledgment of the allegation and is expected to meet with the reporting party within one month. The bishop is also required to meet with the offending cleric to state the allegations and receive a response, if any. The bishop may also choose to meet with or receive statements from any witnesses to the allegation. Finally, the bishop must consult with his superiors and may request assistance in the investigation of the allegation.

After the initial investigation, the allegations of sexual misconduct may be determined to be unsubstantiated. If so, the exonerated party may prepare a statement of innocence to be included in the personnel file. If the allegations appear to be true, a further investigation may proceed. In either case, the victim/person who made the allegation must be advised in writing of the bishop's decision.

When an allegation of clergy sexual misconduct is substantiated, the bishop must remove the offender from the ministry, pending a full investigation. If the allegation relates to a clerical position previously held by the offender, the bishop may remove the offending cleric from the cleric's current ministry, depending upon the seriousness of the allegations and how long ago the incident took place. The offending cleric is then referred for evaluation and treatment. The offending cleric's failure to comply with all such referrals are grounds for long-term suspension or permanent dismissal. In deciding on the future employment of the offender after treatment, the bishop's decision will depend on the advice and opinions of the professionals who provided treatment to the offender. Usually, reinstatement is considered only after a significant period of psychotherapy and employment outside the church.

The Episcopal policy on sexual misconduct also extends to lay employees and volunteers serving in church facilities or at church functions. Congregations are charged with developing clear policies with regard to lay employees and volunteers that include a statement on the reporting and handling of incidents of sexual misconduct, including the requirement that any incident of sexual misconduct by an employee or volunteer must be reported to the local bishop.

The Episcopal policy includes special provisions for the handling of incidents of sexual misconduct that violate criminal law. Allegations of such offenses must be made in writing to the local bishop and must be referred to law enforcement. If the allegations are made to a cleric or a staff member within the church, they are directed to refer the person making the allegation to local law enforcement. In cases of criminal offenses, the ensuing investigation must be conducted by law enforcement, not the bishop, and bishops are mandated to cooperate fully with the investigating agency. Although the bishop lacks authority to investigate criminal matters, the bishop remains responsible for the handling of the alleged offender according to church policy and must respond to concerns expressed by the congregation. As a general rule, a cleric accused of criminal sexual misconduct is removed from the ministry pending the conclusion of the criminal investigation. If found guilty, the offending cleric is subject to the full array of disciplinary provisions provided for by the church, including expulsion from the ministry.

Guidelines are also set forth for the pastoral care of victims of clergy sexual misconduct, including family members and affected congregations. The local bishop must refer the victim who is making an allegation of sexual misconduct to counseling services and is required keep that individual informed of the progress of the investigation. The bishop must be available to meet with and counsel the alleged victim's family members, as well as the family members of the alleged offender. The privacy of the alleged victim must be protected, and his or her identity must remain confidential whenever possible. If an allegation of clergy sexual misconduct is verified, the bishop is required to meet with the lay leadership of the congregation and provide them with a briefing of the allegations and findings, usually after disciplinary action is taken against the offending cleric. In turn, the lay leadership is required to assemble the members of the congregation and inform them of the findings of the investigation and the disciplinary actions taken against the offending cleric.

Because of the unsettling nature of such discussions, the Episcopal policy on sexual misconduct contains a primer on the Congregational Trauma Debriefing Process and a summary of the appropriate protocol, beginning with the following list of symptoms that may be displayed within the affected congregation:

- a loss of energy or a feeling of paralysis;
- distrust of leadership;
- divisions within the congregation regarding the allegations or the disciplinary actions taken;
- isolation and withdrawal by some congregants;
- displays of anger that are disproportionate to the underlying events;
- worry or despair about the parish's future.

Because these reactions can be anticipated, the Trauma Debriefing Process provides a structured process for the congregational meeting that allows congregants to process the events in question, explore the consequences, seek perspective, and plan for the future. This is accomplished by scheduling the debriefing as soon as possible after the event and holding the debriefing in the church, although not as a liturgical event. At the onset, the leader of the meeting should explain the process and guidelines for trauma debriefing and encourage honesty and openness by all participants without fear of reprisal. The facts of the event are presented by the bishop or bishop's representative, without interruption, followed by a period when congregants are free to ask questions and express their feelings. The leader of the meeting then asks congregants to explore repercussions of the incident, such as future leadership in cases where their pastor has been removed or suspended. Counselors and others trained in crisis intervention should be available to help individuals or small groups process the information further. After the meeting, the bishop should meet with the lay leaderships and professional counselors in attendance to discuss their experiences at the meeting.

Finally, the Episcopal policy discusses the prevention of clergy sexual misconduct. Guidelines include providing time off, including at least one uninterrupted day off per week, plus an annual vacation and a period for spiritual retreat in order to cope with the stress of their work. All clergy must receive a certificate of training in the prevention of sexual misconduct. Clergy are responsible to ensure that lay volunteers and staff members who have contact with children are trained in the prevention of sexual abuse and misconduct. Clergy are discouraged from placing themselves in potentially compromising situations, such as one-on-one counseling sessions with a congregant in an isolated setting or an extended period of counseling before referring the congregant to a mental health professional. Background checks are required for all clergy and employees prior to their hiring. Clergy must be aware of warning signs of potential sexual misconduct, including giving or receiving inappropriate gifts, meeting a congregant at an unusual time or location, and keeping secrets that go beyond the requirements of professional confidentiality.

GREEK ORTHODOX ARCHDIOCESE OF AMERICA

Statement of Policy Regarding Sexual Misconduct by Clergy

The Greek Orthodox Archdiocese of America's policy on clergy sexual misconduct set forth three general guides: to treat seriously all allegations of sexual misconduct; to educate its clergy and congregations on the issue and establish screening procedures for incoming clergy; and to cooperate fully with applicable civil laws.

To assist in the implementation of the guidelines, the church established an advisory board composed of a minimum of one bishop and an additional member of the clergy, a female, a licensed mental health professional, and an attorney, each appointed to a renewable term of two years. The advisory board, which reports directly to the archbishop of the Greek Orthodox Archdiocese of America, was established as an independent body to evaluate the effectiveness of the Greek Orthodox policy on clergy sexual misconduct and to propose changes to the policy. The advisory board is precluded from investigating specific allegations of clergy sexual misconduct.

A toll-free telephone number was established to respond to questions about this policy and to take complaints of sexual misconduct and refer them for investigation. As mandated under the policy, the telephone provides access to non-clergy contact persons trained and authorized by the archdiocese to receive reports of clergy sexual misconduct. The list of contact persons must include a minimum of one male, one female, one female fluent in English, and one male and one female fluent in Greek.

Sexual Misconduct and the Clergy

Contact persons selected by the chancellor of the archdiocese are obligated to share information received in their official capacity with the archbishop and other church personnel, as long as that individual is not the perpetrator of the alleged sexual misconduct. In addition, contact persons cannot serve as the counselor, advocate, or attorney for either the alleged perpetrator or victim of sexual misconduct.

The policy of the Greek Orthodox Archdiocese of America is one of zero tolerance for sexual misconduct and requires the archdiocese to implement an ongoing educational program on sexual misconduct for members of its clergy, as well as those in training for ordination. The policy requires verified cases of clergy sexual misconduct to be reported to the cleric's parish, and to "the church community in general." In cases where the cleric is exonerated, no such public airing of the charges is required. In general, disclosures to the parish are not to include the name of the victim, unless the allegation of sexual misconduct is a matter of public records, such as when criminal charges are filed against the offending cleric. The policy forbids retaliation against any individual who cooperates in an investigation of clergy sexual misconduct.

The policy requires any member of the church who knows or suspects a cleric of engaging in sexual misconduct to report the incident to the toll-free hotline or to speak directly with the parish's bishop or the chancellor of the archdiocese by telephone, in writing, or in person. The complainant may remain anonymous. However, when the reporting party is the victim of the alleged sexual misconduct, the complainant must be advised that the failure to disclose identity may impede the investigation. In cases of anonymous complaints, the chancellor is required to conduct an initial inquiry to determine if there is a basis for going forward with a full investigation. A complaining victim must be afforded counseling or pastoral care.

When the initial complaint of sexual misconduct is lodged with a contact person or the local bishop, that individual must immediately notify the chancellor of the archdiocese, who in turn will either initiate an investigation in the allegations or, if the complainant remains anonymous, begin an initial inquiry to determine if any investigation is warranted. In either case, the complainant and the victim must be informed that they may attend all proceedings and that they may be accompanied by a friend or family member, if they choose. In general, when the contact person who received the initial complaint is not a party to the sexual misconduct, the contact person is barred from attending the initial investigatory meetings but must be advised of the results of the investigation. In cases where the alleged incident must be reported to law enforcement, such as in acts of child molestation, the contact person is required to advise the complainant that such a report will be made.

After the complaint is received, the chancellor initiates an investigation, which may include interviews with parties to the sexual misconduct and a review of the offending cleric's personnel file or any other records relating to the parties involved. Consultation with mental health professionals is also permitted during the course of the investigation. The chancellor is required to keep the local bishop apprised of the investigation's progress. While the investigation is ongoing, all parties to the inquiry must keep the process confidential. Initially, the chancellor or his designated representative is required to interview the victim of the alleged sexual misconduct, either by telephone or in person. At that time, the victim can be asked to prepare a written summary of the incident to the chancellor. If the victim is reluctant to put the allegations in writing, the chancellor or his representative may prepare a written report of the allegations, which the victim will be asked to sign. However, refusal to sign the report is not grounds for automatic dismissal of the allegations, and an investigation may still proceed. The initial written report may be supplemented with additional findings. On the basis of the initial information, the chancellor makes a finding if "there is a reasonable basis for conducting further investigation."

If an investigation proceeds, the chancellor or his designee must meet with the accused cleric and inform the cleric of the allegations. The cleric may respond to the allegations at that time. However, any statements made by the cleric can be presented as evidence in a subsequent church hearing, and they may also be turned over to civil authorities in the event of a criminal investigation. In addition, the cleric accused of the misconduct must be offered pastoral or other professional counseling. All products of the investigation, including the complaint, statements, and reports, may be reviewed at any time by the archbishop, the local bishop, and the chancellor if he is not personally conducting the investigation. In addition, the accused cleric may be suspended from the ministry prior to the church hearing if, based on the investigation, the archbishop determines that the immediate suspension of a cleric is necessary.

In the event that the accused cleric admits to the allegations of sexual misconduct, or based on the investigation there is a reasonable possibility that the misconduct occurred, or if the chancellor determines that the accused cleric poses a threat of harm to members of his parish or to the public in general, a church hearing must be convened to make a final ruling on the allegations and to take disciplinary action against the offending cleric. The accused cleric is required to attend the hearing, which must be conducted according to the canons of the Greek Orthodox Church. At the conclusion of the church hearing, the victim and the offending cleric, as well as their families, must be offered ongoing pastoral counseling and support.

Sexual Misconduct and the Clergy

REFORM JUDAISM

Code of Ethics for Rabbis

In its Code of Ethics for Rabbis, the Central Conference of American Rabbis (CCAR) included the addendum Ethics, Guidelines, and Procedures for Responding to Allegations of Sexual Misconduct by CCAR Members. The CCAR's policy on sexual misconduct entrusts rabbis with the responsibility for ensuring that "ethical and sexual boundaries are scrupulously respected" in all rabbinical relationships. The policy states that sexual misconduct by rabbis "is a sin against human beings," and calls upon the CCAR to uphold the sacred calling of the rabbinate by creating just and appropriate responses to sexual misconduct, including responding promptly to all allegations of sexual misconduct. According to the policy, unacceptable behavior includes sexual harassment and intimidation, requests for sexual favors, and unwelcome verbal, physical, or visual conduct of a sexual nature. Even if the offending behavior is consensual, the policy deems the behavior to be unethical for exploiting the vulnerability of the victim and compromising the moral integrity of the rabbi.

Under the policy, the Committee on Ethics and Appeals is charged with investigating and adjudicating allegations of sexual misconduct made against members of the CCAR. When an allegation is made, a gender-mixed fact-finding team composed of two rabbis and a layperson responds to the complaint and conducts the investigation. Professional consultants such as psychologists with expertise in matters of sexual misconduct may also be included in the fact-finding team, as needed.

Anyone with knowledge of a suspected incident of sexual misconduct may report the allegation. Complaints must be in writing and must include the names of all parties involved, as well as specific details of the misconduct. If the complainant is unwilling to make a written complaint, a person may be designated to advise and represent the complainant in order to refer the complaint to the Committee on Ethics and Appeals.

The chairperson of the Committee on Ethics and Appeals is required to respond promptly and in writing to the complainant and to explain the process of investigation. The chairperson must also notify the rabbi against whom the allegation was made as to the nature of the allegations and the pending investigation. Next, the chairperson must assemble the fact-finding team and provide its members with copies of the complaint and the response from the rabbi, if any. However, if the complaint was made by a third party without the consent of the alleged victim, the Committee on Ethics and Appeals has the option of conducting a preliminary investigation into the matter before assembling the fact-finding team.

After consulting with all members of the Committee on Ethics and Appeals, the chairperson has the authority to notify the rabbi's supervisor of the complaint and pending investigation. However, the chairperson may defer to the rabbi accused of the offense and allow the rabbi to personally notify the rabbi's superiors. If the allegation is serious, the Committee on Ethics and Appeals may recommend suspending the accused rabbi pending the completion of the investigation.

Once the fact-finding team is assembled, the team is required to meet separately with the complainant, the rabbi suspected of the offense, and the victim, if the complaint was made by a third party. No more than two people may accompany any party during the meeting with the fact-finding team. Records of all such meetings and a detailed log of all telephone calls relating to the investigation must be maintained by the fact-finding team. During the investigation, and afterward, support services must be offered to the alleged victim, the rabbi accused of the offense, their families, and the affected congregation. When the investigation is completed, the fact-finding team must make one of the following three written recommendations to the chairperson of the Committee on Ethics and Appeals:

- A unanimous finding that there is not sufficient evidence to proceed to adjudication.
- A split finding, in which case the full Committee on Ethics and Appeals must determine whether to proceed to adjudication.
- A unanimous finding of sufficient evidence to proceed to adjudication.

In the event of a unanimous finding to proceed, the chairperson of the Committee on Ethics and Appeals must make a full report to the committee within two weeks of receiving the finding, if possible. The report must also be provided to the complainant and the rabbi accused of the offense. The Committee on Ethics and Appeals may request additional information from the fact-finding team, if necessary. Upon review of all information gathered in the investigation, the Committee on Ethics and Appeals may dismiss the complaint, in which case both the rabbi named in the allegation and the complainant have the right to appeal the committee's decision. However, once the committee confirms its decision, no further appeals are allowed.

If the committee finds that there is a basis for the complaint of sexual misconduct, both the rabbi named in the complaint and the victim are allowed to present their respective cases to the committee and to respond to questions from the committee prior to formal adjudication. Should the accused rabbi resign, the investigation and adjudication may still go forward, and the rabbi will be considered expelled.

If there is a finding of an ethical violation, the Committee on Ethics and Appeals may issue a reprimand, which is a form of admonishment privately communicated to the rabbi for a minor infraction of the rabbi's ethical code. Reprimand requires a two-thirds vote by the committee, with a minimum of six participating members. The rabbi may request to appeal the reprimand. For a more serious violation of the ethical code, the committee may impose a censure, which is a sanction that does not require suspension of the rabbi from rabbinical duties. A censure requires a two-thirds vote by the committee, with a minimum quorum of voting members. An order of censure must include conditions imposed upon the offending rabbi, such as psychological evaluation, counseling, or mentoring, and the order may also impose certain restrictions of the rabbi's rabbinical functions. If the rabbi fails to complete the conditions imposed in the order of censure, the Committee on Ethics and Appeals may recommend removal of the rabbi from all rabbinical functions, and the publication of the censure in the CCAR newsletter. In such cases, the offending rabbi has the right of appeal to the CCAR Board of Trustees. At the appeals hearing, both the offending rabbi and the complainant may present their respective cases and are required to answer questions from the Board of Trustees. If the decision of the Committee on Ethics and Appeals is confirmed by the Board of Trustees, no further appeal is possible.

In order for a rabbi to receive the sanction of suspension, there must be a finding that the rabbi's conduct caused significant harm to the victim or institutions involved, or the rabbi failed to recognize the wrongfulness of what was done and take responsibility for the offending actions, or the rabbi was censured but refused to comply with the conditions of censure, or the rabbi refused to cooperate in the investigation of the complaint. If the adjudication results in suspension, the rabbi has the right of appeal to the Board of Trustees. The board may uphold the suspension by a two-thirds vote or may reject the recommendation without imposing any sanctions. Notice of a rabbi's suspension must be published in the CCAR newsletter with reference to the specific provision of the code of ethics that was violated by the rabbi. The Committee on Ethics and Appeals must also notify the rabbi's supervisor and the rabbi's congregation. Once suspended, the rabbi can no longer work as a rabbi at any other institution. Only when the rabbi has completed all conditions of the suspension can the rabbi be reinstated.

Expulsion, the most serious sanction, is used for repeated violations, failure to comply with conditions of suspension, or willful failure to cooperate during the investigation or adjudication. A recommendation of expulsion requires a two-thirds vote of the members of the Committee on Ethics and Appeals. Upon such a recommendation, the offending rabbi may request to appear before the Board of Trustees and must answer all questions presented by board members. The board may dismiss the expulsion and impose a lesser sanction by a two-thirds vote. Likewise, expulsion of the offending rabbi requires a two-thirds vote by the Board of Trustees. As with a suspension, the rabbi's supervisor and congregation must be notified of the expulsion.

An expelled rabbi may petition the Committee on Ethics and Appeals to be granted the status of suspension. This status change requires a two-thirds vote by the Committee on Ethics and Appeals and by the CCAR Board of Trustees. If a status change is granted, the rabbi shall be subject to the same requirements outlined above for suspended colleagues.

A rabbi may be eligible for reinstatement after fulfilling the following requirements:

- unequivocal acknowledgment of responsibility for harm done to the victim and the congregation as the result of the rabbi's misconduct;
- an expression of remorse to those harmed by the rabbi's misconduct;
- the pledge to never again engage in similar misconduct;
- the making of restitution, which may include expenses incurred by the victim of the rabbi's misconduct;
- mentoring by at least two rabbinic colleagues appointed by the Committee on Ethics and Appeals;
- an appropriate course of therapy or counseling by a professional approved by the Committee on Ethics and Appeals;
- when a colleague is suspended, and sometimes when censured, there is both an intake and a final evaluation rendered to the Committee on Ethics and Appeals by a qualified professional, other than the rabbi's own therapist, chosen by the Committee on Ethics and Appeals.

Reinstatement of a rabbi requires a unanimous recommendation by the mentors, a positive assessment by the professionals involved in administering counseling or therapy, and a recommendation by affirmative vote of at least two-thirds of the Committee on Ethics and Appeals and by the Board of Trustees. As a condition of reinstatement, the rabbi is required to continue meeting with mentors for at least two more years.

PRESBYTERIAN CHURCH U.S.A.

Sexual Misconduct Policy and Its Procedures

According to the basic principles outlined in the policy of the Presbyterian Church U.S.A., sexual misconduct is a violation of trust, a misuse of authority and power that breaches Christian ethical principles and takes advantage of the vulnerability of children and persons who are less powerful to act for their own welfare. The policy acknowledges in cases of sexual misconduct that the needs of the victim, the accused, and the congregation must be met. To that end, an independent response coordination team is charged with coordinating a process to meet the specific needs of all parties to the incident of alleged sexual misconduct.

Members of the response coordination team are drawn from a pool of individuals deemed qualified to handle matters of a sensitive nature, such as sexual misconduct. Ideally, prior to an allegation of sexual misconduct, members should have specific training in how to respond in crisis situations involving alleged sexual misconduct.

The members of a response coordination team (RCT) select their own chairperson. Costs incurred by the RCT must be paid by the governing church body to whom the team reports. Members should serve for no less than three years, in order to build experience and expertise within the group. Each year, members of the RCT are encouraged to assemble for professional training and education on sexual misconduct.

Any individual within the church who becomes aware of an alleged incident of sexual misconduct is required to notify the chairperson of the RCT pool, who must then convene a team consisting of at least five gender-diverse individuals within five days of receiving the complaint. At its first meeting, the RCT receives a report on the nature of the complaint and the identity of the parties to the alleged incident of sexual misconduct. The RCT then notifies those parties of the complaint and of its role in handling the complaint. The RCT must also ensure that, when applicable, civil authorities are notified of the alleged sexual misconduct. The RCT is then charged with assisting the victim, the accused, and the congregation in dealing with the alleged sexual misconduct.

In cases where the victim or family is so outraged or alienated from the church that offers of help are perceived as insincere, the RCT is encouraged to continue offering assistance and discouraged from acting in a self-protective way by ignoring the needs of the alleged victim. The RCT is required to assume that, in all cases of sexual misconduct, the victim was injured, and to acknowledge the victim's feelings of guilt, shame, anger, mistrust, lowered self-esteem, unworthiness, and alienation from God and the religious community. In addition, the RCT is required to take seriously the victim's allegations of sexual misconduct, to offer the victim pastoral and psychological counseling, and to assure the victim that anything divulged in such counseling will remain confidential. The RCT must also inform the victim about church process once an allegation of sexual misconduct is made and to keep the victim apprised at all stages of that process. Also, the victim must be advised that independent legal advice is available and how to obtain such legal advice. Additionally, the RCT must advise the victim that an advocate may be provided to the victim to offer continuing moral support and to represent the victim at church hearings. The advocate may be someone of the victim's choosing, such as a relative, friend, or someone suggested by the RCT. The RCT must also advise the victim that several types of restitution may be available, including financial compensation, removal of the accused from the ministry, or an admission and apology from the accused.

As for the accused, feelings of guilt, shame, anger, mistrust, lowered self-esteem, depression, unworthiness, and feelings of alienation from God, self, the religious community, and family may be experienced by a cleric accused of sexual misconduct. In addition, there may be fear of job loss, incarceration, and indignation if an allegation is false. The RCT is required to recommend seeking legal advice as well as spiritual or professional counseling with someone whose conversations would be recognized by courts as confidential and privileged communication. Information about the allegation of sexual misconduct must be provided to the accused, preferably in writing. In most cases, the written communication must also advise the accused to avoid contact with the accuser, the victim, or the victim's family, and include a warning that any statements made to the RCT may be used against the accused in later proceedings. The RCT must recommend that the accused seek legal counsel, and that the accused has the right to remain silent or have an attorney present during questioning by church personnel about the alleged sexual misconduct.

The RCT must also be aware of the problems that may be experienced by a congregation following allegations of sexual misconduct by a minister, employee, or volunteer. The allegations may polarize the congregation and damage morale. As a result, there may be a need to utilize the services of a consultant or therapist with knowledge and experience in dealing with sexual misconduct, an attorney who can discuss legal aspects of a case, and possibly an insurance agent who can advise the congregation about their exposure to liability or coverage.

Once a special disciplinary committee has been appointed, the RCT closes its work on the matter, although the RCT may remain available to the victim, the accused, and the congregation to provide ongoing assistance. The RCT must maintain records of its proceedings, including detailed accounts of its actions, minutes of its deliberations and its conversations with all affected persons, copies of the initial report, correspondence, and copies of reports to the governing body of the church. When the matter is resolved, the RCT forwards its records to the personnel office of the governing body. Members of the RCT are forbidden from keeping duplicate records of material that has been turned over to the governing body.

In cases of child sexual abuse within the church, all persons covered by the church policy on sexual misconduct are duty-bound to report suspected child sexual abuse to their governing body. All persons should be informed of and must comply with state and local laws regarding incidents of actual or suspected child sexual abuse.

The policy of the Presbyterian Church U.S.A. permits some matters involving sexual misconduct to be resolved outside of the official judicial process of the church. Alternatives to judicial process include arbitration, negotiation, and mediation. Each method has strengths and weaknesses, depending on the nature of the conflict, and each must guarantee confidentiality to the parties, common agreement regarding the admissibility of evidence, and the due process rights of all concerned. In the context of sexual misconduct in the church, success of an alternative judicial process depends upon the degree and kind of injury suffered, the willingness of all parties to remedy that injury, the resources available to assist the processes of healing and remediation, and the expertise of the arbitrators, mediators, or other persons involved in facilitating the process. Informal or secret agreements that do not address the concerns of all parties involved are not considered to be in the best interest of the church.

In the arbitration, the parties to a conflict agree to submit the dispute to an independent person or panel to determine the best resolution. All parties have the opportunity to present their case to the arbitrator, and the arbitrator's decision may be final (binding) or subject to appeal to a higher authority (nonbinding), such as a disciplinary committee.

In negotiation, advocates for the parties are responsible for working out a solution that effectively resolves all issues and protects the interests of all parties. In some cases, a party to the action may serve as his or her own advocate.

In mediation, the parties are assisted by a professional mediator to work out their own agreement. Mediation differs from both arbitration and negotiation in that the power to make the final decisions is retained by the parties themselves. The successful outcome of a mediation depends upon the willingness of the parties to reach agreement, as well as the creativity of the mediator in helping to shape an agreement that is acceptable to all parties.

UNITED METHODIST CHURCH

Council of Bishops' Statement on Sexual Abuse in the Church

The Council of Bishops of the United Methodist Church pledged to prevent and eradicate sexual abuse and misconduct in the church and expressed a commitment to compassion and justice for those injured as the result of clergy sexual misconduct. The council also pledged that clergy and other persons within the church who sexually abuse will not be shielded or protected. Clergy sexual misconduct was framed as an abuse of power that occurs when members of the clergy use their power to gratify their own needs rather than to carry out God's sacred trust. The church has pledged to support equity among all persons without regard to ethnicity or gender and to create an environment of hospitality for all persons, male or female, that is free from misconduct of a sexual nature and encourages respect and equality. The policy recognizes that both clergy and laypersons in positions of authority in the church are vested with a moral responsibility and a sacred trust to maintain a safe environment. Ministerial leaders are cautioned to avoid harmful actions and words, and charged with the duty of those who are vulnerable from harm, including youth and adults who worship, study, and participate in other church-related functions such as camps and retreats.

According to the church policy, sexual misconduct within a ministerial relationship is defined as "a betrayal of sacred trust, a violation of the ministerial role, and the exploitation of those who are vulnerable in that relationship." Those in ministerial roles include clergy, educators, counselors, youth leaders, and others who function in positions of leadership within the church. Sexual abuse within the ministerial relationship occurs when such persons engage in sexual contact or sexualized behavior with a congregant, client, employee, student, staff member, coworker, or church volunteer. The policy defines sexualized behavior as that which communicates sexual interest or conveys sexualized intentions. Examples cited in the policy include displaying sexually suggestive visual materials, making sexual comments or innuendo, inappropriate or uninvited touching of another person, kissing, and sexual intercourse. Sexual harassment is defined as ongoing sexualized behaviors that intimidate, demean, humiliate, or coerce someone, ranging from subtle gestures or looks to stalking, assault, or rape.

The policy cites a 1998 survey authorized by the United Methodist Church's General Council and conducted by the church's General Commission on the Status and Role of Women. The aim of the survey was to assess the church's progress in four key areas of sexual misconduct: prevention, education, intervention, and recovery. Some 51 conferences within the United Methodist Church responded to the internal survey and identified the need for more training on sexual misconduct and the development of models for intervention and healing in order to provide a consistent and thorough response when complaints of lay or clergy sexual misconduct were initiated. In response, in 2000, the United Methodist Church authorized the General Commission on the Status and Role of Women to convene a cooperative work team to address the areas of prevention, education, intervention, and healing in matters of lay and clergy sexual misconduct. The cooperative work team was required to include members of the General Board of Global Ministries, the General Board of Higher Education and Ministry, the General Council on Finance and

Administration, the General Commission on the Status and Role of Women, and the General Board of Church and Society, and up to four additional experts on the prevention and handling of sexual misconduct. The work team was mandated to report its findings, actions, conclusions, and recommendations to the 2004 General Conference, including proposals for legislation if necessary.

The United Methodist Church authorized the General Commission on the Status and Role of Women to provide training on the issue and handling of sexual misconduct for leaders of lay events and programs within the church. The United Methodist Church also mandated the General Commission on the Status and Role of Women to ensure that resources for laity and clergy in ministerial roles are promoted in all church districts and local congregations.

The Council of Bishops reaffirmed its commitment to preventing sexual harassment, abuse, and misconduct within the church through education and training, and charged each episcopal area to develop ongoing plans on the prevention and handling of sexual misconduct. The Council of Bishops requires all United Methodist schools of theology to provide training on the prevention and eradication of sexual harassment, abuse, and misconduct within the ministerial relationship. In addition, annual conference boards of ordained ministers are required to provide annual training on sexual misconduct to all appointed clergy and for all newly appointed clergy.

The United Methodist policy cited the evolution of awareness, laws, and policies since the mid-1970s on the issue of sexual harassment. The policy identified sexual harassment as a type of sexual violence and a high-priority problem identified by the Ecumenical Decade of Churches in Solidarity with Women in 1998, the UN Conference on Women in Beijing in 1995, the reports of the International Labor Organization, in courts-martial in the U.S. military, and position statements of the European Women's Lobby to the European Union.

According to the policy, anyone in the workplace may be a target of sexual harassment, including males and females, as may anyone in an educational setting or in a church setting. The policy explained that the effects of sexual harassment on the victim are demeaning, humiliating, frightening, isolating, and intimidating, and that the experience of being sexually harassed in the workplace may damage the victim's self-esteem and productivity, and may result in illness, absenteeism, and poor performance. Similarly, for students, sexual harassment may led to academic failure, absenteeism, and isolation from peers. According to the policy, the effect of sexual harassment on individuals in a faith community are even more profound and personally devastating because a victim's spiritual life and faith in God and the church is jeopardized and sometimes permanently damaged. As such, the United Methodist Church declared sexual harassment to be "a sin against individuals and communities, and is a chargeable offense for our clergy and laity."

The Council of Bishops called for the elimination of sexual harassment and other forms of discrimination in the workplace. The bishops recognized the need for ongoing vigilance on the issue of sexual harassment in order to maintain effective policies and procedures for the church. The bishops required the regular training of lay and clergy leaders within the church on the issue of sexual harassment and supported the continuing work of intervention teams to respond to incidents of sexual harassment when they occur in a church setting.

The General Conference called for increased efforts worldwide to eradicate sexual harassment within the United Methodist Church and its institutions. It also called upon the General Commission on the Status and Role of Women to develop educational resources to assist United Methodists in understanding the issues of sexual harassment in church and society. The General Commission on the Status and Role of Women was also mandated to identify and develop resources on sexual harassment specific to clergy and lay leaders, students, and faculty. The General Council called for the implementation of plans to eradicate sexual harassment in each episcopal area within the United Methodist Church, with special focus on prevention, education, intervention, and recovery. The bishops called upon the church's annual conferences of ministers to encourage governmental agencies to collect accurate data on the incidence and nature of sexual harassment in church-related workplaces, and to lobby for laws aimed at eradicating sexual harassment. Bishops also mandated the General Board of Church and Society and the General Board of Global Ministries to advocate for federal laws that prohibit sexual harassment in the workplace.

In addressing efforts to reduce the risk of child sexual abuse within the United Methodist Church, the policy cites church law that "children must be protected from economic, physical, emotional and sexual exploitation and abuse." The policy acknowledges that churches have not always been safe places for children and that child sexual abuse and exploitation has occurred in churches large and small, urban and rural, cutting across all economic, cultural, and racial lines. According to the policy, child sexual abuse "is real, and it appears to be increasing." The policy acknowledges that incidents of child sexual abuse "are devastating to all who are involved: the child, the family, the local church, and its leaders," and that congregations run the risk of being divided and even destroyed by the ensuing legal, emotional, and monetary costs following allegations of child sexual abuse.

The General Council issued a series of mandates in 1996 aimed at reducing the risk of child sexual abuse within the church. Local churches are required to develop and implement an ongoing education plan for the congregation and its leaders on the scope of child sexual abuse, risk factors leading to such misconduct, and strategies for its prevention. Local churches are also required to adopt screening procedures for church workers and volunteers who are directly or indirectly involved in the care of children and youth, and to implement safety procedures for church activities, such as requiring two or more nonrelated adults to be present in a classroom or church activity, leaving doors open and installing half-doors or windows, providing hall monitors; and instituting sign-in and sign-out procedures for children ages 10 and younger. The General Council requires churches to advise children and young persons of an agency or a person outside as well as within the local church whom they can contact for advice and help if they have suffered sexual abuse, to carry liability insurance that includes sexual abuse coverage, to implement special curriculum to raise the awareness of children on the issue of sexual misconduct, and to train them in self-protection skills.

The General Conference requires the annual conference of ministers to develop safety and risk-reducing policies and procedures for conference-sponsored events such as camps, retreats, and other youth gatherings, and to develop guidelines and training processes for use by church leaders charged with preventing child sexual abuse in local churches.

---

[1] Winton, Richard, Jean Guccione, and Henry Weinstein, "California Molestation Law Struck Down," *Los Angeles Times*, June 27, 2003, p. A1.

[2] Lerry Drivan, quoted in Guccione, Jean, "Burden of Proof Falls on Victims in Sex Abuse Civil Suits," *Los Angeles Times*, June 28, 2003, p. B1.

[3] Paulson, Michael, and *Boston Globe* staff, "U.S. Bishops OK Revised Policy on Sex Abuse," *Boston Globe*, November 14, 2002, p. A1.

CHAPTER 3

CHRONOLOGY

This chapter presents a chronology of significant developments in the history of clergy sexual misconduct, including the evolution of ideas and policies on human sexuality within religious institutions and the development of laws governing sexual behavior.

circa 2000 B.C.

■ The concept of sexual misconduct is codified in the prohibitions against rape, sodomy, and adultery contained in the Code of Hammurabi, a body of Babylonian laws.

circa 1200 B.C.

■ Moses leads the Israelites out of slavery in Egypt to Sinai and receives moral instructions from God called the Decalogue. More commonly known as the Ten Commandments, these rules formed the foundation for the ethical systems of Judaism, Christianity, and Islam, and contained a prohibition against adultery.

circa 400 B.C.

■ Greek physician Hippocrates (460–370 B.C.) develops an oath of ethics for physicians, known as the Hippocratic Oath, which contains one of the earliest recorded references to the issue of physician-patient sexual misconduct. The oath, later rewritten for Christian physicians, advances a code of conduct applicable to all professionals in the healing arts, including therapists and members of the clergy in their roles as counselors, ministers to the sick, and spiritual advisers.

circa 100 B.C.

■ The Essenes, a small religious sect of ancient Israelites who believed in strict cleanliness and wore only white garments, encourage celibacy.

Sexual Misconduct and the Clergy

A.D. 325

- The Council of Nicaea, known as the First General Council of the Catholic Church, is convened by Roman emperor Constantine. The council forbids priests to marry after ordination. Prior to the ruling, during the first three centuries of Christianity, priests and bishops were allowed to be married at the time of their ordination and to remain married and have children while serving as clerics.

385

- Pope Siricius (pope, 384–399) decrees that after ordination, married men cannot have sexual relations with their wives.

401

- Augustine (354–430), bishop of Hippo Regis in the Roman province Numidia (Algeria), writes the treatise *On the Good of Marriage*, which sets forth the idea that all sexual expression is sinful, except as necessary for procreation within marriage. Augustine writes, "Nothing is so powerful in drawing the spirit of a man downwards as the caresses of a woman." Augustine's views on sexuality and women influence subsequent Catholic Church leaders who view priestly celibacy as a means of preventing the wives and children of clerics from inheriting church assets.

494

- Pope Gelasius I (Pope, 492–496) decrees that women can no longer be ordained to the priesthood, and condemns bishops who allowed the ordination of women.

circa 500

- The Buddhist sects of Zen and Amidism are established.

590

- Pope Gregory I (590–604), known as Gregory the Great, decrees that all sexual desire is sinful, and sexual relations are permissible only between a husband and wife for the sole purpose of having children.

circa 610

- Muhammad receives the first of a series of revelations from Allah and founds Islam. Muslims, or those who practice Islam, believe that Muhammad was the last in a line of prophets that began with Adam.

Chronology

622

- The prophet Muhammad flees Mecca as the result of religious persecution and settles in Medina, marking the beginning of the Muslim era.

731

- An Irish monk, known as Bede, writes *The Penitential of Bede*, in which he advises clerics who sodomize children to repent by subsisting on bread and water for three to 12 years.

753

- The Council of Rome forbids priests and deacons to allow women to live in their households, under punishment of being expelled from the priesthood.

853

- The Council of Rome forbids priests from having sexual relations with women and declares that any priest who does so will be canonically condemned.

1049

- Saint Peter Damian (1007–72) denounces clerical homosexuality and pederasty in *Book of Gomorrah*. In the book, Damian provides penalties for "a cleric or monk who seduces youths or young boys and is found kissing or in any impure situations."

1074

- Pope Gregory VII (pope, 1073–85) requires those who are ordained to take a vow of celibacy.

1095

- Pope Urban II (pope, 1088–99) decrees that married priests who ignore the celibacy laws will be imprisoned "for the good of their souls." The wives and children of those priests are sold into slavery.

1123

- Pope Callistus II (pope, 1119–24) convenes the First Lateran Council, which decrees all clerical marriages invalid and requires all such marriages to be dissolved. Until this time, a married priest was forced to choose between his marriage or his ministry. Now a priest's marriage is automatically invalidated by virtue of his ordination.

1517

- Martin Luther nails a list of criticisms of the Catholic Church, called the 95 Theses, to the door of a Catholic church in Wittenberg, Germany, leading to the Protestant Reformation. Among Luther's objections is the church's requirement of clerical celibacy.

1533

- Henry VIII, king of England, pronounces his divorce from Catherine of Aragon and marries Anne Boleyn. As a result, he is excommunicated from the Catholic Church.

1534

- Henry VIII has Parliament pass an act appointing him and his successors supreme head of the Church of England, establishing an independent national Anglican Church.

1536

- Anne Boleyn is executed for adultery. In 1533, a pregnant Boleyn secretly married King Henry VIII, the Supreme Head of the Church of England.
- John Calvin, Protestant theologian, flees religious persecution in France and settles in Geneva, Switzerland. Like Luther, Calvin objects to the Catholic Church's requirement of clerical celibacy.

1541

- John Calvin establishes a consistory of pastors and church elders in Geneva, Switzerland, to ensure that all aspects of his followers' lives conform to church teachings, including sexual morality.

1563

- The Council of Trent declares that celibacy and virginity are superior to marriage: "If anyone says the married state is to be placed above the state of virginity or of celibacy and that it is not better and more blessed to remain in virginity and celibacy than to be united in matrimony, let him be anathema."

Chronology

1850

- U.S. novelist Nathaniel Hawthorne publishes *The Scarlet Letter*, which tells the story of the illicit affair between a minister and a young woman who became pregnant and is forced to wear a scarlet "A" (for adultery) as punishment for her sexual transgression.

1872

- U.S. journalist Victoria Woodhull publishes an account of the adulterous affair between Henry Ward Beecher, pastor of Plymouth Congregational Church in Brooklyn Heights, New York, and Elizabeth Tilton, who had sought pastoral counseling from Beecher after the death of her infant daughter. In 1878, Elizabeth Tilton is excommunicated. No action is taken against Beecher.

1966

- Pope Paul VI (pope, 1963–78) grants a dispensation from celibacy for Catholic priests. Priests granted such dispensation cannot celebrate the Mass, preach, or administer the sacraments. Nonetheless, thousands of priests worldwide apply for the dispensation.

1967

- A public discussion of the sexual abuse of minors by Catholic priests is sponsored by the National Association for Pastoral Renewal. The conference, held at Notre Dame University in South Bend, Indiana, and called the first of its kind by psychotherapist and former priest A. W. Richard Sipe, invites all U.S. Catholic bishops to attend.

1968

- The National Conference of Catholic Bishops (NCCB) authorizes a series of investigations of the priesthood, including psychological studies. The findings, published in 1972, conclude that one-third of U.S. Catholic priests are underdeveloped emotionally.

1971

- Psychiatrist Conrad Baars presents the first of two studies about the U.S. priesthood to the Synod of Bishops, a group of Catholic bishops from around the world assembled in the Vatican. Baars's report, *The Role of the Church in the Causation, Treatment, and Prevention of the Crisis of the Priesthood*, finds that 20 to 25 percent of American clergy members have serious psychiatric problems, while 60 to 70 percent have an insufficiently developed or distorted emotional life.

1976

■ Servants of the Paraclete, a Catholic monastic order founded in 1949 to serve priests suffering from alcoholism and depression, begins offering treatment programs for sexually abusive priests at its Villa Louis Martin facility in Jemez Springs, New Mexico. Priests treated there include former priests Rudy Kos, James Porter, and David Holley, who was sentenced to 275 years in state prison for molesting children in New Mexico. In 1995, the sex treatment programs are discontinued, in part due to lawsuits against the center for returning unfit priests to dioceses after receiving treatment there.

1977

■ In a study commissioned by the National Conference of Catholic Bishops (NCCB), Father Eugene Kennedy reports that more than half of U.S. Catholic priests are emotionally underdeveloped, and some 8 percent are maldeveloped.

1978

■ Pope John Paul II (elected in 1978) places a freeze on all dispensations from celibacy.

1980

■ The U.S. Equal Employment Opportunity Commission (EEOC) issues guidelines on the identification and elimination of sexual harassment as an illegal form of sex discrimination in workplaces.

1983

■ In a survey conducted for his doctoral dissertation, Richard Blackmon finds that 12 percent of the 300 Protestant clergy surveyed admit to sexual intercourse with a parishioner, and 38 percent admit to other sexualized contact with a parishioner.

1984

■ *January:* Bernard F. Law is named archbishop of Boston.
■ *June:* The Diocese of Lafayette, Louisiana, pays $4.2 million to the families of nine children sexually abused by parish priest Gilbert Gauthe, Jr.

- *October:* Gilbert Gauthe, Jr., is indicted on criminal charges including rape and possession of child pornography involving 11 boys. Gauthe later pleads guilty and is sentenced to 20 years in a Louisiana state prison.

1985

- *May:* The Rev. Thomas Doyle, a canon lawyer for the Vatican embassy in Washington, D.C., writes a confidential report to U.S. Catholic bishops citing 30 cases of sexual misconduct by priests involving some 100 victims. Doyle projects legal costs to the church of $1 billion over the next 10 years. He calls the crisis "the most serious problem that we in the church have faced in centuries."
- *June:* The National Conference of Catholic Bishops (NCCB) meets and establishes five general guidelines for dioceses in cases of alleged sexual misconduct by a priest. The guidelines become known as the Five Principles. Thomas Doyle's memo is considered, but little action is taken by the bishops.

1986

- In a landmark decision, the U.S. Supreme Court in *Meritor v. Vinson* clarifies the concept of "unwanted conduct" sexual harassment as a form of illegal sex discrimination and holds that companies are liable for the conduct of their employees.

1987

- The adulterous affair between evangelical minister Jim Bakker and his former church secretary Jessica Hahn is made public. Bakker attempts to silence Hahn with $265,000 of his ministry's funds and is later accused of defrauding investors of some $158 million by overselling shares in his religious theme park, Heritage USA. In 1989, Bakker is convicted of 15 counts of wire fraud and is sentenced to prison.

1988

- Photographs are released of nationally televised preacher Jimmy Swaggart in a hotel room with a prostitute. Swaggart is summoned by church elders and publicly confesses to the incident. Swaggart later tells reporters that he did not engage in sex with the woman, Catherine Campen. However, in 1989, Campen states in an interview that she and Swaggart "dated" prior to the incident in the hotel room and she performed sadomasochistic acts for Swaggart.

Sexual Misconduct and the Clergy

1989

- A committee of the National Conference of Catholic Bishops (NCCB) formed to investigate allegations of sexual abuse by priests issues a statement that the "problem of priests and child abuse is a serious one but not a very common one."

1990

- *July:* Archbishop Eugene Marino of Atlanta, the first black bishop in the history of the U.S. Catholic Church, resigns amid revelations of his two-year affair with a 27-year-old female parishioner.

1991

- *February:* Alphonsus Penney, archbishop of St. John's, Newfoundland, resigns as the result of findings by a church commission that he failed to prevent the sexual and physical abuse of boys living in Catholic orphanages in Newfoundland.
- *March:* A Colorado jury awards $1.2 million in civil damages to a victim of clergy sexual misconduct, finding that her Episcopal diocese and the presiding bishop of Colorado were liable for covering up the sexual misconduct of her priest. The case demonstrates that church officials, not just the offending clergy member, can be held accountable in cases of sexual misconduct
- *June:* The advocacy group Victims of Clergy Abuse Linkup (VOCAL) is founded. The group later changes its name to Survivors of Clergy Abuse Linkup.
- *October:* Catholic priest Thomas Chleboski is sentenced to eight years in prison for molesting boys in Washington, D.C. He receives an additional 22-year sentence in Virginia for similar offenses.
- *November:* Victims of clergy abuse advocacy group Survivor Connections is founded in Cranston, Rhode Island, by Frank Fitzpatrick, an insurance investigator and childhood victim of former priest James Porter. Fitzpatrick is responsible for tracking down Porter, who allegedly abused more than 100 children in Minnesota, Massachusetts, and New Mexico.

1992

- *February:* The National Conference of Catholic Bishops (NCCB) issues a statement that accusations of child sexual abuse by clergy is to be immediately investigated and reported to law enforcement.
- *March:* The Center for the Prevention of Sexual and Domestic Violence releases the report *Clergy Sexual Misconduct: Sexual Abuse in the Minister-*

ial Relationship. Among the findings, some 48 percent of United Church of Christ female ministers and 77 percent of United Methodist female ministers report being sexually harassed during the course of their ministerial duties.

- *May:* Eamonn Casey, bishop of Galway, Ireland, resigns. Casey admits he fathered the son of a Connecticut woman as the result of an affair with her in 1973 and that he used church funds to pay child support to the woman.
- *June:* The Archdiocese of Chicago releases the results of a review of personnel files for some 2,252 priests who served in the archdiocese from 1951 to 1991. Their findings: Some 39 priests, or 1.8 percent, are guilty of sexual misconduct at some point in their career.
- *September:* Jason Berry publishes *Lead Us Not into Temptation.* The book chronicles the case of Louisiana parish priest James Porter's sexual abuse of children and examines the broader issue of sexual abuse by clergy in the Catholic Church, which Berry estimates involves some 400 priests.
- *October:* Some 300 survivors of clergy sexual abuse attend the first national conference for victims' advocacy group Survivors of Clergy Abuse Linkup. The spin-off group Survivors Network of those Abused by Priests (SNAP) is formed.
- *December:* A settlement is announced in the civil action brought by 68 sexual abuse victims of James R. Porter in the Fall River, Massachusetts, diocese.

1993

- *March:* Archbishop Robert Sanchez of Santa Fe, New Mexico, resigns after he admits to sexual relationships with five women in New Mexico during the 1970s and 1980s.
- *April:* Victims advocacy group Survivors Network of those Abused by Priests (SNAP) sends letters to 172 U.S. bishops requesting them to sign a pledge not to publicly attack victims of clergy sexual misconduct or file countersuits against victims who are suing the church. The bishops refuse to sign the pledge.
- *June:* Reporters Frank Bruni and Elinor Burkett publish *A Gospel of Shame: Children, Sexual Abuse, and the Catholic Church.* The book chronicles and provides historical perspective for the widening clergy sexual abuse scandal in the Catholic Church.
- *July:* Survey by the *Journal of Pastoral Care* finds that 14 percent of Southern Baptist ministers report they engaged in inappropriate sexual behavior with congregants. Seventy percent say they know a minister who has done so, and 80 percent report they lacked written guidelines on clergy sexual misconduct. As a result, training on sexual misconduct is instituted at Southern Baptist seminaries.

- *October:* James R. Porter pleads guilty to 41 counts of molesting some 28 children from August 1961 to September 1967, when Porter served as a priest at three parishes in Massachusetts.
- *November:* Servants of the Paraclete, a monastic order that runs a sex treatment program for priests in Jemez Springs, New Mexico, reaches a settlement in a lawsuit brought by victims of former priest James R. Porter, who reoffended after receiving treatment at the center.

1994

- *February:* Steven Cook recants his claim that Cardinal Joseph Bernardin, archbishop of Chicago, molested him while Cook was a seminary student in Cincinnati. The following year, Bernardin meets Cook, then dying of AIDS, and forgives him.
- *July:* Bishop John Kinney, head of the National Conference of Catholic Bishops' (NCCB's) ad hoc committee on sexual abuse, meets with victims of clergy abuse, who press the bishop to pledge not to countersue victims.

1995

- *April:* Cardinal Hans Hermann Groer of Vienna is forced into retirement by the Vatican as the result of allegations made by a former student that Hermann sexually abused him and other students at an all-male Catholic high school during the 1970s. Groer denies the allegations.
- *June:* Bishop Hansjoerg Vogel of Basel, Switzerland, resigns and admits that he impregnated a woman after his appointment as bishop a year earlier.

1996

- *March:* Historian and religious scholar Philip Jenkins publishes *Pedophiles and Priests: Anatomy of a Contemporary Crisis.* While acknowledging the clergy sexual abuse scandal, Philips blames the media for sensationalized coverage of the scandal and for harboring an anti-Catholic bias.
- *June:* Psychotherapist and former priest A. W. Richard Sipe releases his report, known as the Sipe Report, to the National Conference of Catholic Bishops (NCCB). The report cites the "widespread evidence of sexual misconduct with minors by Catholic priests which was known to the hierarchy of the Catholic Church and concealed from the Catholic public."
- *September 13:* Bishop Hubert O'Connor of Prince George, British Columbia, is sentenced to prison for the sexual assaults of two teenage female students at a boarding school while he was the principal there.

- *September 16:* Bishop Roderick Wright of Argyll and the Isles, Scotland, resigns. Wright admits to having an affair with the mother of three children while counseling her during her divorce. Wright also admits that he fathered a son by another woman earlier in his career.

1997

- A jury in Dallas, Texas, awards damages of $120 million (later reduced to $30 million) to 11 victims who alleged that ex-priest Rudy Kos sexually abused them. In a deposition for the case, psychiatrist Jay Feierman testifies that Kos was among some 1,000 sexually disordered priests treated in the sex treatment program at the Villa Louis Martin, a Catholic-run facility in Jemez, New Mexico. The sex treatment program there was discontinued in 1995.

1998

- *June:* Bishop J. Keith Symons of Palm Beach, Florida, resigns after admitting that he molested five teenage boys at three Florida parishes earlier in his career. The scandal is compounded in 2002 when Bishop Anthony O'Connell, Symons's successor, resigns under similar circumstances.
- *July:* The Central Conference of American Rabbis (CCAR) addresses the issue of clergy sexual misconduct by offering detailed guidelines on how to report, respond to, investigate, and adjudicate allegations of sexual misconduct. Under the CCAR guidelines, suspension or expulsion of rabbis must be publicly reported in the conference newsletter, and offenders are barred from using the rabbinical placement service to look for new appointments.

1999

- *February:* The Hartford Institute for Religion Research interviews 76 clergy members, most of them Protestants, who served more than 500 congregations during their careers. They report 122 cases of clergy sexual misconduct, most involving illicit affairs between adults. Although the study is anecdotal, it provides a window on clergy sexual misconduct in Protestant congregations.
- *July:* Bishop G. Patrick Ziemann of Santa Rosa, California, resigns as the result of allegations by another priest that Ziemann coerced him into sexual acts after learning that the priest had embezzled parish funds. Ziemann admits to the sexual relationship but claims it was consensual.
- *December:* Rabbi Sheldon Zimmerman resigns as the president of Hebrew Union College-Jewish Institute of Religion, a Reform rabbinical

seminary. Earlier, Zimmerman is suspended from the rabbinate for at least two years by the Central Conference of American Rabbis (CCAR), a seven-member ethics committee that found Zimmerman engaged in inappropriate personal relationships prior to 1996. Zimmerman does not contest the findings.

2000

- *April:* A revised edition of Jason Berry's book *Lead Us Not into Temptation* is published, with an introduction by author and sociologist Father Andrew Greeley, who writes that the clergy sex abuse scandal "may be the greatest scandal in the history of religion in America and perhaps the most serious crisis Catholicism has faced since the Reformation."

2001

- Archbishop John Aloysius Ward of Cardiff, Wales, resigns at the urging of the Vatican. Ward is accused of ignoring warnings about two priests under his supervision who were later convicted of child abuse.

2002

- *January:* Voice of the Faithful, a Catholic lay group dedicated to church reform, is founded when some 30 people gather to discuss the clergy sex scandal in the basement of a parish school in Wellesley, Massachusetts. In less than one year, membership grows to some 25,000 Catholics in 21 countries throughout the world.
- *February:* Former parish priest John Geoghan is sentenced to nine to 10 years in a Massachusetts state prison for molesting a 10-year-old boy in Waltham, Massachusetts. Additional prosecutions of Geoghan are hampered because many of his sex crimes against children occurred decades ago, past the applicable statutes of limitation under Massachusetts state law.
- *March 1:* Pope John Paul II makes a public statement that clergy sexual abuse is casting a "dark shadow of suspicion" over all priests.
- *March 8:* Bishop Anthony O'Connell of the Diocese of Palm Beach, Florida, resigns. O'Connell, appointed by the Vatican to "clean house" after Bishop J. Keith Symons's resignation for sexual abuse, admits that he repeatedly sexually abused a teenage boy in Hannibal, Missouri, during the 1970s. In 1996, the victim received a $125,000 settlement from the diocese of Jefferson City, Missouri.
- *March 28:* Archbishop Juliusz Paetz of Poznan, Poland, resigns as the result of allegations that he made sexual advances on young priests. Paetz denies the allegations.

Chronology

- **April 1:** Bishop Brendan Comiskey of Ferns, Ireland, resigns over his mismanagement of accused pedophile priest Sean Fortune, who committed suicide.
- **April 2:** The Archdiocese of New York turns over to the Manhattan district attorney's office a list of priests accused of sexual misconduct with minors. The list is compiled from personnel files for priests serving in the archdiocese of New York for the past 40 years.
- **April 4:** Christian Ministry Resources reports that, based on annual surveys of Protestant denominations on clergy sexual abuse conducted since 1993, there are on average some 70 allegations of child abuse made per week against U.S. churches.
- **April 6:** The *Los Angeles Times* reports on dozens of e-mails to and from Cardinal Roger Mahony and others in the Los Angeles archdiocese regarding the clergy sex scandal. The e-mails, leaked to a local Los Angeles radio station, discuss such subjects as where to place a priest accused of molesting children, whether to start a victims support group, how to respond to media accusations of clergy sex abuse, and how to manage requests from the Los Angeles Police Department for the personnel files of priests suspected of sexual abuse.
- **April 16:** Pope John Paul II summons America's cardinals to the Vatican to discuss the sex scandal and efforts to prevent future cases.
- **April 16:** Auxiliary Bishop Franziskus Eisenbach of Mainz, Germany, resigns after a female university student accuses him of sexually assaulting her during an exorcism. Eisenbach denies the allegation.
- **May 1:** The investigative staff of the *Boston Globe* publishes the book *Betrayal: The Crisis in the Catholic Church*, which chronicles the sexual abuse scandal in the Archdiocese of Boston, Massachusetts.
- **May 23:** Rembert Weakland, archbishop of Milwaukee, Wisconsin, resigns after admitting to an "inappropriate relationship" with a man who, in 1998, was awarded a $450,000 settlement by the Milwaukee archdiocese.
- **June 11:** Bishop J. Kendrick Williams of Lexington, Kentucky, resigns after being named in lawsuits brought by the Archdiocese of Louisville, Kentucky, for sexually abusing two minors decades before. Williams denies the allegations.
- **June 11:** Auxiliary Bishop James McCarthy of New York City resigns after admitting he engaged in sexual relationships with several women.
- **June 14:** U.S. Catholic bishops, meeting in Dallas, Texas, adopt a policy that will strip abusive clergymen of their authority but not automatically oust them from the priesthood. The policy falls short of the "zero tolerance" plan demanded by some abuse victims.

- *July 8:* The Catholic Bishops Conference of the Philippines apologizes for the "grave sexual misconduct" by Filipino priests and promises a protocol to address future cases of abuse.
- *July 28:* Pope John Paul II speaks publicly for the first time about the clergy sex scandals during an outdoor Mass concluding World Youth Day in Toronto, Canada. The pontiff tells the 800,000 Catholics assembled that the harmful actions of some, "fills us all with a deep sense of sadness and shame."
- *August 10:* The Conference of Major Superiors of Men, an association of Roman Catholic religious orders, including the Jesuits and Benedictines, approves a plan at its annual meeting to keep sexually abusive clergy away from children but allow them to remain in the priesthood. The conference acknowledges failures to properly discipline abusive priests in the past.
- *October 1:* Archbishop Edgardo Storni of Sante Fe, Argentina, resigns as the result of allegations that he sexually abused 47 seminarians. Storni denies the allegations.
- *October 18:* The U.S. Roman Catholic Church's new sexual abuse policy is rejected by the Vatican, which says the plan needs to be revised because elements conflict with universal church law.
- *November 7:* U.S. Roman Catholic bishops name the FBI's Kathleen McChesney to head the newly created Office for Child and Youth Protection (OCYP).
- *November 23:* Monsignor Michael Smith Foster, chief canon lawyer for the Boston archdiocese, is cleared of allegations that he molested a teenager from Newton, Massachusetts, during the 1980s.
- *December 12:* The *Boston Globe* reports that a grand jury investigating possible criminal acts by Catholic bishops who failed to prevent acts of sexual abuse has subpoenaed Boston archbishop Bernard F. Law and five subordinates. Law remains in Rome, where he meets with Pope John Paul II.
- *December 13:* Bowing to intense public pressure, Cardinal Bernard F. Law resigns as archbishop of Boston.
- *December 16:* The Vatican approves the revised U.S. bishop's sex abuse policy, allowing bishops to conduct a confidential, preliminary inquiry when a molestation claim is made. The bishop's initial plan permitted pulling priests from their jobs as soon as an accusation is made.

2003

- *January 12:* The *New York Times* release the results of a survey on sexual abuse in the Roman Catholic Church. The survey, which tracked documented reports of sexual misconduct by priests through December 2002 finds that the crisis has "spread to nearly every American diocese and involves more than 1,200 priests" who are responsible for abusing "more than 4,000 minors over the last six decades."

- **February 10:** A Suffolk County, New York, grand jury releases a 180-page report detailing how the diocese of Rockville Centre concealed alleged criminal behavior of its priests and "left thousands of children in the diocese exposed to predatory, serial child molesters working as priests."
- **February 27:** The United States Conference of Catholic Bishops (USCCB) announces that 200 clerical canon lawyers have completed training in the canonical procedures for implementing the Essential Norms for Diocesan/Eparchial Policies Dealing with Allegations of Sexual Abuse of Minors by Priests or Deacons.
- **March 7:** Kathleen McChesney, executive director of the United States Conference of Catholic Bishops' (USCCB's) Office of Child and Youth Protection (OCYP), announces that Safe Environment Programs to protect children in Catholic parishes will be fully implemented for the 2003–04 school year. The program includes a written code of conduct signed by employees and volunteers who have contact with children and requires all such adults to complete training on the issue of sexual abuse.
- **March 31:** Lawyers for the Los Angeles archdiocese appear in California Superior Court and argue against the release of personnel files of priests suspected of sexual abuse. Ten months before, Cardinal Roger Mahony had pledged to turn over all such files to authorities in order to determine if criminal charges will be filed against any of the priests.
- **April 8:** The *Boston Globe* wins the 2003 Pulitzer Prize for meritorious public service for coverage of sexual abuse by Roman Catholic priests. The Pulitzer Prize's board cites the newspaper's "courageous, comprehensive coverage," which "pierced secrecy, stirred local, national, and international reaction, and produced changes" in the Catholic Church.
- **April 15:** The Rev. Ronny E. Jenkins, a priest of the Diocese of Austin, Texas, and an assistant professor of canon law at the Catholic University of America, is appointed by the United States Conference of Catholic Bishops (USCCB) as a consultant on the issue of sexual abuse by clergy.
- **April 21:** The Catholic League issues its 2002 Report on Anti-Catholicism. Among those accused in the report of anti-Catholic bias are Massachusetts attorney general Thomas Reilly, sex abuse victims' attorney Jeffrey Anderson, and the district attorneys of New York, New Hampshire, and Pennsylvania.
- **May 3:** Thomas O'Brien, Roman Catholic bishop of Phoenix, strikes a deal with Maricopa County prosecutor to avoid indictment for sheltering sexually abusive priests. As part of the deal, O'Brien issues a public apology, saying, "I acknowledge that I allowed Roman Catholic priests under

119

my supervision to work with minors after becoming aware of allegations of sexual misconduct." The deal also calls for the diocese of Phoenix to create a victims' compensation fund and a victims' counseling fund.

- **May 10:** "Talking About Touching," a program mandated by the Boston archdiocese for all of its 174 parochial schools from kindergarten through eighth grade, is called "too explicit" by some parents.

- **May 22:** The Roman Catholic Diocese of Manchester, New Hampshire, announces a $6.5 million settlement with 61 victims abused as children by priests at parishes in the diocese. In 2002, the diocese paid some $15.4 million to resolve 176 similar claims.

- **May 24:** Former Catholic priest Sigfried Wideram, facing 42 counts of child molestation, commits suicide by leaping from a hotel in Mazatlan, Mexico, where he is about to be arrested and extradited to the United States. Wideram leaves notes for his victims, it is later reported.

- **May 25:** Cardinal Roger Mahony dedicates a chapel at the Los Angeles Cathedral to the victims of sexual abuse by priests. Abuse victims are not invited to the ceremony. A week later, clergy sexual abuse victims and their supporters enter the chapel and mount a cross with photographs of dozens of victims of clergy sexual abuse.

- **May 29:** The United States Conference of Catholic Bishops (USCCB) announces an audit of all diocesan policies on clergy sexual abuse, conducted by the Gavin Group of Boston, Massachusetts.

- **May 30:** The Archdiocese of Boston announces revised *Policies and Procedures for the Protection of Children*, developed according to guidelines set forth by the United States Conference of Catholic Bishops (USCCB). In announcing the policy, Archbishop Richard G. Lennon states, "We must be ever attentive to the words of Jesus when He said about whoever leads a child astray that it would be better for that person 'to have a great millstone hung about his neck and to be drowned in the depths of the sea' [(Matthew 18:6)]."

- **June 15:** Former Oklahoma governor Frank Keating reports that he will resign as head of a United States Conference of Catholic Bishops (USCCB) lay review panel examining sex abuse by Roman Catholic priests. Keating cites lack of cooperation by church leaders in disclosing information on sexually abusive priests as the chief reason for his departure.

- **June 26:** The U.S. Supreme Court issues a 5-4 ruling in *Stogner v. California*, declaring that California's 1993 law permitting the criminal prosecution of sexual abuse of minors is unconstitutional because the law violates the ex post facto clause of the U.S. Constitution. As a result, pending criminal cases against priests accused of sexual abuse will be dismissed.

- **July 24:** Massachusetts attorney general Thomas F. Reilly releases findings of a 16-month investigation by his office that since 1940 at least 789 minors were victims of sexual misconduct by Roman Catholic priests serving in the Boston archdiocese. The 76-page report was based on a review of some 30,000 pages of church documents and 100 hours of grand jury testimony.

- *July 25:* Some 24 convicted sex offenders are released from California state prisons in the month after the U.S. Supreme Court's decision in *Stogner v. California* that a 1994 California law extending statutes of limitation for sex offenses was unconstitutional.

- *July 31:* The Rev. Sean P. O'Malley, a Capuchian friar, is installed as the new archbishop of Boston, Massachusetts, replacing Cardinal Bernard F. Law, who resigned as archbishop on December 13, 2002, as the result of allegations that Law was aware of sexual misconduct by priests under his supervision but did not act to stop the misconduct.

- *August 8:* The Boston archdiocese offers $55 million to settle some 542 lawsuits brought by alleged victims of sexual misconduct by priests serving in the archdiocese over a period of decades. The offer is increased to $65 million after plaintiffs expressed dissatisfaction with the earlier offer. On September 10, 2003, the offer is again increased to $85 million, and a tentative settlement with plaintiffs is announced by the archdiocese. On December 21, 2003, individual plaintiffs receive notification of their share of the settlement, following an announcement that the archdiocese will sell the archbishop's 75-year-old grand residence to help fund the settlement.

- *September 5:* In Pennsylvania, the Association of Pittsburgh Priests announces plans to collect signatures on a petition supporting optional celibacy for Catholic priests. A month earlier, about one-third of priests in Milwaukee, Wisconsin, sign a letter supporting a change in the church's policy of mandatory celibacy for priests.

- *September 27:* A Massachusetts court vacates the conviction of former Boston priest John Geoghan on charges arising from Geoghan's sexual misconduct with a minor. The conviction is vacated as the result of Geoghan's murder in prison on August 23, 2003, while Geoghan was in the process of appealing the conviction.

- *October 16:* The Diocese of Bridgeport, Connecticut, announces a $21 million settlement with some 40 alleged victims of sexual misconduct by priests serving in the diocese. In announcing the settlement, Bishop William Lori apologizes to victims and asks for their forgiveness.

- *November 6:* The Catholic Communication Campaign of the United States Conference of Catholic Bishops (USCCB) announces 2003 winners of Proclaim Awards honoring excellence in communications. Among the winners is the diocese of Pittsburgh, Pennsylvania, for its multimedia campaign "Commitment and Covenant: Diocese of Pittsburgh Response to National Clergy Misconduct Problem," developed to address concerns of diocesan priests and parishioners on the issue of clergy sexual misconduct.

- *November 21:* David L. Shelter, former pastor of the New Life Fellowship Assembly of God in Redding, California, pleads guilty to 14 counts of sexual misconduct with minors in his congregation. As part of the plea deal, Sheldon agrees to a sentence of 26 years in state prison.
- *December 3:* A civil lawsuit filed in Marshall, Texas, alleges that the former dean of Trinity Lutheran Seminary in Columbus, Ohio, and others allowed the ordination of Lutheran pastor Gerald Patrick Thomas, Jr., despite warnings that Thomas presented a threat to minors. In 2002, Thomas was convicted in Texas of indecent behavior with minors and sentenced to 397 years in state prison.
- *December 15:* Pope John Paul II calls for programs to educate priests-in-training on how to live a celibate life, as mandated for all Catholic priests.
- *December 16:* In Shreveport, Louisiana, former Baptist church youth director Samuel G. Teague is convicted of two counts of sexual molestation of a minor. Teague pleaded guilty in 1991 on similar charges and served time in state prison.

2004

- *January 22:* The Archdiocese of Seattle announces that, to date, a total of $14.3 million was paid in settlements for sexual misconduct by priests in dioceses throughout the state of Washington.
- *January 27:* The Catholic Diocese of Covington, Kentucky, announces it will pay settlements of $8.3 million to 39 victims of clergy sexual misconduct by priests.
- *February 4:* The Catholic dioceses of Helena, Montana, and Great Falls-Billings, Montana, announce collective settlements of $4.3 million paid to victims of clergy sexual misconduct by priests since 1950.
- *February 5:* The Catholic Archdiocese of Detroit, Michigan, releases findings that 63 priests were credibly accused of sexually abusing 116 minors since 1950. On the same day, the Catholic Diocese of Savannah, Georgia, reports 12 verifiable cases of sexual misconduct by six of its priests since 1950.
- *February 27:* The United States Conference of Catholic Bishops (USCCB) releases the research study, "The Nature and Scope of the Problem of Sexual Abuse of Minors by Catholic Priests and Deacons in the United States, 1950–2002," conducted by the John Jay College of Criminal Justice in New York. Among the findings are that allegations of sexual misconduct were made against more than 4,000 U.S. Catholic priests by some 10,667 individuals over the 52-year period of the study.

- *February 27:* The United States Conference of Catholic Bishops' (USCCB's) National Review Board (NRB) for the Protection of Children and Young People issues a companion report, "A Report on the Crisis in the Catholic Church in the United States." The NRB's report discusses the causes and context of the Catholic sexual abuse scandal and proposes recommendations for the prevention of clergy sexual misconduct.
- *April 22:* Nine victims of sexual misconduct by former Evangelical Lutheran Church in America minister Gerald Patrick Thomas, Jr., are awarded $37 million in damages. The lawsuit alleges Thomas's superiors, including former bishop Mark Herbener, ignored warnings about Thomas's behavior. Some $32 million was previously awarded to 16 victims of Thomas, bringing the total damages awarded to $69 million. In 2003, Thomas was sentenced in criminal court to 397 years in state prison for sexually molesting minors while serving as minister from 1997 to 2001 at the Good Shepherd Lutheran Church in Marshall, Texas.
- *July 6:* The Roman Catholic Archdiocese of Portland, Oregon, becomes the first of the 195 Catholic dioceses in the United States to file for bankruptcy. At the time of the bankruptcy filing, some 25 lawsuits alleging incidents of clergy sexual misconduct are pending against the archdiocese. In two of those cases, plaintiffs are seeking $155 million in damages. Since 2000, the Portland archdiocese has paid some $53 million to settle over 130 claims of clergy sexual misconduct.

CHAPTER 4

BIOGRAPHICAL LISTING

Kenneth Angell, Bishop of Burlington, Vermont, and former auxiliary bishop in the Diocese of Providence, Rhode Island, from 1974 to 1992. In 2002, the Providence diocese paid $13.5 million to settle the clergy sexual misconduct claims of 36 victims, who accused Bishop Angell and other diocesan leaders of covering up the sexual misconduct of priests under their supervision.

Jeff Anderson, Minnesota plaintiff's attorney specializing in cases of clergy sexual misconduct.

Augustine, Catholic bishop of Hippo (354–430) whose punitive views on sexual expression influenced church leaders on the imposition of celibacy on Catholic priests, who were allowed to marry and have children during the early history of the church.

Conrad Baars, psychiatrist who in 1971 presented the first of two studies about the U.S. priesthood to the Synod of Bishops, a worldwide group of Catholic bishops. Baars's report, *The Role of the Church in the Causation, Treatment, and Prevention of the Crisis of the Priesthood,* concluded that 20 to 25 percent of American clergy members suffered from serious psychiatric problems, while 60 to 70 percent had an insufficiently developed or distorted emotional life.

Jim Bakker, evangelical minister whose adulterous affair with his former church secretary Jessica Hahn went public in 1987. Bakker, who attempted to silence Hahn with $265,000 of his ministry's funds, was accused of defrauding investors of some $158 million by overselling shares in his religious theme park, Heritage USA, and was later sentenced to prison.

Robert Banks, Catholic bishop of Green Bay, Wisconsin, and former top aide to former Boston archbishop Bernard F. Law. Bishop Banks claimed he was unaware of former priest Paul Shanley's history of sexual misconduct with minors when Banks assisted Shanley in transferring to the Diocese of San Bernardino, California. Since his appointment as bishop of

Green Bay, Wisconsin, Banks suspended one priest accused of sexual misconduct with a minor.

Andrew Barasda, Episcopal priest who, in 2002, resigned from his Massachusetts ministry after admitting to sexual misconduct with a male teenager in 1966.

Bede, Irish monk who in 731 wrote *The Penitential of Bede*, in which he advised clerics who sodomized children to repent by subsisting on bread and water for three to 12 years.

Henry Ward Beecher, pastor of Plymouth Congregational Church in Brooklyn Heights, New York, who engaged in an adulterous affair with Elizabeth Tilton when she sought pastoral counseling from Beecher after the death of her infant daughter. When the affair was publicly revealed in 1872, Beecher was cleared by a congregational investigative committee, whereas Elizabeth Tilton was excommunicated in 1878.

Roy D. Bell, author with Stanley J. Grenz of *Betrayal of Trust: Confronting and Preventing Clergy Sexual Misconduct* (2001), which provides an overview of the issue and presents steps to prevent the occurrence of sexual misconduct among clergy members.

Robert S. Bennett, member of the National Lay Review Board established by the United States Conference of Catholic Bishops (USCCB) in June 2003. An attorney, Bennett served as Special Counsel to the U.S. Senate's Select Committee on Ethics.

Candace R. Benyei, author of *Understanding Clergy Misconduct in Religious Systems: Scapegoating, Family Secrets, and the Abuse of Power* (1998), which examines the dynamics of clergy sexual misconduct within churches.

Jason Berry, reporter credited with bringing the story of sexually abusive priest Gilbert Gauthe, Jr., to national attention through his 1984 reports in the *National Catholic Reporter*, which were later picked up by the *New York Times* and the *Washington Post*. Berry later wrote the book *Lead Us Not Into Temptation* (1992), an in-depth account of the Gauthe story that also examined the wider scandal of sexual abuse by U.S. Catholic priests.

Anthony Bevilacqua, archbishop of Philadelphia, Pennsylvania, who in 2002 dismissed six priests for sexual misconduct with minors over a period of decades. Cardinal Bevilacqua initially refused to identify the dismissed priests, citing concerns about the victims' confidentiality, but later relented under pressure from local prosecutors. The Archdiocese of Philadelphia identified 35 more priests suspected of sexual misconduct with minors since 1950.

Joseph Birmingham, former Catholic priest who allegedly compulsively molested children at six parishes in the Boston archdiocese during his 29-year career, despite complaints to his superiors. Birmingham died in 1989.

Michael J. Bland, member of the United States Conference of Catholic Bishops' (USCCB's) National Review Board (NRB). Bland holds doctorates in psychology and in ministry and served as clinical-pastoral coordinator for the Chicago archdiocese's Victim Assistance Ministry, in which he counseled victims of clergy sexual misconduct.

Anne Boleyn, who in 1533 secretly married King Henry VIII, the eventual Supreme Head of the Church of England. In 1536, Boleyn was executed for adultery.

Paul G. Bootkoski, bishop of the Roman Catholic Diocese of Metuchen, New Jersey, who on January 30, 2003, announced a settlement of $800,000 awarded to 10 victims of diocesan priests accused of sexual misconduct.

Rev. Ronald L. Bourgault, Catholic priest who on February 24, 2003, was reinstated by the Boston archdiocese after being vindicated of allegations that he sexually abused a minor some 30 years earlier.

Stephen G. Breyer, U.S. Supreme Court Justice (since 1994) who wrote the majority opinion in the Court's 5-4 ruling on June 25, 2003, in *Stogner v. California*, which held that a 1993 California law allowing prosecutions of child sex abuse crimes after the statute of limitations expired was unconstitutional under the ex post facto clauses of the U.S. Constitution. Breyer was joined by Justices John Paul Stevens, Sandra Day O'Connor, David Souter, and Ruth Bader Ginsburg.

Frank Bruni and Elinor Burkett, authors of *Gospel of Shame: Children, Sexual Abuse, and the Catholic Church* (1993), one of the earliest books to chronicle the sexual abuse scandal in the U.S. Catholic Church.

Anne M. Burke, member of the United States Conference of Catholic Bishops' (USCCB's) National Review Board (NRB). Since 1995, Burke served as a justice for the Illinois Appellate Court.

William R. Burleigh, member of the United States Conference of Catholic Bishops' (USCCB's) National Review Board (NRB). Burleigh is a journalist and served as president of the American Society of Newspaper Editors Foundation.

Nicholas P. Cafardi, member of the United States Conference of Catholic Bishops' (USCCB's) National Review Board (NRB). A professor of law at Duquesne University School of Law, Cafardi coauthored with Cardinal Adam Maida the book *Church Property, Church Finances, and Church-Related Corporations* and was only the second layman in church history to be elected to the Board of Governors of the Canon Law Society of America, where he served from 1991 to 1993.

Callistus II, Catholic pope (reigned 1119–24) who in 1123 convened the First Lateran Council, which decreed that all clerical marriages were automatically invalid. Previously, a married priest was forced to choose between his marriage or his ministry.

John Calvin, 16th-century French theologian and Protestant reformer who rejected mandatory clerical celibacy, even while advocating strict moral discipline among the laity and clergy.

Matt Carroll, reporter for the *Boston Globe,* who with fellow *Globe* investigative staff members Kevin Cullen, Thomas Farragher, Stephen Kurkjian, Michael Paulson, Sacha Pfeiffer, Michael Rezendes, and Walter V. Robinson was awarded the 2003 Pulitzer Prize for meritorious public service for coverage of sexual abuse by Roman Catholic priests. Carroll, et al., also authored the book *Betrayal: The Crisis in the Catholic Church* (2002), an exhaustive account of the clergy sexual abuse scandal in the Boston archdiocese.

Jane Chiles, member of the United States Conference of Catholic Bishops' (USCCB's) National Review Board (NRB) and vice president of the National Association of State Catholic Conference Directors. Chiles is a graduate of Loyola University in Chicago with a degree in sociology.

Mark Chopko, general counsel for the United States Conference of Catholic Bishops (USCCB) who in 2002 stated that the total expenditures for the U.S. Catholic Church as the result of clergy sexual misconduct was expected to reach $250 million.

David Clohessy, national director of the victims' rights group Survivors Network of those Abused by Priests (SNAP). In the aftermath of the U.S. Supreme Court decision in *Stogner v. California* (2003), which ruled as unconstitutional a California law that extended the statutes of limitations on sex crimes after the original statutes of limitation expired, SNAP called for all Roman Catholic bishops in California to offer rewards for information on priests suspected of sexual misconduct with children.

Steven Colliflower, Methodist minister who engaged in sexual misconduct with congregant Deborah Yardley when she sought counseling for alcoholism and emotional problems. In February 2002, the family of Deborah Yardley was awarded $10 million in damages arising from Colliflower's misconduct.

Thomas Daily, bishop of Brooklyn, New York, who in 1991 endorsed priest Enrique Diaz Jimenez for reassignment in the diocese at a time when Jimenez was indicted on 60 criminal counts involving sexual misconduct with minors. During his previous tenure as auxiliary bishop in the Boston archdiocese, Bishop Daily helped to allow former priest John Geoghan to continue working as a priest despite Geoghan's admission of sexual misconduct with minors. Bishop Daily later said that he regretted that decision.

Peter Damian, 11th-century Catholic saint whose *Book of Gomorrah* denounced clerical homosexuality and pederasty and provided penalties for "a cleric or monk who seduces youths or young boys and is found kissing or in any impure situations."

127

Thomas Doyle, Catholic priest who in 1985, as canon lawyer for the Vatican embassy in Washington, D.C., authored a report to U.S. Catholic bishops citing 30 cases of sexual misconduct by priests involving some 100 victims. Doyle projected that legal costs to the church as the result of clergy sexual misconduct could reach $1 billion, and he called the crisis "the most serious problem that we in the church have faced in centuries."

Edward Egan, archbishop of New York, who in 2003 refused to disclose the results of an internal investigation conducted by the New York archdiocese of priests accused of sexual misconduct with minors. Cardinal Egan was also implicated in sheltering sexually abusive priests while he was bishop of Bridgeport, Connecticut.

David Fellhauer, bishop of Victoria, Texas, and former administrator in the diocese of Dallas, Texas, where in 1997 a jury awarded damages of $120 million (later reduced to $30 million) to 11 individuals who were sexually victimized as minors by former priest Rudy Kos. During the Kos case, Bishop Fellhauer testified that, as early as 1985, he was aware that boys were spending the night with Kos but he did not suspect that Kos was sexually abusing them.

Gerald Fitzgerald, founder in 1947 of the Servants of the Paraclete, a Catholic order dedicated to serving the needs of emotionally and psychologically troubled priests. The Servants of the Paraclete facility in Jemez Springs, New Mexico, ran a treatment program for priests accused of sexual misconduct. The program was discontinued in 1995 as the result of lawsuits alleging that priests were not effectively treated in the program and continued their sexual abuse when returned to their ministries.

Frank Fitzpatrick, Rhode Island insurance investigator and childhood victim of former priest James R. Porter. Fitzpatrick was responsible for tracking down Porter while he was living in Minnesota with a wife and four children.

William A. Fletcher, U.S. circuit judge who delivered the opinion in *Bollard v. The California Province of the Society of Jesus* (1999) that allowed a sexual harassment claim for monetary damages against a religious order to proceed under Title VII despite the ministerial exception. The ruling validated the ministerial exception as it applies to the autonomy of a church or religious organization in choosing members of its clergy. However, because the plaintiff in the case was seeking monetary damages, not reinstatement in the religious order, the court held that the allegations had no impact on the Jesuits' selection of their priests and, therefore, a claim for monetary damages for sexual harassment under Title VII was legitimate.

Harry Flynn, archbishop of St. Paul-Minneapolis, Minnesota, and former bishop of the Diocese of Lafayette, Louisiana, where Flynn was credited with helping to restore credibility in the aftermath of the Gilbert Gauthe scandal in the 1980s. In April 2002, Flynn was appointed by the United States Conference of Catholic Bishops (USCCB) to chair the committee that drafted the church's national policy on clergy sexual misconduct. However, since 1995, Archbishop Flynn allowed five priests accused of sexual misconduct to remain in administrative positions in the archdiocese. Among them were the Rev. Gil Gustafson, who plead guilty to sexually assaulting a boy in the 1970s, and the Rev. Michael Stevens, who plead guilty in the late 1980s to sexual misconduct with a minor.

Monsignor Michael Smith Foster, chief canon lawyer for the Boston archdiocese who in 2003 was exonerated of charges of sexual misconduct and was returned to active duty.

Gilbert Gauthe, former priest in the Diocese of Lafayette, Louisiana, convicted of criminal charges relating to the sexual abuse of minors. In 1984, the Lafayette diocese paid $4.2 million to the families of nine children who were sexually abused by Gauthe.

Gelasius I, Catholic pope (reigned 492–496) who decreed that women can no longer be ordained to the priesthood.

John Geoghan, former priest accused of molesting some 200 children while serving at various parishes from 1962 to 1995 in the Boston archdiocese. In 2002, Geoghan was sentenced to 10 years in state prison where the following year he was murdered by a fellow prison inmate. On September 27, 2003, a Boston court vacated Geoghan's conviction because the case was on appeal at the time of his death.

Gerald Gettelfinger, bishop of Evansville, Indiana, who in March 2002 proclaimed to parishioners a zero tolerance policy for priests who sexually abuse minors in the Evansville diocese. Shortly afterward, news accounts revealed three diocesan pastors with histories of sexual misconduct with minors. They included the Rev. Jean Vogler, who previously served 10 months in federal prison for child pornography; the Rev. Michael Allen, who admitted that in 1974 he had sexual encounters with a 16-year-old boy; and the Rev. Mark Kurzendoerfer, who in 1981 was accused of sexually abusing a 14-year-old student. In May 2002, Bishop Gettelfinger suspended Rev. Kurzendoerfer for conducting private counseling sessions with 11-year-old students at the school where the priest was assigned.

Charles Grahmann, bishop of Dallas, Texas, where in 1997 he was found guilty of conspiracy for his role in allowing former priest Rudy Kos to remain in active ministry despite numerous allegations of Kos's sexual misconduct. Kos was convicted of criminal charges arising from sexual misconduct with minors and sentenced to a life term in state prison.

Andrew M. Greeley, sociologist and Catholic priest who has written extensively on the issue of clergy sexual misconduct in the Catholic Church.

Stanley J. Grenz, author with Roy D. Bell of *Betrayal of Trust: Confronting and Preventing Clergy Sexual Misconduct* (2001), which provides an overview of the issue and presents steps to prevent the occurrence of misconduct among clergy members.

Gregory I, Catholic pope (reigned 590–604), also known as Gregory the Great, who decreed that all sexual desire was sinful, and sexual relations were permissible only between a husband and wife for the sole purpose of procreation.

Gregory VII, Catholic pope (reigned 1073–85) who in 1074 required ordained priests to take a vow of celibacy.

Wilton D. Gregory, bishop of Belleview, Illinois, and president of the United States Conference of Catholic Bishops (USCCB). Gregory presided over the USCCB's 2002 annual meeting in Dallas, Texas, where a zero-tolerance policy on sexual misconduct was drafted by U.S. bishops.

Jessica Hahn, former church secretary whose adulterous affair with evangelical minister Jim Bakker went public in 1987. Bakker attempted to silence Hahn with $265,000 in church funds and was eventually sentenced to prison for defrauding investors by overselling shares in his religious theme park, Heritage USA.

Jerome Hanus, archbishop of Dubuque, Iowa, who in 2000 allowed the Rev. Michael Fitzgerald to remain in active ministry at a rural parish after the diocese was presented with evidence that Rev. Fitzgerald traded sexually suggestive e-mails and arranged a meeting with an investigator posing on the Internet as a 13-year-old boy. Father Fitzgerald died in a car crash in 2001 while training to be a hospital chaplain.

Nathaniel Hawthorne, author of *The Scarlet Letter* (1850), a major American novel that presented a fictional account of clergy sexual misconduct involving a Protestant minister and a woman who bore his illegitimate child and was ostracized by her church and community.

Alice Bourke Hayes, member of the United States Conference of Catholic Bishops' (USCCB's) National Review Board (NRB) and president of the University of San Diego since 1995. Hayes holds a doctorate in biology and has written books and articles on the natural sciences and on Catholic higher education.

Pamela D. Hayes, member of the United States Conference of Catholic Bishops' (USCCB's) National Review Board (NRB). An attorney, Hayes prosecuted cases of child sexual abuse in the Kings County, New York, District Attorney's Office from 1990 to 1992 and is an assistant professor at the John Jay School of Criminal Justice, City University of New York.

Henry VIII, English monarch who, in 1534, developed the Church of England after parting with the Catholic Church in Rome because of the pope's refusal to allow Henry to divorce his wife, Catherine of Aragon. With the adoption of the Thirty-Nine Articles of 1563, the Church of England merged aspects of the Catholic faith, such as holy sacraments, with Lutheran teachings, including the right of clergy to marry and have children.

Hippocrates, Greek physician (460–370 B.C.) who developed an oath of ethics for physicians, known as the Hippocratic Oath. The ethical standards advanced by Hippocrates have been loosely applied as a code of conduct for all professionals in the healing arts, including members of the clergy as counselors and spiritual advisers.

Alfred Hughes, archbishop of New Orleans, Louisiana, and former aide to Cardinal Bernard F. Law in the Boston archdiocese, where in 1991 Hughes failed to take meaningful action after receiving a complaint about John Geoghan having inappropriate conversations with boys at a swimming pool. As archbishop of New Orleans, Hughes suspended at least two priests as the result of allegations of sexual misconduct, and he apologized for the mishandling of sexually abusive priests by Catholic leaders.

Joseph Imesch, bishop of Joliet, Illinois, transferred at least four accused priests within the diocese without alerting parishioners. In addition, the archdiocese of St. Louis, Missouri, removed two priests who transferred from the Joliet diocese because Bishop Imesch did not disclose past allegations of sexual misconduct against them when recommending them for transfers. In 2002, Bishop Imesch supported the church's zero-tolerance policy on clergy sexual misconduct, and he apologized for any past harm he caused to victims of sexual misconduct, their families, and parishioners.

Philip Jenkins, professor of history and religious studies and author of *Pedophiles and Priests: Anatomy of a Contemporary Crisis* (1996), in which he cited anti-Catholic bias in the national media as being partly responsible for driving the extensive coverage of the priest sex abuse scandal in the Catholic Church.

Ronny E. Jenkins, Catholic priest of the Diocese of Austin, Texas, and an assistant professor of canon law at the Catholic University of America who in 2003 was appointed by the United States Conference of Catholic Bishops (USCCB) as a consultant on the issue of sexual abuse by clergy.

John Paul II, Catholic pope (elected in 1978) who in 2002 publicly decried the clergy sexual misconduct scandal in the Catholic Church. After initially refusing to accept the resignation of Cardinal Bernard F. Law for his handling of the sex abuse crisis, Pope John Paul II relented and on December 13, 2002, allowed Law to resign as archbishop of Boston, Massachusetts.

Frank Keating, former head of the United States Conference of Catholic Bishops' (USCCB's) National Review Board (NRB) who in June 2003 resigned after publicly criticizing Cardinal Roger Mahony and other church officials for resisting requests by law enforcement authorities to turn over the names of priests suspected of sex crimes.

Sexual Misconduct and the Clergy

William Keeler, archbishop of Baltimore, Maryland, who in 1993 reinstated the Rev. Maurice Blackwell to active ministry after a child molestation investigation of Rev. Blackwell was dropped. A panel appointed by Cardinal Keeler to review matters of clergy sexual misconduct criticized the reinstatement, saying that the allegations against Rev. Blackwell appeared credible. Rev. Blackwell was suspended in 1998 after admitting to sexual misconduct with another minor. Dontee Stokes, Rev. Blackwell's accuser in the 1993 investigation, was charged in 2002 with shooting and seriously wounding Rev. Blackwell. In the aftermath of the shooting, Cardinal Keeler acknowledged that the 1993 accusation of sexual misconduct against Rev. Blackwell was credible, and he apologized subsequently to Rev. Blackwell's victims.

Thomas Kelly, archbishop of the Archdiocese of Louisville, Kentucky, which in 2003 paid $25.7 million to settle lawsuits brought by 243 alleged victims of sexual abuse by priests and church employees. At the announcement of the settlement, Archbishop Thomas Kelly apologized to victims, including the 29 victims of Louisville priest Louis Miller, who pleaded guilty to 50 criminal counts of sexual abuse and was sentenced to 20 years in state prison.

Anthony M. Kennedy, U.S. Supreme Court justice (since 1988) who wrote the dissenting opinion in the 5-4 decision on June 25, 2003, in *Stogner v. California*, which held that a 1993 California law was unconstitutional because it allowed retroactive prosecution for child sex crimes. Justice Kennedy was joined in the dissent by Chief Justice William Rehnquist and Justices Antonin Scalia and Clarence Thomas. Justice Kennedy wrote the majority opinion in *Burlington Industries, Inc. v. Ellerth* (1998) that an employer is vicariously liable for sexual harassment by an employee who is acting under the authority of the employing company or agency. However, in such cases, the Court ruled that an employer is entitled to present an affirmative defense that fulfills two necessary elements: (1) the employer exercised reasonable care to prevent and promptly correct the sexually harassing behavior, and (2) that the complaining employee unreasonably failed to take advantage of any preventive or corrective opportunities provided by the employer.

Rudy Kos, former Catholic priest convicted of the sexual abuse of minors while serving in Dallas, Texas. In 1997, a jury awarded damages of $120 million (later lowered to $30 million) to 11 victims who alleged that Kos sexually abused them.

Marvin M. Lager, Jr., judge of the Los Angeles Superior Court. On June 17, 2003, Lager was appointed to preside over all civil actions brought by victims of sexual abuse against priests who served in the Los Angeles archdiocese and the dioceses of Orange and San Diego. The litigation was estimated to involve as many as 200 individual cases.

Baruch Lanner, Orthodox rabbi who in 2002 was convicted and sentenced to state prison for sexually abusing minors at an Orthodox youth group in New York over a period of three decades.

Cardinal Bernard F. Law, named archbishop of Boston in 1984, succeeding Cardinal Humberto Medeiros. Law resigned on December 13, 2002, as the result of allegations that for decades he sheltered sexually abusive priests under his authority by transferring them to parishes without notification of the priest's prior misconduct.

Virginia Long, justice of the Supreme Court of New Jersey, who delivered the opinion in *McKelvey v. Pierce* (2002) that the First Amendment of the U.S. Constitution does not place churches or their ministers above the law in claims of sexual misconduct, so long as the claim does not ask the court to interfere with the freedom of a church or religious institution to exercise internal decisions, such as the hiring and firing of clergy members.

William Lori, bishop of the Diocese of Bridgeport, Connecticut, who on October 16, 2003, announced a $21 million settlement with 40 victims of sexual misconduct by 16 priests over a period of four decades, beginning in the 1960s and continuing into the 1990s, when New York archbishop Edward Egan was bishop of the Bridgeport diocese. Previously, the diocese paid out $16.7 million to settle some 47 other claims of sexual misconduct by priests.

Martin Luther, leader in the Protestant Reformation who, in 1517, posted his criticism of the Catholic Church, called the 95 Theses, on the door of a Catholic church in Wittenberg, Germany. Among Luther's later criticisms of the Catholic Church was his rejection of the subordination of marriage to celibacy.

Robert Lynch, bishop of the St. Petersburg, Florida. In 2001, the diocese paid $100,000 to settle claims that Bishop Lynch sexually harassed former diocesan spokesman Bill Urbanski, who said he accepted expensive gifts from Bishop Lynch, including a stereo and a camera, but felt uncomfortable when Bishop Lynch touched and massaged him. Bishop Lynch characterized Urbanski's allegations as a misunderstanding.

Cardinal Roger Mahony, archbishop of Los Angeles since 1985. Mahony resisted requests by prosecutors to turn over personnel files on some 33 priests suspected of sexual misconduct. In 1998, Mahony was a key witness in the civil lawsuit in which two brothers alleged that they were sexually abused by Oliver O'Grady, a priest in the Stockton diocese where Mahony served as bishop before coming to Los Angeles. At the trial, Mahony testified that, despite O'Grady's admission of being a molester, Mahony reassigned O'Grady to another parish, where O'Grady sexually abused more victims. The jury awarded a judgment of $30 million, later reduced to $7 million.

Sexual Misconduct and the Clergy

Adam Maida, archbishop of Detroit, Michigan, who in 2002 provided local prosecutors with the names of 51 clerics accused of sexual misconduct over a period of decades. One of those, the Rev. Walter Lezuchowski, was barred from active ministry due to a finding by the archdiocese that he sexually abused a minor female. According to Cardinal Maida's spokesman, Rev. Lezuchowski remained on restricted duty in 2002. However, the spokesman later acknowledged that Lezuchowski was on active ministry at a diocesan parish since 1997. Father Lezuchowski has since been removed from active ministry, and Cardinal Maida apologized for the mistakes of those priests and bishops who betrayed the trust of parishioners.

Eugene Marino, former archbishop of Atlanta, Georgia, who in 1990 resigned after admitting he had engaged in an intimate relationship with a 27-year-old female parishioner.

Cardinal Humberto Medeiros, predecessor of Bernard F. Law as archbishop of Boston. In 1979, Medeiros acknowledged that Paul Shanley was a "troubled" priest after Shanley had spoken openly about man-boy love. Medeiros nonetheless transferred Shanly to a church in Newton, Massachusetts, where Shanley continued to molest minors.

Kathleen McChesney, former FBI agent who in 2002 was appointed by the United States Conference of Catholic Bishops (USCCB) as the head of the newly created Office for Child and Youth Protection (OCYP). In March 2003, McChesney announced that the Safe Environment Programs to protect children in Catholic parishes will be fully implemented for the 2003–04 school year.

John B. McCormack, bishop of the Diocese of Manchester, New Hampshire, which in 2003 paid $6.5 million to settle claims brought by 61 victims of alleged sexual abuse by priests. McCormack, who served as the director of ministerial personnel under Cardinal Bernard F. Law in the Boston archdiocese from 1984 to 1994, resigned as chairman of a national committee formed by the United States Conference of Catholic Bishops (USCCB) to study the sex abuse scandal.

Rev. Edward McDonagh, Catholic priest in the Boston archdiocese who in 2003 was cleared of allegations of sexual misconduct with a minor 40 years earlier. At the time of McDonagh's suspension from the ministry in 2002, parishioners at his church began holding weekly candlelight vigils for him and expressed the suspicion that McDonagh's suspension was motivated by the priest's outspoken criticism of Cardinal Bernard Law on the issue of sexual misconduct by priests.

Paul R. McHugh, member of the United States Conference of Catholic Bishops' (USCCB's) National Review Board (NRB) and director of the department of psychiatry and behavioral sciences at the Johns Hopkins University School of Medicine. From 1975 to 2001, McHugh was psychiatrist in chief at Johns Hopkins Hospital.

Carl Mengeling, bishop of Lansing, Michigan, who in 1999, with approval from the Vatican, allowed former Palm Beach, Florida, bishop J. Keith Symons to lead spiritual retreats for adults despite Symons's 1998 admission that he engaged in sexual misconduct with altar boys during his career.

Manuel D. Moreno, bishop of Tucson, Arizona, who on January 29, 2002, announced that the Diocese of Tucson paid $15 million to settle 11 civil lawsuits against four diocesan priests who allegedly sexually abused minors. The settlement was paid out to plaintiffs, most of whom were allegedly victimized between 1967 and 1976.

Moses, Jewish prophet who in the 13th century B.C. led the Israelites out of slavery in Egypt to Sinai, where, according to Jewish history, Moses received moral instructions from God called the Decalogue. More commonly known as the Ten Commandments, these rules formed the foundation for the ethical systems of Judaism, Christianity, and Islam, and included a prohibition against adultery.

Muhammad, founder of Islam, who in the seventh century received a series of revelations from Allah. Muslims, or those who practice Islam, believe that Muhammad was the last in a line of prophets that began with Adam.

Tomas J. O'Brien, bishop of the Diocese of Phoenix, Arizona, who on June 2, 2003, agreed to relinquish a substantial portion of his authority in exchange for immunity from prosecution on charges of failing to report priests accused of sexual misconduct with minors and transferring those priests to other parishes without disclosure of the sexual abuse allegations against them. O'Brien later resigned after being charged in a hit-and-run accident that killed a pedestrian.

Anthony O'Connell, bishop of Palm Beach, Florida, who in 2002 resigned after admitting that he had sexually abused a teenage boy at a Missouri seminary during the 1970s. O'Connell succeeded Bishop J. Keith Symons, who resigned in 1998 after he admitted to molesting five teenage boys at three Florida parishes earlier in his career.

Sandra Day O'Connor, U.S. Supreme Court justice (since 1981) who delivered the opinion in *Davis v. Monroe County Board of Education* (1999) that expanded avenues of remedy for victims of sexual harassment under Title IX of the Education Amendments of 1972 and set a new standard of liability for school boards by holding them responsible not only for the actions of their employees but also for the actions of students and others under their authority when the school board demonstrates "deliberate indifference" to sexual discrimination occurring within a school district.

Rev. Sean P. O'Malley, installed on June 30, 2003, as the archbishop of Boston and as the successor to Cardinal Bernard F. Law, who resigned as archbishop on December 13, 2002, as the result of mounting public criticism of his mishandling of sexually abusive priests over a 20-year period. On September 9, 2003, Archbishop O'Malley announced the settlement of some 500 lawsuits pending against the Boston archdiocese as the result of sexual misconduct by priests. O'Malley, a Capuchin friar, was reportedly instrumental in brokering the settlement of some $85 million, the largest single amount ever paid in a case of clergy sexual misconduct.

Leon E. Panetta, member of the United States Conference of Catholic Bishops' (USCCB's) National Review Board (NRB). From 1977 to 1993, Panetta served as a member of the U.S. House of Representatives, and from 1994 to 1997 as chief of staff for President Bill Clinton. Panetta is codirector of the Leon & Sylvia Panetta Institute for Public Policy at California State University, Monterey Bay, California.

Ronald Paquin, former Catholic priest in the Boston archdiocese who in 2002 pleaded guilty and was sentenced to 12–15 years in state prison for raping a boy. Paquin was unique in that he acknowledged having a history of sexually abusive behavior, and he agreed to testify against the Boston archdiocese in other sexual abuse cases involving priests.

Paul VI, Catholic pope (reigned 1963–78) who in 1966 granted a dispensation from celibacy for Catholic priests. Priests granted such dispensation were forbidden from celebrating the Mass or administering the sacraments. Nonetheless, thousands of priests worldwide applied for the dispensation, which was discontinued in 1978 by Pope John Paul II.

James R. Porter, former priest accused of molesting or raping at least 125 children from his graduation from the seminary in 1960 until his resignation from the priesthood in 1974. In 1993, Porter was sentenced to 20 years in prison.

William Rehnquist, Chief Justice of the U.S. Supreme Court since 1986. As an associate justice of the Court (1972–86), Rehnquist delivered the opinion in *Meritor Savings Bank v. Vinson* (1986) that a hostile working environment created by sexually inappropriate behavior constituted sexual harassment and was actionable under Title VII of the Civil Rights Act of 1964. In *Vinson,* the Court also established that the voluntary nature of a sexual relationship between an employee and a supervisor did not preclude a claim of sexual harassment under Title VII.

Thomas Reilly, the attorney general of Massachusetts whose office conducted a 16-month investigation of clergy sexual misconduct of minors in the Boston archdiocese. The Attorney General's Report, released on July 23, 2003, estimated that at least 1,000 children were sexually abused by some 237 priests and 13 other church workers between 1940 and 2000.

Justin F. Rigali, appointed in July 2003 as archbishop of Philadelphia. In October 2003, Archbishop Rigali succeeded Cardinal Anthony J. Bevilacqua, who was criticized for his slow implementation of sexual abuse policies in the archdiocese.

Robert Sanchez, former archbishop of Santa Fe, New Mexico, who in 1993 resigned after he admitted to his sexual involvement with various women.

Antonin Scalia, U.S. Supreme Court justice (since 1986) who delivered the opinion in *Employment Division v. Smith* (1990), clarifying that the First Amendment's guarantee of religious freedom was not intended as a blanket of immunity for individuals who engage in unlawful conduct, as long as the laws that are violated apply to all citizens. In cases of clergy sexual misconduct, courts nationwide have interpreted this ruling to mean that neither individuals nor church officials can claim Fourth Amendment protection to avoid accountability for their illegal conduct. Although the ruling in *Smith* applied to criminal conduct, lower courts have since issued rulings that apply the same reasoning in the civil lawsuits, allowing victims of clergy sexual misconduct to sue churches and the supervisors of offending clergy for monetary damages.

Gary Schoener, psychologist and consultant on some 2,000 cases of clergy sexual misconduct, two-thirds of which involved Protestant ministers.

James M. Shake, Jefferson County, Kentucky, circuit judge who in July 2002, denied arguments made by the Archdiocese of Louisville to seal court documents in 154 civil lawsuits brought against the archdiocese by victims of alleged clergy sexual misconduct who claimed that superiors in the archdiocese were aware of abusive priests but did not take action to remove them from the ministry. Judge Shake's ruling was affirmed in an August 9, 2002, decision by the Kentucky Court of Appeals, which held that the archdiocese failed to show a compelling reason why the court documents should be sealed. On June 10, 2003, the archdiocese of Louisville agreed to pay $25.7 million to settle with 243 plaintiffs in the lawsuits, partly as the result of mounting public criticism of the Kentucky archdiocese based on information disclosed in the court documents.

Paul Shanley, former priest known during the 1960s and 1970s as a "street priest" who ministered to runaways and teenagers questioning their sexual identity. Shanley, a former member of the North American Man-Boy Love Association (NAMBLA), was arrested in 2002 and charged with 10 counts of child rape and six counts of indecent assault and battery.

Anson Shupe, professor of sociology who has written extensively on the issue of clergy sexual misconduct. Shupe, with William A. Stacey and Susan E. Darnell, edited the book *Bad Pastors: Clergy Misconduct in America* (2000), a collection of essays on various aspects of clergy sexual misconduct.

Ray H. Siegfried II, member of the United States Conference of Catholic Bishops' (USCCB's) National Review Board (NRB) and chairman of the board of the NORDAM Group, an international aviation service and manufacturing company.

Anne A. Simpkinson, former producer for Beliefnet.com who has written extensively on the clergy sexual misconduct scandal.

A. W. Richard Sipe, psychotherapist and former priest who has written extensively on issues relating to clergy sexual misconduct, including celibacy in the Catholic priesthood.

Siricius, Catholic pope (reigned 384–399) who decreed that, after ordination, married men cannot have sexual relations with their wives.

Michael Skoor, Lutheran pastor who, in 2002, was sentenced to 29 years in prison for the sexual abuse of an 11-year-old boy and the attempted sexual abuse of the boy's younger brother.

David H. Souter, U.S. Supreme Court justice (since 1990) who wrote the opinion in *Faragher v. City of Boca Raton* (1998) that applied the vicarious liability standard to employers in sexual harassment cases. The ruling clarified that employers have a proactive duty to protect their employees from sexually harassing supervisors or fellow employees, and that it was not sufficient for an employer simply to establish a policy on sexual harassment without appropriate enforcement.

Michael J. Sullivan, U.S. attorney who on August 26, 2003, announced that the U.S. Attorney would review evidence in cases of sexual misconduct by priests in the Boston archdiocese for possible prosecution in federal courts.

Jimmy Swaggart, evangelical preacher who in 1988 was photographed with a prostitute in a hotel room. As a result, Swaggart was summoned by the elders of his church and publicly confessed to the incident.

Constance M. Sweeney, Boston Superior Court judge responsible for several key rulings in the sexual abuse scandal in the Boston archdiocese, including a ruling in January 2003, which denied the Boston archdiocese's request to be removed as a defendant in some 500 civil lawsuits on the grounds that they were immune from litigation under the First Amendment's Free Exercise of Religion clause. On August 13, 2003, Judge Sweeney ordered the Boston archdiocese to turn over thousands of pages of psychiatric records for some 61 priests accused of sexual misconduct with minors.

J. Keith Symons, former bishop of Palm Beach, Florida, who resigned in 1998 after he admitted to molesting five teenage boys at three Florida parishes earlier in his career. Four years later, his successor, Bishop Anthony O'Connell, stepped down after admitting that he had sexually abused a teenage boy at a Missouri seminary during the 1970s.

Elizabeth Tilton, parishioner of Plymouth Congregational Church in Brooklyn Heights, New York, whose adulterous affair with Henry Ward Beecher, her pastor, was publicly revealed in 1872. Tilton, whose affair with Beecher began when she sought counseling from him after the death of her infant daughter, was eventually excommunicated. Beecher was cleared of wrongdoing by a congregational investigative committee.

Anne Underwood, attorney who has written extensively on the issue of clergy sexual misconduct, including the paper "Abuse of Power as a Justice Issue" (2002).

Urban II, Catholic pope (reigned 1088–99) who in 1095 decreed that married priests who ignored the celibacy laws would be imprisoned "for the good of their souls," and that the wives and children of those priests would be sold into slavery.

Rembert Weakland, former archbishop of Milwaukee, Wisconsin. Weakland asked the Vatican to move up his mandatory retirement at age 75 as the result of disclosures that the archdiocese paid $450,000 to Paul Marcoux, who claimed that Weakland sexually assaulted him some 20 years ago when Marcoux was a theology student at Marquette University.

Charles Wells, Chief Justice of the Florida Supreme Court, who on March 15, 2002, wrote the majority opinion in a ruling that churches are not protected by the First Amendment of the U.S. Constitution from lawsuits alleging sexual abuse by members of its clergy. Chief Justice Well, with Justices Leander Shaw, Harry Lee Anstead, Fred Lewis, Barbara Pariente, and Peggy Ann Quince concurring, held that the First Amendment does not provide a shield against liability from a church's negligent hiring or failure to supervise properly clergy members who engage in sexual misconduct. The ruling came in a case filed by two women who accused the Rev. Jan Malicki of sexually assaulting them from 1994 to 1997 while Malicki served at St. David Catholic Church in Davie, Florida. The archdiocese of Miami was also named in the lawsuit for the negligent hiring of Malicki and their failure to do a background check on the priest.

Byron White, U.S. Supreme Court Justice (1962–93) who delivered the opinion in *Franklin v. Gwinnett County Public Schools* (1992) that monetary damages were available in claims of sexual harassment made under Title IX of the Education Amendment of 1972. The ruling expanded the rights of victims of sexual harassment in workplace and educational settings.

Sigfried Widera, former Catholic priest who faced charges of child sex abuse in Wisconsin and California, who on May 27, 2003, committed suicide by leaping from a hotel in Mazatlán, Mexico, where he was hiding from authorities. Widera reportedly left two signed notes apologizing for his actions.

Victoria Woodhull, journalist who in 1872 published an account of the adulterous affair between Elizabeth Tilton and Henry Ward Beecher, pastor of Plymouth Congregational Church in Brooklyn Heights, New York.

Mitchell Blake Young, former Mormon religion instructor who, in 1988, pleaded guilty to criminal charges of sexual misconduct involving four boys at a Salt Lake City youth center, and in 1993 was convicted of similar charges and sentenced to state prison.

G. Patrick Ziemann, former bishop of Santa Rosa, California. In 1999, Ziemann resigned after a priest said he was coerced into sexual acts by Ziemann, who later acknowledged the sexual relationship but claimed it was consensual.

Sheldon Zimmerman, rabbi who in 1999 resigned as the president of Hebrew Union College-Jewish Institute of Religion, a Reform rabbinical seminary. Earlier, Zimmerman was suspended from the rabbinate for two years by the Central Conference of American Rabbis (CCAR), a seven-member ethics committee that found Zimmerman engaged in inappropriate personal relationships prior to 1996. Zimmerman did not contest the findings.

Huldreich Zwingli, early Protestant reformer in Switzerland who released all clerics from the requirement of celibacy.

CHAPTER 5

GLOSSARY

This chapter presents a glossary of terms relevant to understanding the issue of clergy sexual misconduct, including clinical terminology and definitions of religious hierarchy and institutions.

abbot The head of a monastery.

abet To incite, sanction, or help in the furtherance of a crime.

abstinence Avoiding all sexual contact with others, or avoiding certain behaviors, such as sex with minors.

abuse Actions causing physical, emotional, or psychological damage to another person.

accomplice A person who knowingly and voluntarily participates with the principal offender in a criminal act through aiding, abetting, advising, or encouraging the offender. In general, mere presence, acquiescence, or silence, in the absence of a legal duty to act, does not make a person an accomplice.

accountability Taking responsibility for one's actions or behaviors. Accountability is a primary goal in the treatment of sexual offenders.

acquittal The legal certification by a court of the innocence of a person who has been charged with a criminal offense and held to answer to the criminal charge.

adult An individual at least 18 years of age who is not impaired by reason of physical, mental, or emotional handicap.

affiant A person who makes and signs a legal affidavit.

affidavit A written declaration or statement of facts made voluntarily under oath, acknowledged and signed before an official with authority to administer oaths.

allegation The statement of what is expected to be proved in a court of law, contained in a legal complaint made against the offender, such as a complaint of sexual misconduct or sexual harassment.

Anglican Church The Anglican Church of England, known also as the Church of England, split from the Roman Catholic Church in the 15th

Sexual Misconduct and the Clergy

century over the issue of the authority of the bishop of Rome, the pope. In the United States, the church is known as the Episcopal Church, which was formerly the Protestant Episcopal Church in the U.S.A.

answer   The pleading in a civil lawsuit by which the defendant admits, denies, or otherwise responds to the allegations of facts set forth in the plaintiff's complaint.

appeal   A procedure by which a party seeks review by a high court of action taken by a lower court.

appearance   The formal act by which a defendant submits to the jurisdiction of the court.

appellant   The party appealing to the higher court.

appellate court   A court having jurisdiction to review the action taken by the lower court.

appellee   The party against whom an appeal is taken.

archbishop   The highest administrative clergy member or official in a church. The archbishop of the entire Roman Catholic Church is the pope, who appoints subordinate archbishops to govern regional areas, known as archdioceses. In the Anglican Church, the archbishop of Canterbury is afforded informally a special place of honor as leader of the church. Many large churches of a particular organization are administered by archbishops.

archdiocese   The largest administrative unit of a Christian church, generally overseen by an archbishop.

Armenian Church   A branch of the Eastern Orthodox Church of Christianity.

arousal   A state of sexual excitement.

arraignment   A formal proceeding in which a defendant is brought before the court to answer to a criminal charge, usually by entering a plea of guilty or not guilty.

assault   A willful attack or threat to inflict injury upon another person, including a sexual attack on someone who does not or cannot consent to participate in the sexual behavior (such as a minor). A sexual assault may or may not be accompanied by force or violence.

Assemblies of God   Organized in 1914, the largest Pentecostal church in America. The church is considered within the same tradition of evangelical churches and draws its teachings from the Bible as the written Word of God.

auxiliary bishop   A bishop assigned to a Catholic diocese or archdiocese for the purpose of providing assistance to the resident bishop.

Baha'i   A faith founded in 19th-century Persia (now Iran) that emphasizes the unity of all religions and accepts that God has been manifest at many points in history as Moses, Buddha, Jesus, Muhammad, and Baha'u'llah (founder of the Baha'i faith). Adherents believe in the equality of men and

Glossary

women, universal education, world peace, and the creation of a federal system of world government.

bail bond   The financial obligation agreed to by an accused person to secure that person's return to court to face the pending charges. The cash or property posted as bond by the accused person is forfeited if the accused person fails to appear in court.

bail   The release of an arrested person from jail in exchange for cash or property pledged as security to ensure that the person will return to court to face the pending charges.

Baptist church   A major Christian denomination with many associations of Baptist churches, the largest being the Southern Baptist Convention.

bench warrant   An order issued by a judge for the arrest of a person.

beyond a reasonable doubt   The burden of proof of a criminal defendant's guilt to a moral but not absolute certainty.

bishop   The chief priest of a diocese. Bishops are responsible for the pastoral care and supervision of their dioceses. In addition, bishops act in council with other bishops to manage church affairs.

Black Muslims   Associated with the Nation of Islam movement in the United States, made popular through the work of Malcolm X. The name is derived from the 1961 book *The Black Muslims in America* by C. Eric Lincoln.

brief   A written document prepared by an attorney containing a summary of the facts of the case, a statement of pertinent law, and an argument on how the law applies to the facts supporting the attorney's position.

brother   A man who is a member of a religious order but is not ordained or studying for the priesthood.

Buddhism   One of the largest religions of the world with more than 300 million followers. Founded in southern Nepal around 600–500 B.C. by Siddhartha Gautama, who became known as the Buddha (Enlightened One), Buddhism teaches that meditation and the practice of good religious and moral behavior can lead to Nirvana (the state of enlightenment).

burden of proof   The duty to prove a fact in a dispute or a crime. In a criminal proceeding, the government (local, state, or federal) has the burden of proof, not the defendant.

Calvinism   The theological system of John Calvin and his followers emphasizing the omnipotence of God and the attainment of salvation by grace alone.

canon   Greek for rule, norm, standard, or measure. In Catholicism, refers to the Canon of Sacred Scripture—the list of books recognized by the church as inspired by the Holy Spirit.

canon law   The codified body of general laws governing the Catholic Church.

143

cardinal   Appointed by the pope to serve as one of the pope's chief counselors and administrators of church affairs throughout the world. Cardinals are members of the College of Cardinals, a governing body whose duties include the election of a new pope upon the death or incapacitation of the previous pope, usually from among their own members. Cardinals are distinguished by their crimson religious robes and garments.

cathedral   The major church in an archdiocese or diocese.

Catholic   The Greek word that was first used to describe the Catholic Church in a letter written by St. Ignatius of Antioch to the Christians of Smyrna around 107 A.D. In lowercase, catholic means universal or worldwide.

celibacy   The commitment to remain unmarried. Clerical celibates take a religious vow not to marry. Because sexual relations outside of marriage were historically prohibited in Judaism, Christianity, and Islam, celibacy came to imply a life of sexual abstinence. The word *celibacy* is sometimes used interchangeably with chastity, which means abstaining from unlawful or immoral sexual activity.

change of venue   Change in the location of a trial, granted by the court, to ensure a fair trial.

character evidence   Testimony of witnesses who know the general character and reputation of a person in the community. Character evidence is often considered by the court or the jury before imposing a sentence on a criminal defendant.

child   A person under 18 years of age; also referred in courts as a minor.

Christ   The title of Jesus, derived from the Greek translation of the Hebrew term *Messiah*, meaning the Anointed of God.

Christian Science   The denomination founded in 1866 by Mary Baker Eddy. Officially called the Church of Christ, Scientist, Christian Science teaches spiritual healing and promotes the belief that sin, sickness, and death can be destroyed by faith in Jesus Christ. Christian Scientists sometimes refuse medical treatment. Christian Science has no formal clergy. Its leaders are called readers, practitioners, and lecturers. The church also subsidizes the newspaper *The Christian Science Monitor.*

Christianity   The religion that began as a sect of Judaism, whose believers saw Jesus of Nazareth as the fulfillment of Hebrew prophesies that God would send a Messiah. Christians worship Jesus as God's son.

church   Used in Catholicism to describe the universal church spread throughout the world, and the church that is of a particular locality, such as a diocese.

Church of Scientology   A religious group founded in 1954 by writer L. Ron Hubbard, whose teachings, that souls can be cleared of negative en-

144

Glossary

ergy, are based on Hubbard's 1950 book *Dianetics*. Scientology's practices have been investigated by governmental agencies, often because of complaints about its fund-raising practices and recruitment policies. Membership figures are not publicly disclosed, but an estimated 500 Scientology facilities exist around the world.

circumstantial evidence All evidence of an indirect nature, such as fingerprints.

civil action An action between two or more private parties, one of whom (plaintiff) is seeking monetary damages or another remedy for harm or injury done to them by the defendant.

class action A legal action involving a group of persons with a legal interest in a particular matter. For example, victims of sexual abuse by priests serving an archdiocese might file a class action lawsuit to recover damages collectively from the archdiocese.

clergy The plural form of cleric.

clergy sexual misconduct Also known as clergy sexual abuse; unwanted or illegal sexual acts performed by a clergy member upon a victim who is under that clergy member's spiritual leadership or guidance. Clergy sexual misconduct and abuse includes the inappropriate use of the clergy member's power or influence over the victim to gain sexual favors, even if the victim agrees to the sexual contact.

cleric A term denoting a priest, minister, or professional religious leader who administers the rites and promotes the teachings of a church or religious faith. In Catholicism, the term *cleric* comes from the Code of Canon Law and refers to ordained priests.

clerical Referring to the duties and activities of a priest or minister, or of a spiritual leader. For example, clerical duties include conducting religious services and providing spiritual counseling.

cloister Part of a convent or monastery reserved for use by its members.

coercion The use of authority, bribes, threats (real or implied), or force to make someone do something they do not want to do.

College of Cardinals The governing body composed of all cardinals in the Catholic Church that advises the pope, assists in the central administration of the church, and elects a new pope.

collegiality The shared responsibility and authority of the college of bishops, headed by the pope, for the teaching and governing of the church.

common law Legal principles derived from the legal customs of ancient times or from the legal judgments and rulings of other courts, as distinguished from statutory law, which is enacted by a legislative body.

complainant The party bringing or initiating a civil action; synonymous with plaintiff.

145

complaint The document, called a pleading, that is filed with the court to initiate litigation in a civil case. The complaint contains the allegations and the request for monetary damages or other relief by the plaintiff.

concurrent sentences Sentences for two or more crimes ordered by the judge to be served at the same time instead of in sequence.

congregation The members of a church or religious community bound by common rules and beliefs.

consent The agreement to do something without pressure or coercion. The person giving consent must understand what is being agreed to, and have the right to say no or to stop the behavior. Giving permission is not the same as consent. For example, a child who gives permission to engage in a sexual act with an adult is not giving consent, because there is an inequality of age, power, and knowledge, thereby placing the child at a disadvantage in terms of understanding what is being agreed to, or having the power to stop the behavior.

contempt of court An act in the presence or outside the presence of the court that is intended to embarrass, hinder, or obstruct a court in the administration of justice. Direct contempt is committed in the immediate presence of the court, while indirect contempt usually involves the failure or refusal to comply with a court order.

covenant The theological concepts shared by congregants and their clergy that embody the doctrines and teachings of a religious faith or belief system.

crime An act that a legislative body declares contrary to law and is punishable upon conviction.

criminal action An action taken by the government against a private party suspected of possible involvement in the crime.

criminal record check A review of police records to determine if a person has been convicted of a criminal offense or is a known or registered sex offender.

cross-examination The questioning of a witness in a trial by the opposing party.

cycle A repeated pattern of feelings, thoughts, and behaviors that, in the case of a sex offender, often precedes a sexual assault.

damages Money requested or recovered by the plaintiff in a civil action.

deacon An ordained minister who serves as an assistant at a liturgical service, such as a Catholic Mass. In the Catholic Church, a man becomes a deacon prior to taking the sacred vows of the priesthood and may remain a deacon if he does not wish to become a priest. Some churches elect deacons from the laity to serve in worship activities and administrative duties of the church.

dean Also known as a vicar; a priest appointed by the bishop to aid the bishop in administering the parishes in a certain vicinity, called a "deanery."

Glossary

defendant   The party prosecuted in a criminal court, or the party sued in civil court.

deviant   Thoughts or actions outside the normal range of behaviors for most people. For example, the sexual molestation of a child is a deviant act, while the desire to have sex through the use of force or violence is a deviant fantasy.

digital penetration   A sexual act involving the insertion of fingers into the vagina or anus.

diocesan curia   The personnel and offices assisting the bishop in the administration of a diocese.

diocese   An administrative unit of the Christian church that is under the authority of a bishop and usually defined by geographical boundaries. In Roman Catholicism, an ecclesiastical jurisdiction under the pastoral direction of a Catholic bishop, often comprised of multiple parishes.

dispensation   An exemption from church law.

Eastern Orthodox   A group of Christian churches with roots in the earliest days of Christianity that do not recognize the authority of the Roman Catholic pope. Included in the Eastern Orthodox churches are the Greek, Russian, and Armenian Orthodox churches. Eastern Orthodox clergy leaders who function much as do archbishops in the Roman Catholic Church are known as patriarchs or metropolitans in the Orthodox Church.

Eastern Rite Churches   A group of churches that developed in Eastern Europe, Asia, and Africa that function under the Roman Catholic authority but with considerable autonomy in liturgy and the ordination of clergy.

ecclesiastical   Refers to official structures or legal and organizational aspects of a church.

elder   A leader of a religious denomination, usually an older, experienced, and more learned member of a congregation. Some Christian denominations, such as Presbyterians and Congregationalists, give the title to the group of laypeople who run the everyday operation of the church and assist the clergy in worship services.

encyclical   A pastoral letter addressed by the pope to the entire Catholic Church.

episcopal   Refers to a bishop or group of bishops as a form of church government, in which the bishops have ultimate authority. In the Catholic Church, the pope holds all authority and is considered infallible in matters regarding church doctrine.

Episcopal Church   The North American version of the Anglican Church, although without any formal affiliation. An outgrowth of the American Revolution, the Episcopal Church retained all features of the Church of England except fealty to the king.

evangelical   Refers to Christians who emphasize the need for an absolute commitment to faith in Christ and a duty by believers to persuade others to accept Christ as their savior.

evangelical Christianity   A contemporary Christian movement emphasizing conservative biblical scholarship without promoting Fundamentalism.

evangelist   A term from the New Testament referring to a preacher or revivalist who seeks to convert others by preaching to groups.

evidence   Testimony, writings, material objects, or other things presented to prove the existence or nonexistence of a fact in a court proceeding.

exarch   Also known as exarchy; a church jurisdiction, similar to a diocese, established for Eastern Rite Catholics. The head of an exarch, usually a bishop, is also known as an exarch.

excommunication   The penalty of expulsion or exclusion from a church or religious organization, usually as the result of defying teachings that are central to the church or religion.

felony   A more serious crime than a misdemeanor, generally punishable by imprisonment or death.

fine   A monetary penalty imposed in a criminal or civil action.

fondle   The touching of someone's genitals or other body parts in a sexual manner.

forgiveness   An expression of acceptance arising from religious beliefs that does not deny, excuse, or forget another person's offense, but agrees to set it aside in the interest of emotional and spiritual healing.

frottage   The intentional bumping or rubbing of another person's body for sexual gratification, done without the victim's knowledge or consent.

Fundamentalism   Referring to the doctrines set forth in a series of 20th-century Christian writings called *The Fundamentals* that sought to counter the liberal theology of the Enlightenment that gained prominence in 19th-century Europe and the United States. More recently, the term is associated with any type of religious expression perceived as reactionary or conservative, such as Islamic fundamentalism.

gag order   A court's power not to release sensitive information in a trial, such as in a sex offense case. Also, a judge's discretionary power to command attorneys and others involved in a court case not to give interviews or discuss a case publicly.

genitals   The sex organs, including the penis and vagina.

Greek Orthodox Church   One of the churches loosely organized as Eastern Orthodox Christianity. Eastern churches acknowledge Constantinople as their center and follow an ancient liturgical rite known as the Byzantine rite.

Hare Krishna   A sect of Hinduism popularized in North America and Great Britain whose members are called Hare Krishnas.

Glossary

hearsay   Evidence during a trial that is not within the personal knowledge of the witness but was related to the witness by a third party.

hierarchy   The ordered body of clergy within a particular church or religion. In the Catholic Church, the top-to-bottom hierarchy is pope, cardinals and archbishops, bishops, priests, and deacons.

Hinduism   A religion whose adherents, called Hindus, worship the god Krishna (popular deity in Hinduism who represents the eighth incarnation of Vishnu).

Holy Communion   The distribution to congregants of bread and wine consecrated as the body and blood of Jesus Christ during a Catholic Mass and in other Christian liturgies, including Lutheran and Episcopal.

holy orders   In the Catholic Church, the ranks of the clergy as divided into major orders, such as bishops, priests, and deacons.

Holy See   Refers to the diocese of the pope in Rome, and to the pope himself or the various officials and governing bodies of the church's central administration, known as the Roman Curia, which act by authority of the pope.

hung jury   A divided jury that cannot agree upon any verdict.

impeach   To attack the credibility of a witness by the testimony of other witnesses or by other evidence.

incardinated   In the Catholic Church, the legal tie that binds a cleric to a particular diocese.

indictment   A written accusation from a grand jury charging a person with a crime.

indigent   A person without the financial means to hire a lawyer to defend oneself.

information   An accusation of a criminal offense drawn by the prosecuting attorney, not a grand jury.

injunction   A court order directing a person to behave in a certain manner, usually to refrain from doing some act, such as an injunction forbidding a pedophile from associating with minors.

Islam   Religion founded circa 610 by the prophet Muhammad, who received a series of revelations from Allah. Muslims, or those who practice Islam, believe that Muhammad was the last in a line of prophets that began with Adam. Unlike Christianity, which presumes that everyone is born with original sin, the Islamic view is that people are born innocent. Thus, human sexual desire, in and of itself, was not necessarily equated with sinfulness under Islamic tradition, and procreation was not viewed as the sole purpose for sexual relations within marriage, as it was in early Christian teachings.

Jehovah's Witnesses   A denomination classified as Protestant that worships Jehovah, founded in Pittsburgh, Pennsylvania, in 1872 by Charles Taze Russell. Jehovah's Witnesses, sometimes called Russellites, are pacifists who refuse allegiance to any government and sometimes refuse medical treatment. The denomination is organized under three legal corporations: the Watch Tower and Tract Society of Pennsylvania, the Watchtower Bible and Tract Society of New York Inc., and the International Bible Students Association of England.

Jesuits   The religious order known as the Society of Jesus, founded by Ignatius of Loyola. Many Roman Catholic universities in the United States are operated by the Jesuits.

Judaism   The religion of the Jews as recorded in the Torah and the Hebrew books of history and the prophets. Judaism developed a monotheistic religion with a God of compassion, justice, and mercy.

judgment   In a civil case, the official decision of a court determining the rights of the parties.

jury   The group of people selected, usually by the attorneys, to declare truth of evidence in a civil or criminal trial.

Knights of Columbus   Fraternal organization for Catholic men that engages in religious and charitable work in the United States and throughout the world.

Krishna   A popular deity in Hinduism who represents the eighth incarnation of Vishnu. Lord Krishna is a key figure in the epic poem of Hinduism, *The Bhagavad Gita*, and is depicted as one who imparts wisdom that reinvigorates a life of love, selflessness, and devotion.

laicization   The process by which an ordained priest is returned to the status of a lay person.

lay ministries   Ministries within a church that are carried out by laypersons.

layman   Also lay woman, lay person; a church member who is neither ordained nor a member of a religious order.

libel   Material that damages the reputation of a person. Slander is spoken words that damage the reputation of another person.

liturgy   The public prayer of a church or congregation, derived from the Latin and Greek words referring to public service and people. When capitalized, the word refers to the Christian rite of the Divine Liturgy. Christian denominations that de-emphasize formal ritual are sometimes referred to as non-liturgical churches.

Lutheranism   The group of Protestant Christian denominations that trace their roots to Martin Luther and the German Reformation in the early 16th century. In the United States the largest Lutheran denomination is the liberal Evangelical Lutheran Church in America. The second largest is the conservative Lutheran Church—Missouri Synod.

magisterium   The official teaching office of the Catholic Church.

magistrate   An officer of a court authorized with certain powers, such as the ability to accept pleas and adjudicate certain actions.

malicious prosecution A legal action intended to injure the defendant that is without merit and terminates in favor of the person prosecuted.

Mass The common name for the liturgical service of the Catholic Church.

masturbation The use of the hand or an object to sexually arouse oneself or another.

Methodist An individual, congregation, or denomination whose Protestant heritage can be traced to the Christian teachings of John Wesley, an 18th-century English preacher. The term *Methodist* was first used as a derisive title to refer to the very strict daily schedules observed by members of the Holy Club, a religious society Wesley organized in Oxford.

Military Ordinariate Also known as Archdiocese for the Military Services, U.S.A.; nonterritorial diocese for American Catholics and their dependents who are serving in or affiliated with the military.

minister From the Latin word for "servant," an ordained cleric or one who has the authority to minister to others.

misdemeanor Any crime less serious than a felony, usually punishable by a fine and not more than one year in jail.

mistrial A trial declared invalid by the trial judge. Examples include an improperly influenced jury, incapacity of the judge, or misconduct by the parties or counsel. A mistrial is followed by a completely new trial.

mitigating circumstance A factor that does not justify or excuse an offense but that may be considered in reducing the degree of moral culpability.

molest To bother or disturb someone. This includes making sexual contact without the other person's consent, such as touching a child in a sexual manner.

monastery The autonomous community of a religious order, commonly referring to a community of men or women who lead a contemplative life separate from the world.

monk Also known as friar; a man who belongs to a monastic order in a church or religion.

monotheism A religious faith that worships a single god, as opposed to the worship of many gods (polytheism). Greek and Roman cultures were rooted in polytheism. Judaism, Christianity, and Islam are known as the world's three great monotheistic religions.

monsignor An honorary ecclesiastical title granted by the pope to some diocesan priests. In the United States, the title is given to the vicar general of a diocese. In Europe, the title is also given to bishops.

Mormon Church Officially, the Church of Jesus Christ of Latter-day Saints, founded by Joseph Smith. Mormonism is generally considered a branch of Christianity.

mosque A building in which Muslims gather for prayer and worship. Technically, a mosque is not a church, although a mosque serves as a gathering place and as a symbol of the community of faith. The word *mosque* is rooted in the Arabic word for prostrating oneself, which is the primary form of worship and prayer for Muslim men.

Muhammed Sometimes spelled Mohammed; the founder and prophet of Islam.

Muslim A follower of Muhammed and an adherent to the faith of Islam. Literally, the word refers to one who surrenders to God.

Nation of Islam Begun in Detroit in 1930 by Wallace Fard, it claimed direction from Allah to minister to blacks in the United States. In 1934, the Nation of Islam was taken over by Elijah Muhammad, who preached separation of the black race and at one point called for a separate black state. A convert to the Nation of Islam, Malcolm Littler (later known as Malcolm X) became an outspoken activist for the organization and later started a separate organization, the Muslim Mosque Inc., a movement that later became known as the Black Muslims. The Nation of Islam later split. One branch retained the name and came under the leadership of Minister Louis Farrakhan. The other, renamed the American Muslim Mission and led by Wallace D. Muhammad, eventually disbanded.

National Baptist Convention of America An organization of some 5,000 African-American churches with approximately 2.5 million members in the United States.

National Conference of Catholic Bishops (NCCB) Conference of U.S. diocesan and auxiliary bishops that decides matters of ecclesiastical law and issues policy statements on political and social issues.

negligence Failure to do something that would ordinarily be done, or the doing of something that is not ordinarily done, resulting in harm to another. For example, an archbishop's failure to protect minors from a known pedophile priest could be prosecuted as negligence, depending upon the circumstances and state laws.

nolo contendre A plea of no contest that authorizes the court to punish the individual but does not establish guilt for any other purpose.

nun A member of a religious order of women who has taken solemn vows and lives in service to her church or religion.

order Title applied to a particular religious group of men or women who have dedicated their lives in service of a church or religion.

ordinary Diocesan bishops and other church authorities with jurisdiction over the clergy in a specific geographical area or members of a religious order.

ordination A formal process of designating and consecrating individuals to the ministry or priesthood. In Roman Catholicism, the conferral of the sacrament of holy orders to the priesthood.

Glossary

Oriental Orthodox Church   A group of churches including the Armenian, Indian, Ethiopian, Coptic (Egyptian), Syrian, and Eritrean Orthodox churches.

papal infallibility   In Catholicism, the belief that divine assistance precludes the pope from erring in his teachings on faith or morals, thereby conferring ultimate authority to the pope.

parish   A specific community within a diocese with its own church building and under the authority of a pastor who is responsible for providing ministerial services. Most parishes are formed on a geographic basis, but they may be formed along national or ethnic lines.

parish coordinator   A deacon, religious, representative, or layperson who is responsible for the pastoral care of a parish. The parish coordinator is in charge of the day-to-day life of the parish in the areas of worship, education, pastoral service, and administration.

parishioner   A member of a parish.

parole   The conditional release from prison of a convict before the expiration of the sentence imposed by the court. The person paroled (parolee) is under the supervision of a parole officer during the period of parole and can be reincarcerated for violating the conditions of parole.

parties   People actively involved in a legal proceeding.

pastor   A priest or minister in charge of a parish or congregation. The pastor is responsible for administering religious rites and providing religious teaching and spiritual guidance to members of the parish.

pastoral counseling   Advice informed by psychological and theological training given by a clergy member to persons seeking spiritual or emotional guidance.

pedophilia   Sexual interest in children. Pedophiles are adults who are sexually aroused by children and who may act on that arousal by engaging in sexual acts with minors.

penance   The act of showing repentance for some sin or crime.

perjury   The criminal offense of making a false statement under oath.

perpetrator   The person committing an offense or criminal behavior, including a sexual offense.

personal recognizance   A type of bail consisting of a written promise to appear in court as directed by the court.

plaintiff   The party bringing legal action or suing in a civil trial.

plea   A statement of guilt or innocence made in criminal court by the defendant.

plea bargain   An agreement whereby a criminal defendant pleads guilty or no contest to certain charges in exchange for a prearranged sentence agreed to by the prosecutor.

pontiff   A form of reference to the pope.

pornography   Movies, photographs, or other depictions made for the purpose of sexual arousal.

power   Authority over another, including the moral authority of a clergy member in relation to a member of that clergy member's congregation or religious community.

preliminary hearing   The hearing available to a person charged with a crime to determine whether there is enough evidence (probable cause) to hold the person charged for trial.

Presbyterian Church   A Protestant denomination adhering to the teachings of Calvinism.

presumption of innocence   The supposition that a defendant in a criminal trial is innocent until proved guilty in a court of law.

priest   A professed member of a religion who lives according to religious teachings. In the Catholic Church, parish priests are under the direction of their local bishop. A parish priest who is a member of a religious order (for example, a Jesuit) is also supervised by superiors in his religious order. A diocesan, or secular, priest is not a member of a religious order and is solely accountable to his local bishop.

probable cause   The existence of circumstances and facts sufficiently strong to suggest a reasonable belief that the person charged with a crime is guilty but falling short of the burden of beyond a reasonable doubt.

probation   The period of a suspended sentence when a person convicted of a crime is supervised by a probation officer. In some cases, unsupervised probation may be imposed by the court.

prosecutor   A trial lawyer representing the state in a criminal case.

Protestantism   A grouping of thousands of Christian denominations that trace their history back to the Protestant Reformation and the split with the Roman Catholic Church over the authority of the pope. A Protestant church is a Christian denomination that is not Roman Catholic, Eastern Orthodox, or part of the Anglican Communion.

public defender   A trial lawyer employed by the county to represent indigent defendants in criminal cases.

punitive damages   Monetary damages awarded that exceed the amount necessary to compensate a plaintiff in a civil action, often intended to punish the defendant or set an example for wrongdoers.

Quakers   The informal name applied to the Religious Society of Friends. Quakers meet weekly but recognize no rank of clergy.

recidivism   A return to offending behavior.

relapse   A return to a former condition, sometimes after a period of abstinence. For example, a recovering sex offender who molests again has a relapse.

154

Roman Curia   The official collective name for the administrative agencies and courts, and their officials, who assist the pope in governing the Catholic Church. Members are appointed and granted authority by the pope.

Rome   The city of Rome is the diocese of the Catholic pope, who is the bishop of Rome.

sacrament   The Orthodox, Roman Catholic, Anglican, and Episcopal churches recognize seven sacraments: the Eucharist or communion, baptism, confirmation, penance, anointing those who are ill, marriage, and ordination or holy orders. Most Protestant denominations recognize only two sacraments, baptism and marriage.

sanctuary   The part of the church where the altar is located.

search warrant   A document from a judge ordering the search of a property for evidence.

see   Another name for diocese or archdiocese.

seminary   An educational institution for individuals preparing for the priesthood.

sexual abuse   Sexual behaviors that are against the law and violate the rights of another person, such as rape or child molestation. Sexual abuse includes the misuse of power and moral authority by a clergy member to gain sexual favors from another.

sexual behaviors   Actions arising out of sexual arousal or sexual interest that are done with oneself or with others.

sexual exploitation   Inappropriate interaction of a sexual nature between an adult, such as a cleric, and a person who is receiving care from or who is under the authority of that adult.

sexual harassment   The use of words, gestures, or power to suggest unwanted sexual contact with another, including a clergy member's use of authority to suggest sexual contact, regardless of whether the sexual contact that is insinuated or suggested actually occurs.

sexual intercourse   The insertion of the penis into the vagina or anus.

sexual misconduct   Any type of sexual harassment, sexual exploitation, or sexual abuse.

sexual penetration   Inserting an object or an body part, such as the penis or finger, into the mouth, vagina, or anus.

sexually abusive behaviors   Actions arising out of sexual arousal or sexual interest done without the consent of the victim, such as rape or molestation. Sexually abusive behaviors may also include hands-off behaviors such as indecent exposure and obscene phone calls.

sister   A woman belonging to a religion or religious order whose life is lived in service to her faith and religion, whether or not she has taken solemn vows to do so.

slander   Spoken words that damage the reputation of another person. Libel is any material that damages the reputation of another, including written or visual material.

sodomy   The penetration of the anus by a penis, also called anal sex.

statute   A law enacted by the legislative branch of government.

subpoena   An order to a witness to appear and testify at a specified time and place.

subpoena duces tecum   A court order commanding a witness to bring certain documents or records to court.

summons   An order signed by the clerk of the court to a person named as a defendant in a civil action that such an action has commenced in a specified county, and directing the defendant to answer the complaint within an established period of time, usually 30 days.

superior   The head of a religious order or congregation.

survivor   The victim of sexual abuse who has acknowledged the abuse and begun the process of healing and recovery.

synod   A gathering of designated officials and representatives of a church, with legislative and policymaking powers.

temporary restraining order   An emergency remedy of brief duration issued by a court in exceptional circumstances and only until a trial court can determine what relief is appropriate.

testimony   Evidence given by a witness under oath.

tribunal   A type of court that exercises the judicial powers of a church or religious organization.

United Church of Christ   One of the largest of the Congregationalist denominations of Protestantism, formed in 1957 by a merger of the General Council of Congregational Christian Churches and the Evangelical and Reformed Church. The church claims to have approximately 1.7 million members.

United States Catholic Conference (USCC)   Civil executive agency of the National Conference of Catholic Bishops.

unwanted sexual advance   Behavior of a sexual nature that is known by the perpetrator to be offensive to the victim.

Vatican   The headquarters of the Roman Catholic Church and the residence of the pope and his administrative clergy. Vatican City is an independent state of just 100 acres in the heart of Rome, with a resident population of about 1,000.

Vatican council   Called by the pope, a gathering of all bishops of the Catholic Church to discuss matters of interest to the church.

venire   An order summoning prospective jurors, commonly used to designate the panel of prospective jurors.

venue The proper geographical area, county, city, or district in which a court with jurisdiction over the subject may hear a case.

verdict The official decision of a jury or court.

victim A person who has suffered an offense, including sexual abuse or misconduct.

voir dire The examination of prospective jurors by attorneys and the court to determine if they are qualified to sit on the jury in the case being tried.

vow A sacred promise made to God.

voyeur Someone who achieves sexual arousal by watching others, with or without their knowledge. A voyeur is sometimes called a peeping tom.

voyeurism The achievement of sexual arousal by watching others, with or without their knowledge.

witness A person who testifies about what he or she has observed.

World Council of Churches (WCC) An ecumenical organization founded in 1948 to strengthen the relationships between Christian churches and communities worldwide. The Roman Catholic Church is not a member of WCC, although it sends official observers to WCC meetings.

PART II

GUIDE TO FURTHER RESEARCH

CHAPTER 6

HOW TO RESEARCH CLERGY
SEXUAL MISCONDUCT

Beginning in January 2002, with the *Boston Globe*'s reporting of a widening clergy sexual abuse scandal in the Boston archdiocese, the issue of clergy sexual misconduct began to receive unprecedented media attention. As the scandal grew in scope, both print and broadcast news organizations offered in-depth coverage of the issue. The result was a boon to researchers, with the creation of online databases devoted to the topic and the publication of many books on clergy sexual misconduct.

Much of the information on clergy sexual misconduct that was generated in 2002, both online and in print, focused on the U.S. Catholic Church. The fact is that clergy sexual misconduct occurs in virtually all denominations and faiths, including Judaism, Buddhism, and Protestant denominations, to name a few. It is not just a Catholic problem. Furthermore, because sexual misconduct, especially childhood sexual abuse, is a highly charged emotional issue, any source of information must be assessed for its fairness and potential bias. While there are ample sources of reliable information on the scope of clergy sexual misconduct, some sources may present a bias, even unwittingly. Some good questions for the researcher to ask when assessing the fairness and credibility of a particular source are:

- Who is presenting the information? (For example, a newspaper, a victims' advocacy group, an individual with a particular agenda?)

- Does the source deal mainly in allegations of sexual misconduct that have yet to be proved, or more factual information, such as legal settlements or criminal convictions that are a matter of public record?

- Are perpetrators of sexual misconduct identified by name and is their misconduct verifiable in news stories or legal documents, or are they merely identified generically, as in "the pastor of a Baptist church" or "a former priest in the diocese"?

• Is the source linked or referenced by reputable web sites or publications?

In exploring the issue of clergy sexual misconduct, the rule of thumb for the serious researcher is to be cautious and fair-minded.

ONLINE RESOURCES

An excellent starting point for the researcher is a basic online search engine such as Google (http://www.google.com) or Yahoo! (http://www.yahoo.com), which are free to the user and easily accessible from a home computer or computers in schools or public libraries. Because of the abundance of information on clergy sexual misconduct on the World Wide Web, using the appropriate keywords or search phrases becomes especially important. For example, a basic Google search using the keyword phrase *clergy sexual misconduct* or *clergy sexual abuse* will generate many pages of results. It is worth nothing that using the word *abuse* will tend to generate results that are more specific to sexual misconduct in the Catholic Church, as opposed to other denominations. That is because recent allegations of sexual misconduct by Catholic priests often involved minors, which constituted childhood sexual abuse. Search phrases such as *clergy sexual misconduct*, *church sexual misconduct*, or *clergy sexual harassment* tend to generate results that are broader in scope and less focused on the Catholic Church. The lesson for the researcher is to be flexible. Taking the time to modify search terms, even slightly, can bear significantly on the type of information generated by the search engine or database.

In addition to Google and Yahoo!, some of the most widely used search engines are:

• Alta Vista (http://www.altavista.com)

• Excite (http://www.excite.com)

• Go (http://www.go.com)

• Hotbot (http://www.hotbot.com)

• Lycos (http://www.lycos.com)

• Northern Light (http://www.northernlight.com)

• WebCrawler (http://www.webcrawler.com)

It can be useful to enter the same search phrase or keyword in several search engines as a way of readily identifying widely cited sources of information on the topic, which in turn, will provide springboards to further research.

WEB SEARCHES BY SUBJECT CATEGORIES

Many web search engines also allow the researcher to search by subject categories. Among the most popular are Yahoo! and About.com (http://www.about.com). The advantage of category searches is that they quickly produce a collection of links to a topic offering reliable information, often by experts. The disadvantage is that the results are sometimes limited in scope, especially on the issue of clergy sexual misconduct. For example, using the Yahoo! Website Directory (sites organized by subject), then following the links *Society & Culture* to *Sexuality* to *Sex Crimes* generated a link to *Sexual Abuse in the Catholic Church*, which produced a collection of site listings linked to newspapers and broadcast media that covered the scandal, and related organizations such as the United States Conference of Catholic Bishops (USCCB). There was also a category link *Survivors*, which generated links to various advocacy groups for victims of sexual misconduct by Catholic clergy. In addition, the link *Catholic Church Abuse Scandal* generated a page with links to recent articles on the Catholic scandal, as well as more in-depth background information on the scandal. The information generated in this category search was useful as far as sexual misconduct in the Catholic Church. However, it was clearly limited, with little information provided on clergy sexual misconduct in other faiths.

WEB SITES DEDICATED TO THE ISSUE OF CLERGY SEXUAL MISCONDUCT

There are several types of web sites that offer in-depth coverage of the issue of clergy sexual misconduct. Some are offered by newspapers such as the *Boston Globe* and broadcast networks like MSNBC, while others are sponsored by agencies and organizations that provide information on the issue as a public service, including victims' advocacy groups.

A good starting point for news coverage of clergy sexual misconduct is the *National Catholic Reporter*'s Abuse Tracker, which offers recent and archived news articles on the topic of clergy sexual misconduct in all faiths and provides links to various organizations. The URL is http://www.ncrnews.org/abuse/. Prior to January 1, 2004, the Abuse Tracker was sponsored by the Poynter Institute in St. Petersburg, Florida, with the purpose of providing information to journalists covering the topic, as well as to the general public. Following the link *Past Archives for Abuse Tracker* generates the web page as it was previously offered by the Poynter Institute. This is useful to the researcher interested in how the issue of clergy sexual misconduct in the Catholic Church was covered by specific newspapers in the United States. On the right side of the Poynter web page are links to the web sites of 20 major metropolitan newspapers that offered in-depth coverage of the Catholic scandal, including the *Baltimore Sun,* the *Boston Globe,* the *Dallas Morning News,* the *Detroit Free Press,* the *Los Angeles Times,* and the *Washington Post.* To the right of each web link, dates are provided indicating how long the Abuse Tracker has listed articles on clergy sexual misconduct by that particular publication or news organization. Below the links to newspapers, the Abuse Tracker provides additional web links to organizations that offer information on clergy sexual abuse in various denominations. Among the organizations listed are the USCCB, AdvocateWeb, and several victim advocacy groups.

WEB PAGES BY NEWS ORGANIZATIONS

Most major news broadcast organizations such CBS, ABC, and National Public Radio covered the clergy sexual abuse scandal extensively and, as a result, created web pages dedicated to the issue of clergy sexual misconduct. For the most part, the coverage provided by these organizations is focused on sexual misconduct within the U.S. Catholic Church, especially during the height of the Catholic sexual abuse crisis in 2002. While this is valuable from a historical perspective, information on the issue that is both more current and broader in scope as to other religious denominations is available elsewhere, such as the Clergy Abuse Tracker. That said, some valuable background information is provided by news organization on their clergy sex abuse web pages. For example, the NPR site (http://www.npr.org/news/specials/priests) offers links to the Vatican and to an entry on celibacy on the clergy from the *Catholic Encyclopedia.*

The print media also afforded extensive coverage to the 2002 Catholic sexual abuse crisis and, like their broadcast counterparts, they developed web pages dedicated to the issue of clergy sexual misconduct, usually within the Catholic Church. Particularly notable is the web page *Spotlight Investigation: Abuse in the Catholic Church* (http://www.boston.com/globe/spotlight/abuse), created by the *Boston Globe,* which was awarded the 2002 Pulitzer Prize for its investigative reporting on the clergy sexual abuse scandal in the Boston archdiocese. The URL is http://www.boston.com/globe/spotlight/abuse. Although the web page's focus is on the scandal in the Boston archdiocese, the depth of information available is noteworthy. There are interactive features, such as a review of the year of the scandal, a map identifying where accused priests served within the Boston archdiocese, and a video gallery chronicling events in the scandal of 2002. There are links to in-depth information on predator priests, the victims of the scandal, and the financial impact to the Boston archdiocese. Additional links are provided for information on the Catholic Church's response to the sexual misconduct scandal, ongoing investigations, and efforts of congregations to move forward in the aftermath of the scandal. Internal church documents, letters from victims, and excerpts from priests' personnel files are linked, as are the eight court depositions given by Cardinal Bernard F. Law, the former archbishop of the Boston archdiocese.

Of particular use is the extensive listing of links to organizations with information on clergy sexual abuse provided on the link *Other sites on the web*. Links include official church web sites, church reform groups, victims' advocacy and support groups, and legal documents relating to court cases arising from clergy sexual misconduct. There is also a link to the *Catholic press* that provides the following listing of links to Catholic publications that provide a range of perspectives on clergy sexual misconduct in the Catholic Church.

- *America Magazine, a national weekly Catholic magazine* (URL: http://www.americapress.org)

- *The Catholic Free Press, the official newspaper of the Diocese of Worcester* (URL: http://www.worcesterdiocese.org/news/cfp/CFP.html)

- *Catholic News Service, the official news arm of the American Catholic Church, operated by the United States Conference of Catholic Bishops* (URL: http://www.catholicnews.com)

- *Catholic Press Association, member organization for American and Canadian Catholic media* (URL: http://www.catholicpress.org)

- *Catholic World News, an independent news organization, affiliated with the Catholic World Report, that reports on news of the Catholic Church* (URL: http://www.cwnews.com)

- *Catholic World Report, a magazine affiliated with the Catholic World News web site* (URL: http://www.catholic.net/rcc/Periodicals/Igpress/cwr2.html)

- *Catholic.net, a clearinghouse for leading Catholic magazines, newspapers, and other resources* (URL: http://www.catholic.net)

- *Commonweal Magazine, an independent, liberal opinion review of religion, politics, and culture, edited by Catholics* (URL: http://www.commonwealmagazine.org)

- *Crisis Magazine, a monthly lay Catholic magazine* (URL: http://www.crisismagazine.com)

- *Crossroads Independent, a Catholic student newspaper at Boston College* (URL: http://www.bccrossroads.com)

- *Latin Mass Magazine, a magazine dedicated to the preservation of the Latin Mass and traditional Catholic thought* (URL: http://www.latinmassmagazine.com)

- *National Catholic Register,* an independent weekly Catholic newspaper (URL: http://www.ncregister.com)
- *National Catholic Reporter,* a weekly lay Catholic newspaper (URL: http://www.natcath.com)
- *Our Sunday Visitor,* a weekly Catholic newspaper (URL: http://www.osvpublishing.com)
- *The Pilot,* the official newspaper of the Archdiocese of Boston (URL: http://www.rcab.org/pilot.html)
- *The Tablet,* a weekly lay Catholic newspaper from Great Britain (URL: http://www.thetablet.co.uk)
- *The Wanderer,* a national weekly lay Catholic journal (URL: http://www.thewandererpress.com)

Another valuable resource provided by the *Boston Globe's* web page on clergy sexual misconduct in the Catholic Church is the link *related books,* which offers an excellent listing of dozens of books about clergy sexual misconduct and other related issues. Titles are often accompanied with links to book reviews. There are also links to background issues, including *Homosexuality and the church* and *Should celibacy be reconsidered?*

VICTIMS' ADVOCACY GROUPS

Survivors Network of those Abused by Priests (SNAP) hosts a web site with extensive information on clergy sexual misconduct, primarily involving the Catholic Church. Their web site address is http://www.snapnetwork.org. Among the links provided are *Online support, Emotional healing, Spiritual healing,* and *Headlines,* which provides links to news stories on clergy sexual abuse from across the United States.

The victims' advocacy group Survivors First hosts a web site that provides detailed information on Catholic priests in dioceses nationwide accused of sexual misconduct. Their web site address is http://www.survivorsfirst.org. Links allow access to information on allegations against priests in a variety of ways. For example, it is possible to focus on particular types of legal actions pending against priests by using the links *Criminal Conviction, Civil Settlement or Judgement, Pending Criminal Action,* and *Pending Civil Litigation.* This information is accessible alphabetically by priest or by diocese.

The Survivors First web site also offers links to news articles relating to clergy sexual misconduct, as well as other information, such as the grand jury report by the attorney general of Massachusetts on the estimated number of cases of clergy sexual misconduct in the Boston archdiocese over a period of several decades.

CATHOLIC WEB SITES AND ONLINE RESOURCES

Most Catholic dioceses in the United States have developed their own policies on clergy sexual misconduct, in compliance with the U.S. Catholic Church's national standards. A listing of all dioceses and archdioceses in the United States is available on the USCCB's web site at http://www.usccb.org. Dioceses may be contacted by U.S. mail or by telephone to request copies of their policy on clergy sexual misconduct, or other information on the issue. Also, entering the name of a particular diocese in a standard search engine will usually generate a link to their web site. For example, a Google search for *Diocese of Santa Rosa, CA*, generated a link to the web site for the Diocese of Santa Rosa at http://www.santarosacatholic.org. From their home page, the link *a safe environment* generated a page with the *Summary of Policies and Procedures Regarding Sexual Misconduct* for that diocese. Similarly, the home page of the web site for the Diocese of Knoxville, Tennessee, located at http://www.diocese.net/site/home/knoxville, offered the link *View the diocese's revised Policy and Procedure Relating to Sexual Misconduct*, and the home page of the web site for the Archdiocese of Chicago, Illinois, at http://www.archdiocese-chgo.org, offered an entire section entitled *Keeping Children Safe*, with links to policies, the national charter, victims assistance, and a report on sexual misconduct in the Archdiocese of Chicago.

WEB RESOURCES ON CLERGY SEXUAL MISCONDUCT IN OTHER DENOMINATIONS

AdvocateWeb is a nonprofit organization for the promotion of awareness and understanding of issues relating to the exploitation of individuals by trusted helping professionals, including clergy. Their web site address is http://www.advocateweb.org. On the left side of the web site's home page, the link *Information* generates a page with links to articles, books, law and ethics, victims' support groups, mental and spiritual health resources for victims, resources for family members and friends of victims, and research studies on issues related to clergy sexual misconduct.

Selecting the link *Articles*, then *Clergy/Religious Community*, generates a page with links to dozens of articles on the issue of clergy sexual misconduct in various denominations, including Judaism, Buddhism, Southern Baptist, and Presbyterian, to name a few. Similarly, the link *Advocate Support Groups* produces a page with web links for dozens of organizations. Some provide support to victims within a particular religion, such as SNAP at http://www.snapnetwork.org, and the Awareness Center, at http://www.theawarenesscenter.org, which is dedicated to addressing sexual abuse in Jewish communities.

Sexual Misconduct and the Clergy

The Interfaith Sexual Trauma Institute (ISTI) at St. John's Abbey and University, Collegeville, Maryland, also provides myriad resources on their web site, located at http://www.csbsju.edu/isti. Clicking on the link *ISTI Newsletter Articles* generated a listing of dozens of articles on clergy sexual misconduct in many denominations. Clicking on the link *Treatment Programs* generated a listing of organizations that provide counseling and other assistance to victims of clergy sexual misconduct, as well as to congregations and perpetrators. The listing included the address, telephone number, and e-mail contact for each organization. In addition, ISTI provides an extensive online bibliography on the issue of clergy sexual misconduct that is available in its entirety free of charge.

An excellent web site for news accounts of clergy sexual misconduct among Protestant denominations is provided by Reformation.com at http://www.reformation.com. Summaries of more than 800 articles are categorized by denomination, including Baptist, Bible Church or Evangelical, Episcopalian, Lutheran, Methodist, and Presbyterian. Each summary is linked to the full article.

The American Association of Pastoral Counselors (AAPC) is a professional association whose web site at http://www.aapc.org/ethics.htm offers information of clergy sexual misconduct in Protestant denominations.

In addition, most major U.S. religious denominations sponsor web sites with useful links to church policies, statistics, and other information on clergy sexual misconduct. Among them:

- African Methodist Episcopal (AME) Church (http://www.abc.usa.org)
- African Methodist Zion Church (http://www.amezionchurch.com)
- American Baptist Churches in the USA (http://www.abc.usa.org)
- Baptist Bible Fellowship International (http://www.bbfi.org)
- Central Conference of American Rabbis (http://www.ccarnet.org)
- The Churches of Christ (http://www.church-of-christ.org)
- Churches of God General Council (http://www.cggc.org)
- The Church of God in Christ, Inc. (http://www.cogic.org)
- The Church of Jesus Christ of Latter-day Saints (Mormon Church) (http://www.lds.org)
- Evangelical Lutheran Church in America (http://www.elca.org)
- The General Council of the Assemblies of God (http://www.ag.org)
- Greek Orthodox Archdiocese of America (http://www.goarch.org)
- Jehovah's Witnesses (http://www.watchtower.org)
- The Lutheran Church—Missouri Synod (http://www.lcms.org/cic)

- National Baptist Convention of America (http://www.nbcamerica.org)
- National Baptist Convention, U.S.A., Inc. (http://www.nationalbaptist.com)
- National Missionary Baptist Convention of America (http://www.nmbca. com)
- Pentecostal Assemblies of the World (http://www.pawinc.org)
- Presbyterian Church U.S.A. (http://www.pcusa.org)
- The Progressive National Baptist Convention, Inc. (http://www.pnbc.org)
- The Rabbinical Assembly (http://www.rabassembly.org)
- Rabbinical Council of America (http://www.rabbis.org)
- The Southern Baptist Convention (http://www.sbc.net)
- Union of American Hebrew Congregations (http://www.uahc.org)
- United Church of Christ (http://www.ucc.org)
- United Methodist Church (http://www.umc.org)

Smaller denominations may also have web sites that usually can be located via Internet searches. In addition, contact information for a particular denomination is usually available through telephone directories, available online, or in one's local library.

ONLINE BIBLIOGRAPHIES

Bibliographies are another way to locate books, articles, and other materials on issues relating to clergy sexual misconduct. Two extensive annotated bibliographies on the issue are available online, free of charge, from ISTI at http://http://www.csbsju.edu/isti, and AdvocateWeb at http://www. advocateweb.org/hope/bibliographyje/default.asp. Both are user-friendly, but AdvocateWeb's annotated bibliography is especially well organized by the following categories:

    I. Books, Book Chapters, Monographs, Booklets, and Packets
   II. Journal and Internet Articles, Papers, Book Reviews, Newsletter Articles, and Pamphlets
  III. Unpublished Papers
  IV. Articles from Secular Newspapers, Magazines, and Newsweeklies
   V. Reports Issued by Formal Inquiries
  VI. Novels, Fiction, Plays, Art, Photography, and Poetry
 VII. Theses and Dissertations
VIII. Videotapes, DVDs, and Audiotapes
  IX. Training Materials

In addition, the Sexual Information and Education Council of the United States (SIECUS), a national nonprofit organization providing information on sexuality, offers several smaller annotated bibliographies on issues relating to sexual misconduct and religion. Their web site address is http://www.siecus.org. From the SIECUS home page, follow the *Publications* link to *Annotated Bibliographies*. Topics covered include Sexual Abuse and Religion, Spirituality, and Sexuality.

BOOKSELLER CATALOGS

Another convenient and useful source of bibliographic information is online booksellers, such as Amazon.com and Barnes & Noble (http://www.barnesandnoble.com). A simple search under the category *Bookstore* using the search term *clergy sexual misconduct* generated more than 20 titles, each with links for more detailed information and, in some cases, book reviews.

LIBRARY RESOURCES

Books on clergy sexual misconduct are plentiful, and even small libraries will often carry one or more titles on the issue. Most such books include many references that are jumping-off points for further research. A good place to start is the book's index, which will provide names of individuals and organizations relevant to the topic. In addition, local libraries will typically carry published reference works, which can be useful, including bibliographies on subjects such as crime or religion. Telephone directories may provide useful contact information for local or regional offices of various denominations, government agencies, and victims' support groups. Among other useful reference books is *The New Catholic Encyclopedia*, which contains historical and biographical information relevant to Catholicism as well as other world religions.

LIBRARY CATALOGS

Access to the Library of Congress, with the largest library catalog in the world, is available at http://catalog.loc.gov and accessible from any home, library or school computer with an Internet connection. From the opening page it is possible to conduct a basic search by title, author, subject, call number, keywords, and by LCCN, ISSN, or ISSN, or ISBN publishing numbers. A more advanced guided search is also possible, and its search parameters are explained on the web page.

A good starting point is to conduct a basic search using the *keywords* category and entering a search phrase. Once again, the choice of the search phrase is critical. For example, the phrase *clergy sexual misconduct* generated only three hits, and the search phrase *clergy sexual abuse* generated only four results, including one already provided under the previous search phrase. However, entering the keyword phrase *religion + sexual misconduct* generated 10,000 results. From there, it was possible to refine the search. For example, when reorganized by date, the most recently published titles were listed first.

University libraries and law libraries, as well as an increasing number of local libraries, offer similar electronic catalogs that can be efficiently searched by using the same techniques and keywords utilized in a web-based search engine.

PERIODICAL INDEXES

General periodical indexes provide another good source of information on the issue of clergy sexual misconduct. Many public libraries subscribe to such electronic databases, and computer access is available at the library or from a personal computer by using a password or library card number. Among the more popular periodical indexes is Info Trac, which provides coverage for about 1,000 general-interest magazines. Depending upon the publication, it may be possible to view abstracts (brief summaries of articles) or complete articles. In addition, helpful tips are provided on how to efficiently search the database.

LEGAL RESEARCH

There are at least two web sites that offer pertinent and quickly accessible information on laws relating to clergy sexual misconduct.

A state-by-state survey of statutes of limitation applicable to civil claims of childhood sexual abuse, compiled by attorney Susan K. Smith, is available at http://www.smith-lawfirm.com/statutestable.html. The opening page provides a link to each of the 50 U.S. states, plus the District of Columbia, containing that state's statute of limitations for civil cases relating to clergy sexual abuse and often additional information. The web site's home page also includes the links *Remedies for Victims of Sexual Abuse*, a lengthy article with sub-links, and a link for additional *Legal Resources for Victims of Sexual Abuse*.

The National Clearinghouse on Child Abuse and Neglect Information, a service provided by the Administration for Children and Families, U.S. Department of Health and Human Services, offers a web site with mandatory reporting laws at http://nccanch.acf.hhs.gov/general/legal/statutes/sag/manda_search.cfm. The opening page presents the search options that generate mandatory reporting laws nationwide, on a state-by-state basis, or by regions, as defined by the U.S. Department of Health and Human Services.

Another option available to the researcher are online legal databases, such as Westlaw, LexisNexis, and FindLaw. Westlaw and LexisNexis are for use by paid subscribers; however, one or both may be freely available at one's local library or a law library. On the other hand, FindLaw is accessible to the general public and allows users to retrieve legal statutes and case law. The web site address is http://www.findlaw.com. Findlaw's database includes federal and state cases and codes. Under U.S. Laws it is possible to search for U.S. Supreme Court decisions, as well as U.S. courts of appeal and district courts. Cases can be searched by the year in which they were decided. However, a more efficient way to search is by citation or party name. For example, the U.S. Supreme Court case *Meritor Savings Bank v. Vinson* (1986) is cited at 477 U.S. 57, meaning that the case is published in volume 477 of *U.S. Reports* at page 57. The year of the U.S. Supreme Court's decision (in this case, 1986) is placed either before or after the citation. The parties to the case are listed as the plaintiff or appellant (Meritor Savings Bank) versus the defendant (Vinson).

In addition to online searches, it is also possible to review published federal and state cases and statutes at most law libraries.

CHAPTER 7

ANNOTATED BIBLIOGRAPHY

This chapter provides an extensive bibliography for clergy sexual misconduct and related issues and topics. The works presented range from books by clinicians in the field of sexual abuse to articles that offer first-person accounts of victims of clergy sexual misconduct. Whenever possible, Internet links are provided for articles, especially those that may be difficult to find. Some documents listed are available only on the World Wide Web.

The bibliography is divided into the following three sections:

- Reference and Professional Literature
- General Interest
- Victims and Congregations

Each section is further divided as follows:

- Books and book chapters
- Articles and papers
- Web documents

In addition, because clergy sexual misconduct encompasses related topics, including spirituality and issues of gender, the following sections are also included in this chapter:

- Books on Religion and Sexuality
- Books on Sexual Harassment

The materials presented in this bibliography are broad in scope in order to provide the reader with a range of options for further study and research.

REFERENCE AND PROFESSIONAL LITERATURE

BOOKS AND BOOK CHAPTERS

Beintema, William J. *Clergy Malpractice: An Annotated Bibliography.* Buffalo, N.Y.: William S. Hein Co., 1990. Provides a compilation of 104 annotated books and articles related to clergy sexual misconduct.

Brooke, Stephanie L. *Art Therapy with Sexual Abuse Survivors.* Springfield, Ill.: Charles C. Thomas Publishers, Ltd., 1997. Discusses art therapy as a component of treatment for victims of sexual exploitation or sexual abuse. Also includes information on repressed memory.

Bryant, Curtis. "Psychological Treatment of Priest Sex Offenders." From Plante, Thomas G., ed. *Bless Me Father for I Have Sinned: Perspectives on Sexual Abuse Committed by Roman Catholic Priests.* Westport, Conn.: Praeger, 1999, pp. 87–110. Provides a broad overview of the treatment of sexual offenders from the perspective of a Roman Catholic Jesuit priest and licensed psychologist who was the former director of inpatient clinical services at the Saint Luke Institute.

Camino, Lisa. *Treating Sexually Abused Boys: A Practical Guide for Therapists and Counselors.* San Francisco: Jossey-Bass Publishing, Inc., 2000. Clinical discussion of the treatment of sexually abused boys between seven and 17 years of age. Includes activities designed to help such victims overcome feelings of helplessness, fear, and vulnerability.

Chaffee, Paul. *Accountable Leadership: A Resource Guide for Sustaining Legal, Financial, and Ethical Integrity in Today's Congregations, Revised Edition.* San Francisco: Jossey-Bass, 1997. Includes a section with three chapters on managing incidents of clergy sexual misconduct.

Courtois, Christine A. *Recollections of Sexual Abuse Treatment Principles and Guidelines.* Scranton, Pa.: W. W. Norton & Company, 1999. Clinical discussion of delayed or repressed memory of sexual abuse that includes treatment guidelines and an overview of the controversy surrounding the issue of repressed memory.

Cumming, Georgia, and Maureen Buell. *Supervision of the Sex Offender.* Brandon, Vt.: The Safer Society Press, 1997. Discusses techniques and guidelines for the clinical management and treatment of sexual offenders, and includes chapters on the psychological and social theories of sexual deviance and relapse.

Edmunds, Stacey Bird, ed. *Impact: Working with Sexual Abusers.* Brandon, Vt.: The Safer Society Press, 1997. Presents data on the effects on clinicians working with sexual offenders, including chapters on burnout and identifying factors that contribute to stress on the clinician.

Annotated Bibliography

Eldridge, Hillary. *Therapist's Guide for Maintaining Change: Relapse Prevention for Adult Male Perpetrators of Child Sexual Abuse.* Thousand Oaks, Calif.: Sage Publications, 1998. Clinical discussion of therapeutic techniques designed to reduce the incidence of relapse in adult male sexual offenders.

Gartner, Richard B. *Betrayed as Boys: Psychodynamic Treatment of Sexually Abused Men.* Examines the impact on adult males of sexual abuse suffered as minors, and provides guidelines for treatment. New York: The Guilford Press, 1999.

Gasker, Janice A. *I Never Told Anyone This Before: Managing the Initial Disclosure of Sexual Abuse Recollections.* Binghamton, N.Y.: The Haworth Press, 1999. Clinical discussion of the techniques for handling the disclosure of sexual abuse in a therapeutic setting.

Gonsiorek, John C. "Forensic Psychological Evaluations in Clergy Abuse." From Plante, Thomas G., ed. *Bless Me Father for I Have Sinned: Perspectives on Sexual Abuse Committed by Roman Catholic Priests.* Westport, Conn.: Praeger, 1999, pp. 27–57. Describes the clinical components of a forensic psychological evaluation of clergy involved in or suspected of sexual misconduct, including a discussion of the potential for rehabilitation based on the results of the assessment, potential, the assessment process, and issues and controversies.

Irons, Richard. "Inpatient Assessment of the Sexually Exploitative Professional." From Gonsiorek, John C., ed. *Breach of Trust: Sexual Exploitation by Health Care Professionals and Clergy.* Thousand Oaks, Calif.: Sage Publications, 1995, pp. 163–175. Provides guidelines for the clinical psychological assessment of professionals who engaged in sexual misconduct, including clergy, based on 150 formal assessments of clergy, attorneys, and health professionals.

Jackson, Helen, and Ronald Nuttall. *Childhood Abuse: Effects on Clinicians' Personal and Professional Lives.* Thousand Oaks, Calif.: Sage Publications, 1997. Discusses potential bias toward sex offenders among clinicians who are providing treatment for victims of sexual misconduct. Discusses age, gender, and the spiritual beliefs of the clinician as potential factors for forming bias.

Lewis, Alvin D. *Cultural Diversity in Sexual Abuse Treatment: Issues and Approaches.* Brandon, Vt.: The Safer Society Press, 1999. Discusses treatment processes for victims of sexual abuse from culturally diverse populations, including Native Americans, African Americans, and Hispanics.

Lothstein, Leslie. "Neuropsychological Findings in Clergy Who Sexually Abuse." From Plante, Thomas G., ed. *Bless Me Father for I Have Sinned: Perspectives on Sexual Abuse Committed by Roman Catholic Priests.* Westport, Conn.: Praeger, 1999, pp. 59–85. A discussion of the neuropsychological underpinnings of sexual deviancy as it relates to clergy sexual misconduct.

175

Luepker, Ellen Thompson. "Helping Direct and Associate Victims to Restore Connections After Practitioner Sexual Misconduct." From Gonsiorek, John C., ed. *Breach of Trust: Sexual Exploitation by Health Care Professionals and Clergy.* Thousand Oaks, Calif.: Sage Publications, 1995, pp. 112–128. Examines the effects of sexual misconduct by mental health practitioners, including clergy, from a clinician's perspective.

Margolin, Judith A. *Breaking the Silence: Group Therapy for Childhood Sexual Abuse: A Practitioner's Manual.* Binghamton, N.Y.: The Haworth Press, 1999. Outlines a 15-step group therapy program for adult survivors of sexual abuse.

Milgrom, Jeanette Hofestee, and Gary R. Schoener. "Responding to Clients Who Have Been Sexually Exploited by Counselors, Therapists, and Clergy." From Pellauer, Mary D., et al., eds. *Sexual Assault and Abuse: A Handbook for Clergy and Religious Professionals.* San Francisco: Harper & Row, 1987, pp. 209–218. Discusses sexual exploitation by trusted professionals, including clergy, and provides guidelines for clergy on how to respond when a confessor or congregant confides about an incident of sexual misconduct by a trusted professional.

Ormerod, Neil, and Thea Ormerod. *When Ministers Sin: Sexual Abuse in the Church.* Alexandria, Australia: Millennium Books (E.J. Dwyer), 1995. Frames the issue of clergy sexual misconduct for those who develop church policies and procedures. The authors discuss a range of related topics, including celibacy in the Roman Catholic priesthood, responding to victims of sexual misconduct, and understanding the legal consequences of clergy sexual misconduct.

Peterson, Marilyn R. *At Personal Risk: Boundary Violations in Professional-Client Relationships.* New York: W.W. Norton & Co., 1992. A discussion of so-called boundary violations in relationships between professionals and clients, including examples of clergy sexual misconduct. The book also provides detailed accounts of the impact of boundary violations on victims.

Prentky, Robert, and Stacey Bird Edmunds. *Assessing Sexual Abuse: A Resource Guide for Practitioners.* Brandon, Vt.: The Safer Society Press, 1997. Presents clinical assessment guidelines for assessing sexual offenders and victims of sexual abuse.

Salter, Anna C. *Transforming Trauma: A Guide to Understanding and Treating Adult Survivors of Child Sexual Abuse.* Thousand Oaks, Calif.: Sage Publications, 1995. Discusses common problems experienced by adult survivors of child sexual abuse. The book includes information on psychological factors that increase the risk of sexual offending among victims of sexual abuse.

Sanders, Randolph K., ed. *Christian Counseling Ethics: A Handbook for Therapists, Pastors & Counselors.* Downers Grove, Ill.: InterVarsity Press, 1997.

Offers guidelines for clergy and other professionals in Christian counseling settings.

Shackelford, John F., and Randolph K. Sanders. "Sexual Misconduct and Abuse of Power." From Sanders, Randolph K., ed. *Christian Counseling Ethics: A Handbook for Therapists, Pastors & Counselors.* Downers Grove, Ill.: InterVarsity Press, 1997, pp. 295–317. Discusses clergy sexual misconduct in Christian counseling settings as violations of professional boundaries. The chapter includes references for further study.

ARTICLES AND PAPERS

Cobble, James F., Jr. "Screening Children's Workers: How to Protect Your Church Kids from Sexual Abuse," *Leadership*, vol. 23, Summer 2002, p. 72. Presents guidelines for the pre-screening of church volunteers and staff workers who have contact with children, including Sunday school teachers, primarily in Protestant settings.

Deibel, David L. "Saving Grace: Defending Priests Accused of Sexual Misconduct," *San Francisco Attorney*, vol. 24, February–March 1998, p. 14. Discusses legal defense strategies and points of law relevant to cases involving clergy sexual misconduct.

Haywood, Thomas W., et al. "Psychological Aspects of Sexual Functioning Among Cleric and Non-cleric Alleged Sex Offenders." *Child Abuse and Neglect*, vol. 20, June 1996, p. 527. Discusses a study by the authors of 30 Roman Catholic priests and 39 non-clerics accused of sexual misconduct. Among the findings: Clerics may be less seriously psychologically disordered than non-cleric offenders.

Ruzicka, Mary F. "Predictor Variables of Clergy Pedophiles," *Psychological Reports*, vol. 81, October 1997, p. 589. Presents data, including familial traits and past sexual experience as a victim, identified in clinical literature as risk factors for pedophilia among 10 clerics convicted of sexual misconduct with minors.

Saradjian, Adam, and Dany Nobus. "Cognitive Distortions of Religious Professionals Who Sexually Abuse." *Journal of Interpersonal Violence*, vol. 18, August 2003, p. 905. Discusses a self-report study of 14 male clergy who sexually abused minors and were confined to a treatment center for sexual offenders. Among the findings: Clergy used their religious role and relationship with God to rationalize their sexual misconduct by giving themselves permission to offend and to assuage their guilt after offending.

Schaefer, Arthur Gross. "Combating Clergy Sexual Misconduct," *Risk Management*, vol. 41, May 1994, p. 32. Discusses how risk management techniques for the prevention of clergy sexual misconduct should focus on education and response, including training at the seminary level on factors that may lead to intimacy between a minister and congregant. The article also presents a discussion of measures to reach an internal resolution of allegations of sexual misconduct as a means of avoiding legal action.

Young, John L., and Ezra E. H. Griffith, "Regulating Pastoral Counseling Practice: The Problem of Sexual Misconduct." *Bulletin of the American Academy of Psychiatry and the Law*, vol. 23, September 1995, p. 421. A discussion of the prevention and management of clergy sexual misconduct in a variety of denominational settings. Available on line. URL: http://www.emory.edu/AAPL/journal.htm.

GENERAL INTEREST

BOOKS AND BOOK CHAPTERS

Aitken, Robert. "Brahmadana, Intervention, and Related Considerations: A Think Piece." From Aitken, Robert, ed. *Original Dwelling Place: Zen Buddhist Essays.* Washington, D.C.: Counterpoint, 1996, pp. 160–170. Essay explores the spiritual and social ramifications of a Buddhist teacher's sexual exploitation of his students.

Anderson, Bill. *When Child Abuse Comes to Church: Recognizing Its Occurrence and What to Do About It.* Minneapolis: Bethany House Publishers, 1992. Recounts the experiences of a Michigan pastor newly appointed to a church where, prior to his arrival, some 64 children were sexually molested and abused by a teenage congregant.

Anderson, Lavina Fielding, and Janice Merrill Allred. *Case Reports of the Mormon Alliance, Volume 1, 1995.* Salt Lake City: Mormon Alliance, 1996. A discussion of child sexual abuse within the Church of Jesus Christ of Latter-day Saints by two former trustees of the church who were excommunicated prior to the book's publication.

Armstrong, John H. *Can Fallen Pastors Be Restored? The Church's Response to Sexual Misconduct.* Chicago: Moody Press, 1995. Discusses the impact of clergy sexual misconduct from a conservative evangelical perspective.

Barnett, Barbara. *The Truth Shall Set You Free: Confessions of a Pastor's Wife.* Mukilteo, Wash.: WinePress Publishing, 1996. Recounts the impact of sexual misconduct by the minister of a Pentecostal church and Bible college, as told by the pastor's wife.

Barrie, Iain A. G. "A Broken Trust: Canadian Priests, Brothers, Pedophilia, and the Media." From Claussen, Dane S., ed., *Sex, Religion, Media.* Lanham, Md.: Rowman & Littlefield Publishers, Inc., 2002, pp. 65–77. A discussion of a clergy sexual misconduct scandal at St. Joseph's Training School in Ontario, Canada, where some 177 minors were the victims of sexual abuse by Roman Catholic brothers from 1941 to 1971.

Annotated Bibliography

Benyei, Candace Reed. *Understanding Clergy Misconduct in Religious Systems: Scapegoating, Family Secrets, and the Abuse of Power.* Binghamton, N.Y.: The Haworth Press, 1998. Discusses clergy sexual misconduct from the perspective of the congregation as a family system.

Berry, Jason. *Lead Us Not into Temptation: Catholic Priests and the Sexual Abuse of Children.* New York: Doubleday, 1994. Chronicles the case of pedophile Gilbert Gauthe, a former Catholic priest, and explores the broader issue of clergy sexual misconduct within the U.S. Catholic Church. Berry, a journalist, was twice awarded by the Catholic Press Association for his reporting on sexual misconduct by Roman Catholic priests.

Berry, Jason, and Gerald Renner. *Vows of Silence: The Abuse of Power in the Papacy of John Paul II.* New York: Free Press, 2004. Discusses the culture of secrecy in the Roman Catholic clergy as a possible impediment to reforms proposed by U.S. bishops in 2002 to prevent clergy sexual abuse. Includes profiles of Catholic clergy, including priest and canon lawyer Thomas Doyle, whose attempts to bring reform to the church on the issue of clergy sexual misconduct were thwarted by church hierarchy.

Booker, Janet A. *Unholy Orders: Abuse of Power That Tempts Us All: The Identification and Recovery Process from Sexual Harassment and Assault by Clergy and Other Religious Leaders, Revised Edition.* St. Catherine's, Ontario: FreedomLine Enterprises, 1996. Provides general information on clergy sexual misconduct, including identifying and handling incidents of clergy sexual misconduct within the Canadian Roman Catholic Church.

Boucher, Sandy. *Turning the Wheel: American Women Creating the New Buddhism, Updated Edition.* Boston: Beacon Press, 1993. Discusses issues relevant to women Buddhists in the United States and includes examples of sexual misconduct by male Buddhist teachers with female students.

Brennan, Carla. "Sexual Power Abuse: Neglect and Misuse of a Buddhist Precept." From Deborah Hopkinson, et al., eds., *Not Mixing Up Buddhism: Essays on Women and Buddhist Practice.* Fredonia, N.Y.: White Pine Press, 1986. Discusses examples of Buddhist teachers in the United States who engaged in sexual relationships with female students.

Brown-Nolan, Virginia A. *Toward Healing and Wholeness: Facing the Challenge of Sexual Misconduct.* Cincinnati: Forward Movement Publications, 1994. Booklet designed as an educational and study guide, with suggestions for future reading, written by an Episcopalian vicar.

Burkett, Elinor, and Frank Bruni. *A Gospel of Shame: Children, Sexual Abuse and the Catholic Church, Revised Edition.* New York: Viking, 2002. Discusses clergy sexual misconduct, primarily within the U.S. Catholic Church, based upon interviews with sexually abusive priests, victims and their family members, attorneys, and Roman Catholic bishops.

Chirban, John T., ed. *Clergy Sexual Misconduct: Orthodox Christian Perspectives.* Brookline, Mass.: Hellenic College Press, 1994. Discusses clergy sexual misconduct in Orthodox Christian settings in four essays.

Coldrey, Barry M. *Religious Life without Integrity: The Sexual Abuse Crisis in the Catholic Church.* Thornbury, Victoria, Australia: Tamanaraik Press, 1999. Includes a discussion and commentary on sexual misconduct in Australian Catholic settings, including a summary of child sexual abuse by Roman Catholic priests in Australia since 1980.

Couser, Richard B. *Ministry and the American Legal System: A Guide for Clergy, Lay Workers, and Congregations.* Minneapolis: Fortress Press, 1993. Provides background and guidelines on the legal aspects of clergy sexual misconduct, including litigation and the management of incidents of sexual misconduct in religious settings.

Damian, Peter. *Book of Gomorrah: An Eleventh-Century Treatise against Clerical Homosexual Practices.* Waterloo, Ontario: Wilfrid Laurier University Press, 1982. Originally published in Latin circa 1049. The book is a discussion of clergy sexual misconduct within Catholic settings in the Middle Ages, including punishments for offenders, written by the monk Damian (1007–72), who rose to the rank of cardinal and worked to promote church reform.

Dietrich, Donald J. "Abusing the Faith: Crisis in the Church." From Jeanrond, Werner G., and Lisa Sowle Cahill, eds. *Religious Education of Boys and Girls.* London: SCM Press, 2002. Chronicles the clergy sexual abuse scandal in the Boston archdiocese, written by a professor of theology at Boston College.

Echols, Mike. *Brother Tony's Boys: The Largest Case of Child Prostitution in U.S. History. The True Story.* Amherst, N.Y.: Prometheus Books, 1996. Chronicles the true story of a traveling evangelical minister who engaged in sexual misconduct and sexual exploitation of minors, involving some 800 victims in 20 states until his conviction in 1988.

Fortune, Marie M. *Is Nothing Sacred? When Sex Invades the Ministerial Relationship.* San Francisco: Harper & Row, 1989. Discusses sexual misconduct by ministers. The book was named the 1990 book of the year by the Academy of Parish Clergy.

France, David. *The Secret Life of the Catholic Church in an Age of Scandal.* New York: Broadway Books, 2004. Provides an in-depth discussion of the clergy sexual abuse scandal in the U.S. Catholic Church and includes profiles of former priests involved in the scandal, including Joseph Birmingham, John Geoghan, and Paul Shanley from the Boston archdiocese. Written by a reporter who covered the clergy sexual abuse scandal in 2002 for *Newsweek* magazine.

Freeman-Longo, Robert E., and Gerald T. Blanchard. *Sexual Abuse in America: Epidemic of the 21st Century.* Brandon, Vt.: The Safer Society

Press, 1998. Discusses the issue of sexual abuse as a public-health matter and includes chapters on recovery and prevention.

Friberg, Nils C., and Mark R. Laaser. *Before the Fall: Preventing Pastoral Sexual Abuse.* Collegeville, Minn.: The Liturgical Press, in association with the Interfaith Sexual Trauma Institute, 1998. Discusses clergy sexual misconduct from the perspective of prevention, including factors that contribute to the occurrence of clergy sexual misconduct.

Gafke, Arthur, and Lynn Scott, eds. *Living the Sacred Trust: Clergy Sexual Ethics. A Resource on Clergy Misconduct of a Sexual Nature for Cabinets and Boards of Ordained Ministry of the United Methodist Church.* Nashville: General Board of Higher Education and Ministry, United Methodist Church, 1998. Presents an overview of clergy sexual misconduct within Methodist Church settings, including church policy on clergy sexual ethics, the reporting of incidents of clergy sexual misconduct, and services to victims and congregations.

Grenz, Stanley J., and Roy D. Bell. *Betrayal of Trust: Confronting and Preventing Clergy Sexual Misconduct, Second Edition.* Grand Rapids, Mich.: Baker Books, 2001. Discusses the scope of clergy sexual misconduct, the response to victims, congregations, and perpetrators, and presents guidelines for the prevention of clergy sexual misconduct.

Gulla, Richard M. *Ethics in Pastoral Ministry.* Mahwah, N.J.: Paulist Press, 1996. Discusses professional ethics in the ministry, including the areas of sexual abuse and sexual harassment, and offers guidelines for the prevention of clergy sexual misconduct.

Haliczer, Stephen. *Sexuality in the Confessional: A Sacrament Profaned.* New York: Oxford University Press, 1996. Chronicles the sexual solicitation in the confessional by Catholic priests in Spain from 1530 to 1819, and the ensuing 223 tribunal cases in which 80 percent of victims were females.

Harris, Michael. *Unholy Orders: Tragedy at Mount Cashel.* Marham, Ontario: Viking, 1990. Chronicles the scandal involving the sexual abuse of minors during the 1970s and 1980s at Mount Cashel Orphanage in St. John's, Newfoundland, by members of the Irish Congregation of Christian Brothers.

Harvey, John F. "The Moral Aspects of Addiction." From Smith, Russell E., ed. *The Twenty-Fifth Anniversary of Vatican II: A Look Back and a Look Ahead. Proceedings of the Ninth Bishops' Workshop, Dallas, Texas.* Braintree, Mass.: The Pope John XXIII Medical-Moral Research and Education Center, 1990. Discusses the issue of clergy sexual abuse and pedophilia from the perspective of sexual addiction, written by a Catholic priest.

Hausken, Terje C. *Peacemaking: The Quiet Power. Conflict Resolution for Churches Through Mediation.* West Concord, Minn.: CPI Publishing, 1992. Chronicles the case of a pastor arrested for sexual misconduct with a minor and the role of mediation bringing resolution to the victim and congregation through an agreement to drop criminal charges in exchange for the pastor leaving the community.

Hedin, Raymond. *Married to the Church*. Bloomington: Indiana University Press, 1995. Presents interviews with current and former Roman Catholic priests and provides insights into their reasons for entering, or leaving, the priesthood.

Heggen, Carolyn Holderread. "Pastoral Abuse." From Heggen, Carolyn Holderread, ed. *Sexual Abuse in Christian Homes*. Scottdale, Pa.: Herald Press, 1993, pp. 98–120. Discusses the issue of clergy sexual misconduct in a Mennonite setting, beginning with the first person account of a survivor of such misconduct.

Henton, Darcy, and David McCann. *Boys Don't Cry: The Struggle for Justice and Healing in Canada's Biggest Sex Abuse Scandal*. Toronto, Ontario: Mc-Clelland and Stewart, Inc., 1996. Chronicles the scandal involving the sexual abuse of minors by Brothers of the Christian Schools at St. Joseph's Training School for Boys in Alfred, Ontario, based on articles published in the *Toronto Star* beginning in the early 1990s. The author was cited for excellence in investigative reporting by the Canadian Association of Journalists.

Hopkins, Harold. "The Effects of Clergy Sexual Misconduct on the Wider Church." From Hopkins, Nancy Meyer, and Mark Laaser, eds. *Restoring the Soul of a Church: Healing Congregations Wounded by Clergy Sexual Misconduct*. Bethesda, Md.: The Alban Institute, Inc., in association with the Interfaith Sexual Trauma Institute, 1995. Discusses the impact of clergy sexual misconduct on non-offending clergy, church staff, and congregants, including the financial impact on the church.

Horst, Elisabeth A. *Questions and Answers about Clergy Sexual Misconduct*. Collegeville, Minn.: The Liturgical Press, in association with the Interfaith Sexual Trauma Institute, 2000. Booklet provides an overview of the issue of clergy sexual misconduct, presented in a question-and-answer format.

Houts, Donald C. "Training for Prevention of Sexual Misconduct by Clergy." From Gonsiorek, John C., ed. *Breach of Trust: Sexual Exploitation by Health Care Professionals and Clergy*. Thousand Oaks, Calif.: Sage Publications, 1995. Presents resources for the prevention of clergy sexual misconduct, drawn from training conferences on clergy sexual misconduct by the United Methodist Church in Illinois.

Hulme, William E. "Sexual Boundary Violations of Clergy." From Gabbard, Glen O., ed. *Sexual Exploitation in Professional Relationships*. Washington, D.C.: American Psychiatric Press, Inc., 1989. Presents an overview of the issue of clergy sexual misconduct among Protestant congregations occurring between male ministers and adult female congregants.

Annotated Bibliography

Investigative staff of the *Boston Globe*. *Betrayal: The Crisis in the Catholic Church*. Boston: Little, Brown and Company, 2002, revised with new afterword in 2003. Chronicles the clergy sexual abuse scandal in the Boston archdiocese, drawn from articles beginning in January 2002, by the investigative staff of the *Boston Globe*, which was awarded a 2003 Pulitzer Prize for their coverage of the scandal.

Irons, Richard, and Katherine Roberts. "The Unhealed Wounder." From Hopkins, Nancy Meyer, and Mark Laaser, eds. *Restoring the Soul of a Church: Healing Congregations Wounded by Clergy Sexual Misconduct*. Bethesda, Md.: The Alban Institute, Inc., in association with the Interfaith Sexual Trauma Institute, 1995. Discusses the psychological profiles of 25 male clergy who committed acts of sexual misconduct and were then assessed during a five-day multidisciplinary program.

Jacobs, Janet. "Charisma, Male Entitlement, and the Abuse of Power." From Shupe, Anson, William Stacey, et al., eds. *Bad Pastors: Clergy Misconduct in Modern America*. New York: New York University Press, 2000. Discusses the issue of clergy sexual misconduct by tracing the connection between charismatic authority and male entitlement in patriarchal church organizations.

Jenkins, Philip. "Clergy Sexual Abuse: The Symbolic Politics of a Social Problem." From Best, Joel, ed. *Images of Issues: Typifying Contemporary Social Problems, Second Edition*. New York: Aldine de Gruyter, 1995. A professor of history and religious studies argues that a general social concern over clergy sexual misconduct with minors was transformed into an attack on the Roman Catholic Church by, among others, victim advocacy groups, attorneys, and feminists.

———. *Pedophiles and Priests: Anatomy of a Contemporary Crisis*. New York: Oxford University Press, 1996. Discusses the extensive news coverage of clergy sexual misconduct involving minors by Roman Catholic priests as a manifestation of anti-Catholic bias by the media and others.

King, Sharon E. "Clergy Sexual Abuse." From Francoeur, Robert T., ed. *Sexuality in America: Understanding Our Sexual Values and Behaviors*. New York: Continuum Publishing Co., 1998. Summarizes recent events related to clergy sexual misconduct, with focus on pedophilia and sexual abuse of minors by U.S. Roman Catholic priests.

Kitchens, Ted. *Aftershock: What to Do When Leaders (and Others) Fail You*. Portland, Ore.: Multnomah Press, 1992. Discusses the issue of clergy sexual misconduct as a sin, using biblical references as a blueprint for a church's recovery from clergy sexual misconduct and for disciplining the offender.

Küstermann, Gabriele. "Sexual Conduct and Misconduct: Buddhist Ethics in the West." From Tsomo, Karma Lekshe, ed. *Innovative Buddhist*

Sexual Misconduct and the Clergy

Women: Swimming against the Stream. Richmond, Surrey, England: Curzon Press, 2000. Discusses Buddhist sexual ethics and the potential for sexual misconduct in Buddhism, including cultural differences between Asian teachers and Western practitioners.

Laeuchili, Samuel. *Power and Sexuality: The Emergence of Canon Law at the Synod of Elvira.* Philadelphia: Temple University Press, 1972. Discusses the sexual edicts promulgated by the Roman Catholic Church's Synod of Elvira in southern Spain in 309, and how the Spanish Catholic Church sought to control its faithful through sexual behavior. The book offers a historical perspective on how attitudes on sexuality were formed in the Catholic Church.

LaHaye, Tim. *If Ministers Fall, Can They Be Restored?* Grand Rapids, Mich.: Zondervan, 1990. Explores factors that contribute to clergy sexual misconduct in conservative Christian churches.

Langberg, Diane. "Clergy Sexual Abuse." From Kroeger, Catherine Clark, and James Beck, eds. *Women, Abuse and the Bible: How Scripture Can Be Used to Hurt or Heal.* Grand Rapids, Mich.: Baker Books, 1996, pp. 58–69. Explores issues of pastoral leadership and charisma as factors that may contribute to clergy sexual misconduct, written by a psychologist.

Lebacqz, Karen. *Professional Ethics: Power and Paradox.* Nashville: Abingdon Press, 1985. Examines ethical issues for ministers, including sexual ethics, written by a professor of ethics.

Lebacqz, Karen, and Ronald G. Barton, eds. *Sex in the Parish.* Louisville, Ky.: Westminster/John Knox Press, 1991. Argues that a romantic relationship between pastor and congregant is possible, but only under a set of controlled circumstances.

———. "Boundaries, Mutuality, and Professional Ethics." From Ragsdale, Katherine Hancock, ed. *Boundary Wars: Intimacy and Distance in Healing Relationships.* Philadelphia: Westminster Press, 1996, 96–110. Explores issues of friendship, intimacy, and sexual boundaries within a therapeutic relationship, including the relationship between a congregant and minister during spiritual counseling.

Lebacqz, Karen, and Joseph D. Driskill. "Ethics for Clergy." From Lebacqz, Karen, and Joseph D. Driskill, eds. *Ethics and Spiritual Care: A Guide for Pastors, Chaplains, and Spiritual Directors.* Nashville: Abingdon Press, 2000, pp. 37–55. Discusses the basic ethical obligations of parish clergy and the types of behavior that violate those ethics.

———. "Pastoral Care and Spiritual Direction." From Lebacqz, Karen, and Joseph D. Driskill, eds. *Ethics and Spiritual Care: A Guide for Pastors, Chaplains, and Spiritual Directors.* Nashville: Abingdon Press, 2000, pp. 59–83. Examines clergy sexual misconduct within the context of the Code of Ethics for the American Association of Pastoral Counselors.

Annotated Bibliography

Leberg, Eric. *Understanding Child Molesters: Taking Charge.* Thousand Oaks, Calif.: Sage Publications, 1997. Includes information on the criminal justice system and legal means of obtaining information on sexual offenders.

Linnane, Brian F. "Celibacy and Sexual Malpractice: Dimensions of Power and Powerlessness in Patriarchal Society." From Macy, Gary, ed. *Theology and the New Histories.* Maryknoll, N.Y.: Orbis, 1999, pp. 227–244. Discusses sexual misconduct by Roman Catholic priests in relation to the patriarchal power structure of the Catholic Church.

Loftus, John Allan. *Understanding Sexual Misconduct by Clergy: A Handbook for Ministers.* Washington, D.C.: Pastoral Press, 1996. Based on workshops for Roman Catholic priests and deacons conducted by the author, a Jesuit priest and professor of psychology.

Melton, Joy Thornburg. *Safe Sanctuaries: Reducing the Risk of Child Abuse in the Church.* Nashville: Discipleship Resources, 1998. Discusses the prevention of child abuse, including child sexual abuse, in a United Methodist setting, in response to a 1996 resolution adopted by the General Conference of the United Methodist Church.

Miles, Rebekah L. "Keeping Watch Over the Shepherds by Day and Night: Sexual Misconduct and Accountability among Moral Guides." From Miles, Rebekah L., ed. *The Pastor as Moral Guide.* Minneapolis: Augsburg Fortress, 1999, pp. 103–122. Presents a practical guide to the issue of clergy sexual misconduct, including information on prevention, ministerial accountability, and congregational response to clergy sexual misconduct.

Mitchell, Timothy. *Betrayal of the Innocents: Desire, Power, and the Catholic Church in Spain.* Philadelphia: University of Pennsylvania Press, 1998. Chronicles cases of sexual misconduct with minors by Roman Catholic priests in Spain during the 16th and 17th centuries, and includes a chapter on similar transgressions by priests in Spain during the 20th century.

Moore, Chris. *Betrayal of Trust: The Father Brendan Smyth Affair and the Catholic Church.* Dublin, Ireland: Marino Books, 1995. Chronicles the sexual abuse of minors by John Gerard Brendan Smyth while he was a Roman Catholic priest in Belfast, Ireland, over a period of four decades, beginning in the early 1960s. Smith, who victimized both boys and girls as young as six years of age, was convicted in 1994 on 17 counts relating to sexual misconduct with minors and sentenced to four years in prison.

Moore, N. "Dr. Jekyll and Rev. Hyde." From *Pulpit Confessions: Exposing the Black Church.* New York: Exodus Books, 1998, pp. 81–90. Discusses clergy sexual misconduct among African-American clergy, written under a pseudonym by an African-American pastor.

Morey, Ann-Janine. "A Tradition of Divine Lechery: Men Write about the Ministry." From Gelpi, Albert, and Ross Posnock, eds. *Religion and Sexuality in American Literature.* Cambridge, England: Cambridge University

Press, 1992, pp. 75–103. Discusses clergy sexual misconduct as an outgrowth of the tension between sexuality and religion within institutional settings, as portrayed in literature, including the novels *The Scarlet Letter* (1850) by Nathaniel Hawthorne, *The Damnation of Theron Ware* (1896) by Harold Frederic, and *A Month of Sundays* (1974) by John Updike.

Muck, Terry, ed. *Sins of the Body: Ministry in a Sexual Society.* Carol Stream, Ill.: Christianity Today, Inc., 1989. Presents a variety of viewpoints on the issue of clergy sexual misconduct in various denominations and the handling of incidents of sexual misconduct by clergy.

Muse, Steven J. "The Distorted Image: Clergy Sexual Abuse in an Orthodox Context." From Chirban, John T., ed. *Clergy Sexual Misconduct: Orthodox Christian Perspectives.* Brookline, Mass.: Hellenic College Press, 1994, pp. 19–43. Discusses the issue of clergy sexual misconduct in Orthodox Christian settings as violations of vocation, intimacy, and power.

Muster, Nori J. *Betrayal of the Spirit: My Life behind the Headlines of the Hare Krishna Movement.* Urbana: University of Illinois Press, 1997. An insider's account of sexual misconduct by male leaders within the Hare Krishnas, including child sexual abuse.

Neustein, Amy, and Michael Lesher. "The Silence of the Jewish Media on Sexual Abuse in the Orthodox Jewish Community." From Claussen, Dane S., ed. *Sex, Religion, Media.* Lanham, Md.: Rowman & Littlefield Publishers, Inc., 2002, pp. 79–87. Discusses the social and religious factors that hinder reporting in the Jewish press on sexual misconduct by rabbis within the Orthodox Jewish community in the United States and Israel.

O'Connor, Alison. *A Message from Heaven: The Life and Crimes of Father Sean Fortune.* Dingle, County Kerry, Ireland: Brandon-Mount Eagle Publications, 2000. Presents the account of Sean Fortune, a Roman Catholic priest in Ireland, who committed suicide in 1999 at age 45 during his trial on 66 counts of sexual abuse of minors between 1981 and 1987.

O'Grady, Ron. *The Hidden Shame of the Church: Sexual Abuse of Children and the Church.* Geneva, Switzerland: WCC Publications, 2001. Focuses on criminal acts of sexual abuse of minors by Christian clergy and lay workers, written by a pastor for the World Council of Churches (WCC). Offers an international perspective on the issue of clergy sexual misconduct.

Ohlschlager, George, and Peter T. Mosgofian. *Sexual Misconduct in Counseling and Ministry.* Waco, Texas: Word Books, 1995. Discusses the prevention of clergy sexual misconduct by thoroughly screening applicants to the ministry, and presents guidelines on providing assistance to victims and offenders.

Parkinson, Patrick. *Child Sexual Abuse and the Churches.* London: Hodder & Stoughton Ltd., 1997. Presents statistics on victims of clergy sexual misconduct, discusses theological issues related to clergy sexual abuse and offers guidelines for churches, primarily in Australia and England.

186

Annotated Bibliography

Parris, Matthew. *The Great Unfrocked: Two Thousand Years of Church Scandal.* London: Robson Books Ltd., 1998. A somewhat irreverent discussion of church scandals, including sexual scandals, written by an English radio commentator and newspaper columnist who was a former member of the British Parliament. The book is well researched, with extensive references.

Payer, Pierre J. *Sex and the Penitentials: The Development of a Sexual Code, 550–1150.* Toronto, Ontario: University of Toronto Press, 1984. Provides an academic survey of European Roman Catholic penitentials during the sixth through 12th centuries. Penitentials were akin to personal handbooks for clergy that set forth guidelines on sins, including sexual behavior, and penances (prayers offered for forgiveness). Useful in understanding the historical underpinnings of sexual attitudes in the modern Roman Catholic Church.

Plante, Thomas G., ed. *Bless Me Father for I Have Sinned: Perspectives on Sexual Abuse Committed by Roman Catholic Priests.* Westport, Conn.: Praeger, 1999. Offers perspectives by various contributors on clergy sexual misconduct and related issues, such as the psychology of pedophilia and the emotional components of victimization.

Poling, James Newton. "Sexual Abuse as a Theological Problem." From Fortune, Marie M., and James N. Poling. *Sexual Abuse by Clergy: A Crisis for the Church. Monograph No. 6.* Decatur, Ga.: Journal of Pastoral Care Publications, Inc., 1994, pp. 35–48. Discussion of clergy sexual misconduct from a theological perspective that equates clergy sexual abuse to incest.

Poloma, Margaret M. *The Assemblies of God at the Crossroads: Charisma and Institutional Dilemmas.* Knoxville: University of Tennessee Press, 1989. Discusses scandals within Pentecostal religious denominations, including sexual scandals, from a sociological perspective.

Puttick, Elizabeth. "The Problem of Sexual Abuse in New—and Old—Religions." From Hayes, Michael A., et al., eds. *Religion and Sexuality.* Sheffield, England: Sheffield Academic Press, 1998. Examines sexual relationships between male clergy and female congregants or followers in Western and Eastern religious traditions, including New Age religions.

Rediger, G. Lloyd. *Ministry and Sexuality: Cases, Counseling, and Care.* Minneapolis: Augsburg Fortress Press, 1990. Presents case studies of clergy sexual misconduct, and discusses clergy sexual ethics and related issues, such as sexual addiction, sexual harassment, and pedophilia.

Rossetti, Stephen J. *A Tragic Grace.* Collegeville, Minn.: The Liturgical Press, 1996. Examines the impact of sexual misconduct with minors by Roman Catholic priests, including 1992 research findings on the effects of clergy sexual abuse of minors on parishioners. The book also presents treatment options for offenders and related issues, such as recidivism and criteria for returning to the ministry.

Rutter, Peter. *Sex in the Forbidden Zone: When Men in Power—Therapists, Doctors, Clergy, Teachers, and Others—Betray Women's Trust.* Los Angeles: Jeremy P. Tarcher, Inc., 1989. A psychiatrist discusses sexual misconduct by clergy and other professionals as an abuse of power.

Scheper-Hughes, Nancy. "Institutionalized Sex Abuse and the Catholic Church." From Scheper-Hughes, Nancy, and Carolyn Sargent, eds. *Small Wars: The Cultural Politics of Childhood.* Berkeley: University of California Press, 1998, pp. 295–317. Discusses clergy sexual misconduct by Catholic clergy and challenges the church's assertion that such abuse is unrelated to priestly celibacy.

Schoener, Gary R., and Jeanette Hofstee Milgrom. "Sexual Exploitation by Clergy and Pastoral Counselors." From Schoener, Gary R., et al., eds. *Psychotherapists' Sexual Involvement with Clients: Intervention and Prevention.* Minneapolis: Walk-In Counseling Center, 1989. Presents case studies of clergy sexual misconduct referred for treatment at psychologist Schoener's Walk-in Counseling Center in Minneapolis. Examines the issue of sexual misconduct from the perspectives of the victim, the offender, and the church or religious organization.

Schwab, Charlotte Rolnick. *Sex, Lies and Rabbis: Breaking a Sacred Trust.* Bloomington, Ind.: 1st Books Library, 2002. Discusses sexual misconduct by rabbis, including the extent of the problem within congregational Judaism, guidelines for the prevention of sexual misconduct, and outreach to victims. Presents examples of rabbis who engaged in sexual misconduct.

Sennott, Charles M. *Broken Covenant.* New York: Simon & Schuster, 1992. Chronicles the allegations of sexual misconduct of minors made against Catholic priest Bruce Ritter, founder of Covenant House, a refuge for homeless and disenfranchised youth in New York City.

Shupe, Anson D. *In the Name of All That's Holy: A Theory of Clergy Malfeasance.* Westport, Conn.: Praeger, 1995. Examines systemic issues within religious organizations, such as opportunities for sexual exploitation by clergy as members of a trusted hierarchy, from a sociological perspective.

———. *Wolves within the Fold: Religious Leadership and Abuses of Power.* New Piscataway, N.J.: Rutgers University Press, 1998. Offers a collection of essays organized around the issue of clergy sexual misconduct, particularly in Roman Catholic settings. Topics include pedophilia, homosexuality, and celibacy.

Sipe, A. W. Richard. "The Problem of Prevention in Clergy Sexual Abuse." From Plante, Thomas G., ed.. *Bless Me Father for I Have Sinned: Perspectives on Sexual Abuse Committed by Roman Catholic Priests.* Westport, Conn.: Praeger, 1999, pp. 59–85. Examines the institutional impediments within the Roman Catholic Church for implementing programs for the prevention of sexual abuse of minors by priests.

188

————. *A Secret World: Sexuality and the Search for Celibacy.* New York: Brunner/Mazel, 1990. Examines the sexual adjustment of men who become Roman Catholic priests and take a vow of celibacy, written by a retired Catholic priest who later married.

————. *Sex, Priests, and Power: Anatomy of a Crisis.* New York: Brunner/Mazel Publishers, 1995. Discusses the sexual abuse of minors by Catholic priests and examines the backgrounds of priests who sexually abused minors, identifying four categories of offenders predisposed to commit sexual abuse.

Stacey, William A., et al. "How Much Clergy Malfeasance Is Really Out There? A Victimization Survey of Prevalence and Perceptions." From Shupe, Anson, et al., eds. *Bad Pastors: Clergy Misconduct in Modern America.* New York: New York University Press, 2000, pp. 187–213. Presents preliminary findings from a study undertaken by the authors to determine through statistical extrapolation the prevalence of clergy sexual misconduct in the United States.

Steed, Judy. *Our Little Secret: Confronting Child Sexual Abuse in Canada.* Toronto, Canada: Random House of Canada, 1994. Chronicles the account of sexual misconduct by John Ballienne, choirmaster of St. George's Cathedral, an Anglican church in Ontario Province, beginning in 1974. In 1992, Ballienne pleaded guilty to multiple counts of sexual abuse of minors and was sentenced to 18 months in prison. Ten victims of Bellienne were later awarded a $9 million judgment in a civil lawsuit.

Stockton, Ronald R. "The Politics of a Sexual Harassment Case." From Shupe, Anson, et al., eds. *Bad Pastors: Clergy Misconduct in Modern America.* New York: New York University Press, 2000, pp. 131–154. Presents a case study of clergy sexual misconduct within the Presbyterian Church (U.S.A.)., in which a female church elder filed a formal ecclesiastical complaint of verbal and physical sexual harassment and was joined by five more women, four of whom were church employees.

Tabachnick, Joan, ed. *Because There Is a Way to Prevent Child Sexual Abuse: Facts about Abuse and Those That Might Commit It.* Brandon, Vt.: The Safer Society Press, 1998. This booklet presents an overview of the issue of sexual abuse of minors, including brief chapters on defining sexual abuse, responding to allegations of sexual abuse, and the warning signs in children who are victims of such abuse.

Taylor, Catherine, and Lisa Aronson Fontes. "Seventh Day Adventists and Sexual Child Abuse." From Fontes, Lisa Aronson, ed. *Sexual Abuse in Nine North American Cultures.* Thousand Oaks, Calif.: Sage Publications, Inc., 1995, pp. 176–199. Discusses child sexual abuse within Seventh Day Adventist settings and examines issues including the culture of the church and the closed family systems among Seventh Day Adventists.

Sexual Misconduct and the Clergy

Thigpen, Thomas Paul, ed. *Shaken by Scandals: Catholics Speak Out about Priests' Sexual Abuse.* Ann Arbor, Mich.: Servant Publications, 2002. Catholics from various walks of life speak out on the sexual abuse scandal in the U.S. Catholic Church and discuss what should be done to prevent clergy sexual misconduct by priests.

Van der Zee, John. *Agony in the Garden: Sex, Lies, and Redemption from the Troubled Heart of the American Catholic Church.* New York: Thunder's Mouth Press/Nation Books, 2002. Discusses the need for reform in the Roman Catholic Church and chronicles case studies of clergy sexual misconduct by U.S. Catholic priests.

Waller, Altina L. *Reverend Beecher and Mrs. Tilton: Sex and Class in Victorian America.* Amherst: University of Massachusetts Press, 1982. Historian's analysis of the adulterous relationship, made public in 1872, between Elizabeth Tilton, a parishioner at Plymouth Church in Brooklyn, New York, and her pastor, Henry Ward Beecher, a prominent 19th-century Protestant clergyman.

Weiser, Conrad W. *Healers—Harmed and Harmful.* Minneapolis: Fortress Press, 1994. Examines the issue of clergy sexual misconduct as a manifestation of unresolved personal issues by clergy.

Whetsell-Mitchell, Juliann. *Rape of the Innocent: Understanding and Preventing Child Sexual Abuse.* Florence, Ky.: Taylor & Francis, 1995. Provides an overview of the issue of child sexual abuse, including information on developmental psychology and guidelines on the prevention of sexual abuse of minors. The book includes chapters on minority children and children with special needs who may be at risk.

Winebrenner, Jan, and Debra Frazier. *When a Leader Falls: What Happens to Everyone Else?* Minneapolis: Bethany House Publishers, 1993. Discusses clergy sexual misconduct in Christian settings and includes case studies using pseudonyms.

Yantzi, Mark. *Sexual Offending and Restoration.* Waterloo, Ontario: Herald Press, 1998. Discusses the issue of clergy sexual misconduct from the perspective of the offender, while integrating accounts of victims of clergy sexual misconduct. Uses a restorative justice model as a means of reconciling the needs of victims and offenders.

ARTICLES AND PAPERS

Allen, John L., Jr. "Secret Vatican Norms on Abuse Show Conflicts with U.S. Policy." *National Catholic Reporter,* vol. 39, November 29, 2002, p. 5. Available online. URL: http://www.natcath.com/NCR_Online/archives/112902/112902f.htm. Downloaded on February 20, 2004. Discusses agreements and potential conflicts between norms on clergy sexual misconduct with minors promulgated by Pope John Paul II on April 30, 2001, and those adopted by the U.S. Conference of Catholic Bishops at their June 2002 meeting in Dallas, Texas. The Vatican document, "Vatican Norms Governing Grave Offenses Including Sexual Abuse of Minors," is available online at URL: http://www.natcath.org/NCR_Online/documents/index.htm.

Australian Catholic Bishops Conference. "Integrity in Ministry: A Document of Principles and Standards for Catholic Clergy and Religious in Australia." Report, National Committee for Professional Standards, Australian Catholic Bishops Conference and the Australian Conference of Leaders of Religious Institutes, Melbourne, Australia, 1999. Presents guidelines for clergy, particularly Roman Catholic priests, for the prevention of clergy sexual misconduct, presented from a theological perspective.

Belluck, Pam. "Boston Sexual Abuse Report Breaks Down Accusations." *New York Times*, vol. 24, February 26, 2004, p. A1. Presents statistics on sexual misconduct by Catholic clergy in the Archdiocese of Boston, Massachusetts, and makes comparisons with findings contained in the national survey "The Nature and Scope of the Problem of Sexual Abuse of Minors by Catholic Priests and Deacons in the United States, 1950–2002," released on February 27, 2004, by the United States Conference of Catholic Bishops (USCCB).

Berry, Jason. "Why I Am (Still) Catholic." *National Catholic Reporter*, vol. 36, September 1, 2000, p. 14. Presents statistics on U.S. Catholics that signify their enduring faith in the Catholic Church and clergy despite sexual abuse scandals.

Burke, Anne, et al. "A Report on the Crisis in the Catholic Church in the United States." Report, National Review Board for the Protection of Children and Young People, United States Conference of Catholic Bishops (USCCB), February 27, 2004. Available online. URL: http://www.catholicreviewboard.com/Report.pdf. Posted on February 27, 2004. Provides a detailed analysis of findings presented in "The Nature and Scope of the Problem of Sexual Abuse of Minors by Catholic Priests and Deacons in the United States," a research study conducted by the John Jay College of Criminal Justice, as commissioned by the USCCB. The report also provides recommendations for further study of the issue of sexual misconduct by Catholic clergy and suggests guidelines for the prevention of such misconduct.

Butterfield, Fox, "789 Children Abused by Priests since 1940, Massachusetts Says." *New York Times*, vol. 23, July 24, 2003, p. A1. Available online. URL: http://www.yourlawyer.com/practice/news.htm?story_id=6368&topic=Clergy%20Abuse. Discusses the 2003 report released by the attorney general of Massachusetts on the scope of clergy sexual abuse by Catholic priests serving in Massachusetts dioceses over a period of some 60 years.

Cagney, Mary. "Sexual Abuse in Churches Not Limited to Clergy." *Christianity Today*, vol. 41, October 6, 1997, p. 90. Presents statistics that approximately half of church sexual misconduct cases involve allegations made against clergy, according to findings in a survey of 1,700 congregations of various denominations, and that the remaining cases involve church staff members and church volunteers.

Canadian Conference of Catholic Bishops. "From Pain to Hope: Report from the Canadian Catholic Bishops' Ad Hoc Committee on Child Sexual Abuse." Report, Canadian Conference of Catholic Bishops, 1992. Presents recommendations by a seven-member committee on how the Canadian Catholic Church should respond to victims of clergy sexual misconduct, their families, priest offenders, and affected congregations, and proposes steps for prevention of sexual misconduct by priests.

Catholic League for Religious and Civil Rights. "Sexual Abuse in a Social Context: Catholic Clergy and Other Professionals." Special Report, *The Catholic League*, February 2004. Available online. URL: http://www. catholicleague.org/research/abuse_in_social_context.htm. Posted on February 21, 2004. Compares the extent of sexual misconduct by U.S. Catholic priests to the incidence of such misconduct among other professionals, including Protestant ministers, Jewish rabbis, and teachers.

Catholic News Service. "Some Bishops Release 50-Year Recaps of Clergy Sexual Abuse." *The Tiding*, vol. 38, January 14, 2004, p. 1. Available online. URL: http://www.the-tidings.com/2004/cns/cns0114.htm. Reviews statistics on sexual misconduct by Catholic clergy between 1950 and 2002 in various U.S. dioceses, including some in California, Indiana, Iowa, Florida, Louisiana, New York, North Dakota, and Texas.

Clayton, Mark, "Sex Abuse Spans Spectrum of Churches." *Christian Science Monitor*, vol. 21, April 5, 2002, p. A1. Provides an overview of clergy sexual misconduct occurring in religious denominations other than Catholic.

Colbert, Chuck. "Parishioners, Priests Search for Solutions." *National Catholic Reporter*, vol. 38, March 15, 2002, p. 12. Special report on the impact of the clergy sexual abuse scandal by U.S. priests on local parishes and on pastors in ministering to their congregations.

Dart, John. "Risk Management: Protestants Confront Sexual Abuse." *The Christian Century*, vol. 119, June 5, 2002, p. 8. Presents measures for preventing clergy sexual misconduct and for managing allegations of such misconduct in Protestant denominational settings.

Donovan, Gill. "Expert Says Abuse Policy Should Extend to Bishops." *National Catholic Reporter*, vol. 38, August 16, 2002, p. 10. Presents opinions on the causes and consequences of clergy sexual misconduct in Catholic and Protestant denominations by the director of a Connecticut mental health network that treats both victims of clergy sexual misconduct and offenders.

————. "Religious Orders Take Different View of Abuse Policy." *National Catholic Reporter*, vol. 38, August 16, 2002, p. 10. Discusses different viewpoints on the Catholic sexual abuse scandal presented at the annual meeting of the Conference of Major Superiors of Men, a group of leaders of Catholic religious orders, held on August 7, 2002, in Philadelphia, Pennsylvania.

————. "Some See Big Reforms on Horizon: Conservatives and Liberals Align in Call for Lay Involvement," *National Catholic Reporter*, vol. 38, July 19, 2002, p. 3. Discusses reforms implemented by the U.S. Conference of Catholic Bishops (USCCB) in June 2002 and the appointment of conservative and liberal Catholics as members of the National Lay Review Board to oversee the implementation of those reforms.

Ferder, Fran, and John Heagle. "Clerical Sexual Abuse: Exploring Deeper Issues." *National Catholic Reporter*, vol. 68, May 10, 2002, p. 6. Discusses reforms aimed at preventing clergy sexual misconduct by U.S. Catholic priests and the impact such reforms may have on celibacy and other aspects of the Catholic priesthood.

Filteau, Jerry. "Understanding of Child Sexual Abuse Has Evolved in Last 50 Years." Story of the Day, *Catholic News Service*, February 23, 2004. Available online. URL: http://www.catholicnews.com/data/stories/cns/20040223.htm. Posted on February 23, 2004. Discusses the evolution in the awareness of child sexual abuse as a serious problem and the responsiveness to incidents of such abuse by law enforcement, social service agencies, and others, from 1950 to the present day.

Fortune, Marie M. "Is Nothing Sacred? The Betrayal of the Ministerial or Teaching Relationship," *Journal of Feminist Studies in Religion*, vol. 10, Spring 1994, p. 17. A basic primer on clergy sexual misconduct that defines clergy sexual misconduct and discusses how such misconduct may occur in a variety of religious and educational settings.

————. "Spare Us the False Shepherds, *SIECUS Report*, vol. 28, February–March 2000, p. 14. Discusses the occurrence of clergy sexual misconduct since the mid-1980s in various denominational settings, including the Jewish, Roman Catholic, Buddhist, and Protestant religions. The article presents data on the rise in lawsuits as a result of allegations of clergy sexual misconduct and discusses the concept of religious freedom as guaranteed by the First Amendment.

Gilbert, Natasha. "Darkness in the Catholic Confessional." *The Times Higher Education Supplement*, vol. 10, August 22, 2003, p. 18. Discusses clergy sexual abuse, primarily in the Roman Catholic Church, and examines limited statistical research on the issue.

Golway, Terry. "Dangerous Sentiments?" *America*, vol. 187, August 26, 2002, p. 7. Discusses the emergence and rise in membership of Voice of the Faithful, a group of Catholics organized in the wake of the sex abuse scandal in the Boston archdiocese, and the group's advocacy for sweeping reforms within the U.S. Catholic Church.

Goodstein, Laurie. "Abuse Scandal Is Now History, Top Bishops Say." *New York Times*, vol. 24, February 28, 2004, p. A1. Discusses comments by leaders in the United States Conference of Catholic Bishops (USCCB), the National Review Board (NRB) for the Protection of Children and Young People, and U.S. religious scholars on the report "The Nature and Scope of the Problem of Sexual Abuse of Minors by Catholic Priests and Deacons in the United States, 1950–2002," released on February 27, 2004, by the USCCB.

Goodstein, Laurie. "Celibacy Issue Flares Again within Ranks of U.S. Priesthood." *New York Times*, vol. 23, September 5, 2003, p. A5. Discusses the debate over celibacy as a factor in clergy sexual misconduct by U.S. Catholic priests.

Goodstein, Laurie, and Anthony Zirilli. "Decades of Damage: Trail of Pain in Church Crisis Leads to Nearly Every Diocese." *New York Times*, vol. 23, January 12, 2003, p. A1. Discusses findings of a comprehensive study by the *New York Times* on the prevalence of sexual misconduct within the U.S. Catholic Church.

Grabowski, John S. "Clerical Sexual Misconduct and Early Traditions Regarding the Sixth Commandment," *The Jurist*, vol. 55, Summer 1995, p. 527. Presents clergy sexual misconduct from a canonical legal perspective and includes a discussion of the history of the Sixth Commandment against adultery.

Guccione, Jean, and William Lobdell. "Law Spurred Flood of Sex Abuse Suits." *Los Angeles Times*, vol. 123, January 1, 2004, p. A1. Discusses how some 800 civil lawsuits alleging sexual misconduct by Catholic clergy were filed in California during 2003, when the statute of limitations for filing claims was extended for a 12-month period.

Hall, Dinah. "It's Not Just Happening in Boston." *Working Together to Prevent Sexual and Domestic Violence Newsletter*, vol. 22, Spring 2002, p. 1. Discusses the scope of clergy sexual misconduct within Catholic and other denominations.

Jones, Arthur. "Church in Crisis: A Chronology of Sex Abuse in Southern California." *National Catholic Reporter*, vol. 19, January 31, 2003, p. 14. Provides a useful chronology from March 2002 through January 2003 of sexual misconduct by Catholic priests in several dioceses in Southern California, including the Los Angeles archdiocese.

Kennedy, John W. "$1.75 Million Paid to Abuse Victims." *Christianity Today*, vol. 38, June 20, 1994, p. 56. Discusses the sexual misconduct case of former Assemblies of God minister Dalton Webber and the legal settlement reached with plaintiffs who accused Webber of sexually molesting them from 1971 to 1985, while Webber was pastor of Good Shepherd Worship Center in Carlsbad, California.

Kichline, Kathleen MacInnis. "Footnotes that Determine History: Sex Scandals Grab Headlines While Liturgical Directives Ritualize Clerical Separation." *National Catholic Reporter*, vol. 39, November 15, 2002, p. 21. Available online. Discusses the liturgical direction to reinstate the communion rail in churches, made by Catholic bishops in June 2002, as a symbol of a growing separation between parishioners and priests as a result of the clergy sexual abuse scandal in the Catholic Church.

Knott, J. Ronald. "Collateral Damage: How One Priest Feels These Days." *America*, vol. 187, July 29, 2002, p. 20. First-person account by a Catholic priest on the impact of the clergy sexual abuse scandal on his ministry.

Lobdell, William. "27-Year Abuse Tally Released by O.C. Church." *Los Angeles Times*, vol. 123, January 3, 2004, p. B1. Presents statistics released by the diocese of Orange, California, on the incidence of sexual misconduct by Catholic clergy serving in Orange County (O.C.) from 1976 to 2002.

Lobdell, William, and Larry B. Stammer. "Mahony Criticized by National Review Panel." *Los Angeles Times*, vol. 123, February 28, 2004, p. A1. Discusses the criticism of Los Angeles archbishop Roger Mahony, New York archbishop Edward M. Egan, former Boston archbishop Bernard F. Law, and others for their reluctance to disclose information on allegedly sexually abusive priests under their supervision, as expressed in "A Report on the Crisis in the Catholic Church in the United States," released on February 27, 2004, by the United States Conference of Catholic Bishops' (USCCB's) National Review Board (NRB) for the Protection of Children and Young People.

Martin, Michelle. "Chicago Archdiocese Gives Accounting of Sex Abuse Costs." *National Catholic Reporter*, vol. 39, February 7, 2003, p. 10. Discusses financial costs of clergy sexual misconduct in the Chicago archdiocese, including legal settlements and jury awards to victims, psychological treatment for offenders, and declines in contributions by parishioners in the aftermath of a sexual abuse scandal.

"Massachusetts Attorney General Grand Jury Report." June 23, 2003. Available online. URL: http://www.survivorsfirst.org/downloads/Crimine.pdf. Downloaded on February 20, 2004, from the web site of Survivors First. Presents findings of a grand jury investigation of sexual misconduct by Catholic priests serving in Massachusetts since 1950.

Matovina, Timothy. "A Fundamental Gap: Conservatives, Progressives and Hispanic Catholicism." *America*, vol. 188, March 17, 2003, p. 6. Examines differing perspectives on clergy sexual misconduct in the Catholic Church.

Minnesota Interfaith Committee on Sexual Exploitation by Clergy. "Entrusted to Our Care: Reflections and Guidelines for Religious Leaders." Report, Minnesota Interfaith Committee on Sexual Exploitation by Clergy, 1989. Discusses the issue of clergy sexual misconduct in a legal and social context, written by one of eight subcommittees on the Task Force on Sexual Exploitation by Counselors and Therapists created by the Minnesota State Legislature in 1984.

Moore, Art. "Megachurch Pastor Resigns but Denies Sexual Misdeeds." *Christianity Today*, vol. 42, July 13, 1998, p. 26. Presents the case of Bob Moorehead, who resigned as pastor of a nondenominational evangelical church in Redmond, Washington, as the result of accusations of sexually molesting some 17 minors. Moorehead was subsequently exonerated of all allegations by church elders, who cited a scriptural mandate for a witness other than the accuser to be present at the time of the offense.

Morey, Ann-Janine. "The Reverend Idol and Other Parsonage Secrets: Women Write Romances about Ministers, 1880–1950," *Journal of Feminist Studies in Religion*, vol. 6, Spring 1990, p. 87. Reviews romance literature from the 19th and 20th centuries for stories about illicit affairs between clergy and female congregants.

O'Neill, John, "For Sex Addiction, Too, Answers Will Be Found." *National Catholic Reporter*, vol. 31, July 28, 1995, p. 21. Discusses clergy sexual misconduct as a manifestation of a sexual addiction and describes the work of Wounded Brothers, an organization that provides counseling and support for sex-addicted clerics.

O'Neill, Robert. "Priests' Rights Could Be the Next Victim of Church's Scandal." Beliefnet.com. Posted in 2002. Discusses the rights of priests and other clergy faced with allegations of sexual misconduct and how those rights may be put at risk when public allegations are generated by media coverage.

Ostling, Richard N. "Protestant Clergy Sex Abuse Issue Murky." *Associated Press*, as published in the *Boston Globe*, vol. 77, February 22, 2004, p. A1. Discusses the difficulty in quantifying the extent of clergy sexual misconduct in Protestant denominations, due to factors including the diffuse structure of many such congregations, as compared with the more centralized hierarchical structure of the Catholic Church.

Patterson, Margot. "Call to Action Proposes Sex Abuse Guidelines." *National Catholic Reporter*, vol. 38, June 7, 2002, p. 8. Available online. Presents recommendations by the Catholic reform advocacy group Call to Action on the prevention and elimination of sexual misconduct by U.S. Catholic priests.

Paulson, Michael. "Scandal Eclipses a Far-Reaching Record." *Boston Globe*, vol. 27, December 14, 2002, p. A1. Available online. Discusses the career accomplishments of Cardinal Bernard F. Law, who on December 12, 2003, submitted his resignation as archbishop of the Boston archdiocese in the wake of widespread allegations that Law concealed the pasts of sexually abusive priests from parishes to which they were later transferred.

Peterson, Michael R., et al. "The Problem of Sexual Molestation by Roman Catholic Clergy: Meeting the Problem in a Comprehensive and Responsible Manner." Report, United States Conference of Catholic Bishops (USCCB), 1985. Available online at http://www.natcath.com/NCR_ Online/documents. Provides a comprehensive evaluation of clergy sexual misconduct as it existed within the U.S. Roman Catholic Church in 1985. Initially prepared as a private document for the USCCB, the report's key recommendation to establish an impartial national review committee to investigate allegations of sexual misconduct by Roman Catholic clergy was essentially ignored by U.S. Catholic bishops.

Pfeiffer, Sacha. "Memos Reveal Trail of Charges." *Boston Globe*, vol. 36, June 5, 2002, p. A16. Discusses the Boston archdiocese's release of internal memos that reveal a pattern of covering up allegations of sexual misconduct by former priest Joseph Birmingham while he was assigned to the archdiocese.

Raushenbush, Paul B. "Questions and Answers about Clergy Sexual Misconduct." Beliefnet.com. Posted in 2002. Presents an overview of clergy sexual misconduct in a question-and-answer format, utilizing three experts on the issue: Robert Clark of Clergy Consultation Service, the Rev. Thelma B. Burgonio-Watson of Training and Education at the Center for the Prevention of Sexual and Domestic Violence, and the Rev. Bud Holland of the Ministry Development Office of the Episcopal Church in New York.

Shelley, Marshall. "Forty Years before Churches Were Articulating Vision and Values, There Was Modesto." *Leadership Journal*, vol. 24, Winter 2003, p. 3. Discusses evangelist Billy Graham's 1948 meeting in Modesto, California, with officials from his organization to formulate a policy on clergy sexual misconduct, and the success of Graham's policy in the ensuing years of his ministry.

Simpkinson, Anne A. "Who Abuses?" Beliefnet.com. Posted in 2002. Discusses research findings on risk factors and traits common among clergy who engaged in sexual misconduct and compares those findings to sexual offenders in other professions, such as physicians and psychotherapists.

Staff of the *Cleveland Plain Dealer* and Wire Reports. "Dioceses across U.S. Sell Land, Borrow Money." *Cleveland Plain Dealer*, vol. 22, March 11, 2002, p. A1. Discusses financial consequences of large legal settlements due to clergy sexual misconduct scandals in Catholic dioceses throughout the United States. The article is part of the series "The Cost of Abuse," available online at http://www.cleveland.com/abuse.

Stammer, Larry B. "L.A. to Disclose Clergy Abuse." *Los Angeles Times*, vol. 123, February 17, 2004, p. A1. Presents statistics released by the Los Angeles archdiocese on February 17, 2004, on the extent of sexual misconduct by priests and other clergy serving in the archdiocese from 1950 to 2000.

Stevenson, Michael R. "Understanding Child Sexual Abuse and the Catholic Church: Gay Priests Are Not the Problem." *Angles*, the Policy Journal of the Institute for Gay and Lesbian Strategic Studies, vol. 6, September 2002, p. 1. Available online. URL: http://www.iglss.org/media/files/angles_62.pdf. Downloaded on February 10, 2004. Presents findings from several studies that pedophilia is a mental illness that is unrelated to sexual orientation.

Suffolk County, New York, Office of the District Attorney. "Grand Jury Report." Suffolk County, New York, Office of the District Attorney, May 6, 2002. Available online. URL: http://www.co.suffolk.ny.us/da/ DRVC%20GRAND%20JURY%20REPORT.pdf. Downloaded on February 20, 2004. Presents the findings of a nine-month grand jury investigation of clergy sexual misconduct in the diocese of Rockville Centre, New York.

Terry, Karen, et. al. "The Nature and Scope of the Problem of Sexual Abuse of Minors by Catholic Priests and Deacons in the United States. "Research Study, John Jay College of Criminal Justice, The City University of New York, February 27, 2004. Available online. URL: http://www. catholicreviewboard.com/johnjaypdfindex.html. Posted on February 27, 2004. Presents findings on the incidence of sexual abuse of minors by Catholic clergy from 1950 to 2002, in a study commissioned by the United States Conference of Catholic Bishops (USCCB), as mandated by the Charter for the Protection of Children and Young People that was adopted by the USCCB at its meeting in Dallas, Texas, in June 2002.

United States Conference of Catholic Bishops (USCCB). "Canonical Delicts Involving Sexual Misconduct and Dismissal from the Clerical State." Report, USCCB (formerly National Conference of Catholic Bishops), Washington, D.C., 1995. Presents guidelines for the dismissal of a Catholic cleric who has sexually abused a minor, in violation of canon 1395. The report includes a list of frequently asked questions and information on statutes of limitation set forth in canon law.

Watanabe, Teresa, "A Crisis of Many Faiths." *Los Angeles Times*, vol. 22, March 3, 2002, p. A1. Available online. URL: http://www.latimes.com/ news/nationworld/nation/la-032502punish.story. Downloaded on February 19, 2004. Discusses clergy sexual misconduct and ensuing legal settlements in various religious denominations.

Wirpsa, Leslie, "Blowing Whistle on Sex Abuse Means New Career for Priest." *National Catholic Reporter*, vol. 31, September 15, 1995, p. 5. Profiles the Rev. Thomas Doyle, Catholic priest and former canon lawyer for the Vatican embassy, and discusses the 1985 report Doyle coauthored with attorney F. Ray Mouton, "The Problem of Sexual Molestation by Roman Catholic Clergy." The report, which included the recommendation of establishing a centralized national review board to investigate all diocesan allegations of sexual misconduct by priests, was largely ignored by the United States Conference of Catholic Bishops (USCCB), and Doyle subsequently left his post as canon lawyer for the Vatican embassy.

Woodward, Kenneth L. "Sex, Morality and the Protestant Minister: What Sexual Standards Should the Clergy Obey?" *Newsweek*, vol. 130, July 28, 1997, p. 62. Discusses attempts by the United Church of Christ, the Presbyterian Church (USA), and the Episcopal Church to implement guidelines for appropriate sexual conduct by clergy.

WEB DOCUMENTS

Beliefnet.com. "Religious Views of Sodomy: A Look at How World Religions View Non-procreative Sexual Acts." Beliefnet.com. Posted in 2002. Presents a historical overview of teachings on sexuality by major religions, including Judaism, Catholicism and other Christian denominations, Islam, Buddhism, Hinduism, and Mormonism.

Survivors First, Inc., "Interim Report of Number of Allegedly Abusive Priests in the United States," 2003. Available online. URL: http://www. survivorsfirst.org. Provides an extensive database on U.S. Catholic priests accused of sexual misconduct. The report includes sections on criminal convictions, civil settlements and judgments, and pending civil actions and criminal prosecutions. The site permits access to the database by the name of the accused priest or by diocese. Downloaded on February 19, 2004.

Underwood, Anne, "Abuse of Power as a Justice Issue." 2002. Available online. URL: http://www.votf.org/papers/AbuseofPowerasJusticeIssue.html. Downloaded on February 19, 2004, from the web site of Voice of the Faithful. A discussion of clergy sexual abuse within all denominations as an issue of public justice, and not purely as an issue of morality to be dealt with internally by religious organizations.

VICTIMS AND CONGREGATIONS

BOOKS AND BOOK CHAPTERS

Allender, Dan B. *The Wounded Heart: Hope for Adult Victims of Childhood Sexual Abuse*. Colorado Springs, Colo.: Navpress, 1990. Discusses the topic of child sexual abuse and recovery from a conservative evangelical point of view.

Bass, Ellen, and Laura Davis. *The Courage to Heal: A Guide for Women Survivors of Child Sexual Abuse, 3rd Edition.* New York: Harper & Row, 1994. Provides a comprehensive discussion of the effects of child sexual abuse on women and provides guidance and resources for surviving such abuse.

Bera, Walter H. "Betrayal: Clergy Sexual Abuse and Male Survivors." From Gonsiorek, John C., ed. *Breach of Trust: Sexual Exploitation by Health Care Professionals and Clergy.* Thousand Oaks, Calif.: Sage Publications, 1995, pp. 91–111. Focuses on clergy sexual abuse of minors, drawn from the professional experiences of a psychologist who treated male victims of clergy sexual abuse.

Block, Heather. *Advocacy Training Manual: Advocating for Survivors of Sexual Abuse by a Church Leader/Caregiver.* Winnipeg, Manitoba: Mennonite Central Committee Canada, 1996. Provides guidelines and resources for advocates of victims of clergy sexual misconduct among Canadian Mennonites and other religious settings.

Burroughs, Margaret G. *The Road to Recovery: A Healing Journey for Survivors of Clergy Sexual Abuse.* Chatham, Mass.: Island Scribe, 1992. Booklet offers guidance and resources for female victims of clergy sexual misconduct, written by a survivor.

Carlson, David, and Margaret Carlson. "Child Molestation: One Family's Experience." From Chirban, John T, ed. *Clergy Sexual Misconduct: Orthodox Christian Perspectives.* Brookline, Mass.: Hellenic College Press, 1994, pp. 62–79. Chronicles the experiences of the parents of a girl who was sexually abused by a man who recently joined their church congregation, written under pseudonyms.

Center for Women and Religion. *A Clergy Abuse Survivors' Resource Packet, Third Edition.* Berkeley, Calif.: Center for Women and Religion, Graduate Theological Union, 1993. Provides guidance and resources for victims of clergy sexual misconduct, from a nondenominational perspective.

De Fuentes, Nanette. "Hear Our Cries: Victims-Survivors of Clergy Sexual Misconduct." From Plante, Thomas G., ed. *Bless Me Father for I Have Sinned: Perspectives on Sexual Abuse Committed by Roman Catholic Priests.* Westport, Conn.: Praeger, 1999, pp. 135–170. Discusses responses by church officials to victims of clergy sexual misconduct, written by a psychologist who is a consultant to the Roman Catholic archdiocese of Los Angeles, California.

Erickson-Pearson, Jan. *Safe Connections: What Parishioners Can Do to Understand and Prevent Clergy Sexual Abuse.* Minneapolis: Augsburg Fortress, Evangelical Lutheran Church in America, 1996. Booklet provides a discussion of clergy sexual misconduct within the Evangelical

Lutheran Church of America, including the prevention and consequences of such misconduct.

Flanagan, Eamonn. *Father and Me: A Story of Sexual Abuse at the Hands of a Priest.* North Blackburn, Victoria, Australia: HarperCollins Publishers (Australia), 1995. Provides a first-person account of a survivor of clergy sexual misconduct who was sexually abused from the age of 12 by a Roman Catholic priest in Australia.

Friberg, Nils. "Wounded Congregations." From Hopkins, Nancy Meyer, and Mark Laaser, eds. *Restoring the Soul of a Church: Healing Congregations Wounded by Clergy Sexual Misconduct.* Bethesda, Md.: The Alban Institute, in association with the Interfaith Sexual Trauma Institute, 1995, pp. 55–74. Discusses the impact of clergy sexual misconduct on congregations, including the spiritual dimensions as well as practical concerns such as media coverage and dealing with the perpetrator's spouse and family.

Hamilton, Phyllis, and Paul Williams. *Secret Love: My Life with Father Michael Cleary.* Edinburgh, Scotland: Mainstream Publishing Co., 1995. First-person account of a woman's 26-year romantic relationship with a Catholic priest, beginning in 1967 when she was a patient in a psychiatric hospital as the result of sexual abuse by her father and physical abuse by her mother.

Hanna, Jeffrey W. *Safe and Secure: The Alban Guide to Protecting Your Congregation.* Bethesda, Md.: The Alban Institute, Inc., 1999. Includes three chapters on issues related to clergy sexual misconduct, written by a United Methodist minister who was a former sheriff's deputy.

Haskin, Darlene K. "Afterpastors in Troubled Congregations." From Hopkins, Nancy Meyer, and Mark Laaser, eds. *Restoring the Soul of a Church: Healing Congregations Wounded by Clergy Sexual Misconduct.* Bethesda, Md.: The Alban Institute, Inc., in association with the Interfaith Sexual Trauma Institute, 1995, pp. 155–164. Discusses the impact of clergy sexual misconduct on congregations, based on interviews with ministers who assumed their pastorships in the aftermath of an incident of clergy sexual misconduct.

Hoertdoerfer, Patricia, and William Sinkford, eds. *Creating Safe Congregations: Toward an Ethic of Right Relations. A Workbook for Unitarian Universalists.* Boston: Unitarian Universalist Association, 1997. Discusses clergy sexual misconduct in a Unitarian setting and provides resources for further study and guidance.

Hopkins, Nancy Meyer, and Mark Laaser, eds. *Restoring the Soul of a Church: Healing Congregations Wounded by Clergy Sexual Misconduct.* Bethesda, Md.: The Alban Institute, Inc., in association with the Interfaith Sexual Trauma Institute, 1995. Provides guidance and resources for congregations dealing with an incident of clergy sexual misconduct, from the discovery of the allegation through the resolution of the crisis and its aftermath.

Horst, Elisabeth A. *Recovering the Lost Self: Shame-Healing for Victims of Clergy Sexual Abuse.* Collegeville, Minn.: The Liturgical Press, in association with the Interfaith Sexual Trauma Institute, 1998. Booklet on the spiritual healing and psychological recovery of victims of clergy sexual misconduct.

Jenkins, Clare. *A Passion for Priests: Women Talk about Their Love for Roman Catholic Priests.* London: Headline Book Publishing, 1995. Presents the accounts of women romantically involved with Roman Catholic priests, based on interviews with more than 50 women in England, France, Germany, and the United States.

Keene, Jane A. *A Winter's Song: A Liturgy for Women Seeking Healing from Sexual Abuse in Childhood.* New York: Pilgrim Press, 1991. Discusses spiritual healing from child sexual abuse, using masculine and feminine images of God.

Kelly, Andrew F. "Clergy Offenders." From Marshall, William Lamont, et al., eds. *Sourcebook of Treatment Programs for Sexual Offenders.* New York: Plenum Press, 1998, pp. 303–318. Provides an overview of the treatment of sex offenders, including assessment and aftercare.

Kennedy, Margaret. *The Courage to Tell: Christian Survivors of Sexual Abuse Tell Their Stories of Pain and Hope.* London: Churches Together in Britain and Ireland (CTBI), 1999. Presents the issue of clergy sexual abuse through first-person accounts of victims of such abuse, and offers guidelines and resources for victims, congregations, and offenders.

Knight, Ivor A. *Out of Darkness: Growing Up with the Christian Brothers.* South Fremantle, Western Australia: Fremantle Arts Centre Press, 1998. Autobiographical account of sexual abuse in a Catholic orphanage for boys run by the Christian Brothers in Australia.

Knudsen, Chilton R. "Understanding Congregational Dynamics." From Hopkins, Nancy Meyer, and Mark Laaser, eds. *Restoring the Soul of a Church: Healing Congregations Wounded by Clergy Sexual Misconduct.* Bethesda, Md.: The Alban Institute, Inc., in association with the Interfaith Sexual Trauma Institute, 1995. Offers a case study of an incident of clergy sexual misconduct in the Episcopal diocese of Chicago, Illinois, written by an Episcopal priest.

Laaser, Mark R. "Long-Term Healing." From Hopkins, Nancy Meyer, and Mark Laaser, eds. *Restoring the Soul of a Church: Healing Congregations Wounded by Clergy Sexual Misconduct.* Bethesda, Md.: The Alban Institute, Inc., in association with the Interfaith Sexual Trauma Institute, 1995, pp. 232–250. Discusses recovery from clergy sexual misconduct in the context of the four stages of grief—shock, searching, disorientation, and reorganization.

Langelan, Martha J. *Back Off!: How to Confront and Stop Sexual Harassment and Harassers.* New York: Simon & Schuster, 1993. Presents a first-person account of a woman who was sexually abused as a minor by a youth pastor at her church and her recovery from the sexual misconduct.

Lovelace, Marian E. *Remembering and Recovering: One Clergy Abuse Survivor's Pathway to Spiritual Renewal.* Las Vegas: Writing Unlimited Publishers, 1996. Autobiographical account of a victim of clergy sexual misconduct by a Roman Catholic priest and her process of recovery. The book is designed as a self-help tool for victims of clergy sexual misconduct.

Maes, Yvonne, with Bonita Slunder. *The Cannibal's Wife: A Memoir.* New York: Herodias, 1999. Firsthand account of a former Roman Catholic nun's sexual exploitation by a priest in Vancouver, British Columbia, with a discussion of the broader social and religious implications.

Maris, Margo E., and Kevin M. McDonough. "How Churches Respond to the Victims and Offenders of Clergy Sexual Misconduct." From Gonsiorek, John C., ed. *Breach of Trust: Sexual Exploitation by Health Care Professionals and Clergy.* Thousand Oaks, Calif.: Sage Publications, 1995, pp. 348–367. Discusses the response of churches to victims of clergy sexual misconduct, including the role of a church-designated victims' advocate and the handling of the disclosure of the incident to a congregation, written by an Episcopal priest and a Catholic priest.

Mellody, Pia. "Physical, Sexual, or Emotional Abuse from a Religious Representative." From Mellody, Pia, and Andrea Wells Miller. *Facing Codependence.* New York: HarperCollins Publishers, 1989, pp. 190–192. Discusses the impact on victims of sexual misconduct by religious leaders, including denial and repression of the misconduct.

Miller, Dee. *How Little We Knew: Collusion and Confusion with Sexual Misconduct.* Lafayette, La.: Prescott Press, 1993. First-person account of a victim of clergy sexual misconduct while serving as a missionary for the Southern Baptist Convention.

O'Doherty, Iseult. *Stolen Childhood: Testimonies of the Survivors of Child Sexual Abuse.* Dublin, Ireland: Poolbeg Press Ltd., 1998. Presents first-person accounts of victims of child sexual abuse by Catholic priests in Ireland and a follow-up on what happened to the priests involved in the sexual misconduct.

Pellauer, Mary D., et al. "Resources for Ritual and Recuperation." From Pellauer, Mary D., et al., eds. *Sexual Assault and Abuse: A Handbook for Clergy and Religious Professionals.* San Francisco: Harper & Row, 1987, pp. 209–218. Provides a variety of liturgical services and prayers for victims and congregations recovering from an incident of clergy sexual misconduct.

Poling, Nancy Werking, ed. *Victim to Survivor: Women Recovering from Clergy Sexual Abuse.* Cleveland, Ohio: United Church Press, 1999. First-person accounts by six women victims of clergy sexual misconduct from various Christian denominations.

Van Dyke, Beth. *What About Her?* Mukilteo, Wash.: WinePress Publishing, 1997. First-person account of a victim of sexual misconduct by her pastor, told with pseudonyms.

Willerscheidt, Phyllis A. "Healing for Victims." From Hopkins, Nancy Meyer, and Mark Laaser, eds. *Restoring the Soul of a Church: Healing Congregations Wounded by Clergy Sexual Misconduct*. Bethesda, Md.: The Alban Institute, in association with the Interfaith Sexual Trauma Institute, 1995, pp. 23–32. Discusses the recovery of victims of clergy sexual misconduct, written by an executive director of the Commission on Women, Roman Catholic Archdiocese of St. Paul and Minneapolis, Minnesota. The book has an overview that draws upon the author's experience facilitating a support group for women sexually exploited by clergy.

Women's Ministries Program Area. *Hearing the Silence, Healing the Pain: Stories of Professional Misconduct through Sexual Abuse in the Church*. Louisville, Ky.: Office of Women's Advocacy, Presbyterian Church (U.S.A.), 1995. Booklet drawn from the experiences of victims of clergy sexual misconduct in Presbyterian settings. The booklet includes questions for further discussion.

ARTICLES AND PAPERS

Boodman, Sandra G. "How Deep the Scars of Abuse?" *Washington Post,* vol. 34, July 29, 2002, p. A1. Available online. URL: http://www. washingtonpost.com/ac2/wp-dyn/A14253-2002Jul28?language=printer. Downloaded on February 21, 2004. Profiles victims of clergy sexual misconduct by Catholic priests and examines the varying effects of childhood sexual abuse on victims as adults.

Bruni, Frank. "Am I My Brother's Keeper?" *New York Times Magazine*, vol. 40, May 12, 2002, p. 12. Profiles David Clohessy, president of the victims' advocacy group Survivors Network of those Abused by Priests (SNAP), and discusses Clohessy's sexual abuse by a Catholic priest in the diocese of Jefferson City, Missouri, beginning in 1969, when Clohessy was 12 years of age, and continuing until 1973.

Clarke, Kevin. "Broken Trust, Broken Lives; Survivors of Priest Sexual Abuse Speak Out." *U.S. Catholic*, vol. 67, June 2002, p. 12. In-depth profiles of victims of clergy sexual misconduct by U.S. Catholic priests, with emphasis on the ramifications of childhood sexual abuse in adult life.

Goodstein, Laurie. "Victims' Group Uses Spotlight to Seek Changes in the Law." *New York Times*, vol. 107, May 10, 2002, page A10. Discusses the work of the victims' advocacy group Survivors Network of those Abused by Priests (SNAP) since its founding in 1992.

Fernadez, Elizabeth. "A Chance to Be Heard." *San Francisco Chronicle*, vol. 26, May 10, 2002, p. A27. Chronicles the impromptu meeting on May 9, 2002, of officials from the Archdiocese of San Francisco, California, with a group of alleged victims of clergy sexual misconduct by priests.

Kissinger, Meg. "Voices from the Pews Are Full of Anger, Hurt," *Milwaukee Journal Sentinel*, vol. 53, May 5, 2002, p. A1. Discusses the impact, both spiritually and in terms of church donations, on Catholics in Wisconsin in the wake of allegations of clergy sexual abuse against priests in the state.

Lenning, Chris. "Mending a Congregation's Heart," *The Lutheran*, vol. 6, June 2002, p. 20. Available online. URL: http://www.thelutheran.org/0206/page20.html. Downloaded on February 21, 2004. Discusses the shame and embarrassment often experienced by congregations in the aftermath of an incident of clergy sexual misconduct and provides guidelines and resources for recovery to congregations.

Solomonson, Sonia C. "I Could Heal or Die," *The Lutheran*, vol. 6, June 2002, p. 12. Available online. URL: http://www.thelutheran.org/0206/page12.html. Downloaded on February 21, 2004. Profiles the psychological and spiritual recovery of Linda Maue, who in 1992 was the victim of clergy sexual misconduct by her pastor in the Evangelical Lutheran Church of America.

Stamberg, Susan. "Sex Scandal's Impact: Life in Parishes Changes in Subtle but Real Ways." Transcript of broadcast on National Public Radio, May 9, 2002, p. 1. Available online. URL: http://www.npr.org/programs/morning/features/2002/may/priests/index.html. Posted May 9, 2002. Priests from several parishes in Massachusetts discuss the impact of the clergy sexual misconduct scandal in the Catholic Church on their ministries and on their congregations.

Strong, Barry R. "When the Pastor Is Removed: Lessons from a Grieving Parish." *America*, vol. 187, August 26, 2002, p. 8. The author recounts his Catholic parish's experience following the removal of its pastor as the result of allegations of sexual misconduct.

WEB DOCUMENTS

Blaine, Barbara A. "Survivors Wisdom." 2002. Available online. URL: http://www.snapnetwork.org/survivors_wisdom/Survivors_wisdom_1.htm. Downloaded on February 21, 2004. Presents guidelines for emotional growth for victims of clergy sexual misconduct and includes a step-by-step discussion of actions to redress the harm. Survivors Network of those Abused by Priests (SNAP).

"Choosing the Right Therapist." The Linkup—Survivors of Clergy Abuse. 2002. Available online. URL: http://www.thelinkup.org/. Downloaded on February 21, 2004. Presents an overview of types of therapists and how they are qualified to treat victims of sexual abuse, and discusses aspects of therapy, including confidentiality and various therapeutic modes.

Delaplane, David, and Anne Delaplane. "Victims of Child Abuse, Domestic Violence, Elder Abuse, Rape, Robbery, Assault, and Violent Death: A Manual for Clergy and Congregations." The Spiritual Dimensions in Victims Services, Denver, Colorado, 2001. Available online. URL: http://www.ojp.usdoj.gov/ovc/publications/infores/clergy/welcome.html. Downloaded on February 21, 2004. Discusses the role of congregations when a congregant becomes a victim of a crime, including clergy sexual misconduct.

Fortune, Marie M. "How Congregations Can Keep Young Members Safe from Abuse." Center for the Prevention of Sexual and Domestic Violence 2002. Available online. URL: http://www.cpsdv.org/Articles/how-congregations-keepsafe.htm. Downloaded on February 21, 2004. Presents guidelines for congregations in preventing clergy sexual misconduct and managing incidents of clergy sexual misconduct.

"Hearing and Being Heard: Boys Dealing with Sexual Abuse." Treating Abuse Today, Survivors and Victims Empowered, 2003. Available online. URL: http://child-abuse.com/SAVE/abouttat.html. Downloaded on February 21, 2004. Discusses the importance of validation in the process of recovery for male victims of childhood sexual abuse.

Miller, Dee Ann. "Spiritual Healing for Survivors of Clergy Sexual Abuse." Advocate Web. Posted in 1998. Available online. URL: http://advocateweb.org/hope/spiritualhealing.asp. Downloaded on February 21, 2004. Presents guidelines on the recovery process for victims of clergy sexual misconduct, written from the perspective of a registered nurse who is also a victim of clergy sexual abuse.

Polin, Victoria, and Gail Roy. "Common Coping Mechanisms Used by Adult Survivors of Sexual Abuse." The Awareness Center. 1994. Available online. URL: http://www.theawarenesscenter.org/copingmechanisms.html. Downloaded on February 21, 2004. Discusses coping mechanisms of victims of childhood sexual abuse, including minimizing or denying the sexual abuse, escapism through work, drugs, and alcohol, and suicidal attempts or ideation.

Polin, Victoria, et al. "When a Family Member Molests: Reality, Conflict, and the Need for Support." The Awareness Center. Posted. Available online. URL: http://www.theawarenesscenter.org/familymembermolests.html. Downloaded on February 21, 2004. Discusses the victimization of spouses and family members of sex offenders and provides guidance on coping with allegations of sexual misconduct made against a family member.

Smith, Susan K. "Civil Remedies for Victims of Sexual Abuse." Susan K. Smith, Attorney-Mediator, 2003. Available online. URL: http://www. smith-lawfirm.com/remedies.html. Downloaded on February 21, 2004. Presents an overview of remedies for victims of sexual misconduct and abuse who are considering filing civil lawsuits for damages. The document also presents information on practical and legal considerations, such as statutes of limitation and the availability of victim compensation funds provided by some states. The site was written by an attorney.

———. "First Steps". Susan K. Smith, Attorney-Mediator 2003. Available online. URL: http://www.smith-lawfirm.com/First_Steps.htm. Downloaded on February 21, 2004. Presents guidelines for victims of sexual misconduct and abuse who are considering legal action, including helpful links to statutes of limitations.

RELIGION AND SEXUALITY

BOOKS

Boyarin, Daniel. *Carnal Israel: Reading Sex in Talmudic Culture*. Philadelphia, Pa.: California-Princeton Press, 1993. Discusses the belief in Judaism that human sexuality is an mutual expression of the physical and spiritual.

Cabezón, Jose Ignacio, ed. *Buddhism, Sexuality, and Gender*. Ithaca, N.Y.: State University of New York Press, 1992. Provides historical and contemporary analysis of issues of sexuality in Buddhism, including the role of women in Buddhist culture.

Comstock, Gary David. *Unrepentant, Self-Affirming, Practicing Lesbian/Bisexual/Gay People within Organized Religion*. Herndon, Va.: Continuum International, 1996. Examines findings of various empirical studies on homosexuals who are practicing members in organized religions, including Islam, Judaism, and Christianity.

Foote, Catherine J. *Survivor Prayers: Talking with God about Childhood Sexual Abuse*. Louisville, Ky.: Westminster John Knox Press, 1994. Examines the effect of childhood sexual abuse on the spirituality of victims of abuse.

Fortune, Marie M. *Love Does No Harm: Sexual Ethics for the Rest of Us*. Herndon, Va.: Continuum International, 1998. Discusses how sexual ethics guide decisions on sexual behavior. Includes a foreword by former U.S. surgeon general M. Jocelyn Elders, M.D.

Fox, Thomas C. *Sexuality and Catholicism*. Scranton, Pa.: W.W. Norton, 2000. Examines the theme of sexuality and sin in the Roman Catholic Church, with emphasis on the impact of papal encyclicals on church teachings.

Gomes, Peter J. *The Good Book: Reading the Bible with Mind and Heart.* Scranton, Pa.: HarperCollins Publishers, 1998. Examines biblical teachings on a variety of subjects, including sexuality.

Gudorf, Christine E. *Body, Sex, and Pleasure: Reconstructing Christian Sexual Ethics.* Berea, Ohio: The Pilgrim Press, 1995. Discusses the historical development of traditional Christian sexual ethics, drawing from Christian theology and social sciences.

Hisel, Lisa M. *Sexuality and Christianity: A Bibliography Focusing on the Catholic Experience.* Washington, D.C.: Catholics for a Free Choice, 1998. Booklet containing references to works on Christian views of sexuality in the Catholic Church and non-Catholic Christian denominations.

Lebacqz, Karen, and David Sinacore-Guinn, eds. *Sexuality: A Reader.* Berea, Ohio: The Pilgrim Press, 1999. An anthology of essays examining sexuality from various religious perspectives. Contributing authors include John D'Emilio, James B. Nelson, Leonore Tiefer, and Naomi Wolf.

Monti, Joseph. *Arguing about Sex: The Rhetoric of Christian Sexual Morality.* Ithaca, N.Y.: State University of New York Press, 1995. Examines evolving Christian views on sexuality and presents a discussion of sexual ethics in the modern era.

Nelson, James B., and Sandra P. Longfellow, eds. *Sexuality and the Sacred: Sources for Theological Reflection.* Louisville, Ky.: Westminster John Knox Press, 1994. The relationship between spirituality and sexuality is explored in a collection of essays. Contributors include Carter Heyward, Lisa Sowle Cahill, L. William Countryman, Margaret Farley, and Audre Lorde.

Nugent, Robert, and Jeannine Gramick. *Building Bridges: Gay and Lesbian Reality and the Catholic Church.* Mystic, Conn.: Twenty-Third Publications, 1992. Examines issues of sexual orientation among practicing Roman Catholics, including clergy.

Parrinder, Geoffrey. *Sexual Morality in the World's Religions.* Newark, N.J.: Penguin Putnam, Inc., 1996. Discusses sexual morality within world religions in the modern era, including Buddhism, Christianity, Islam, and Judaism, and traces historical evolution of sexual morality within each faith.

Phipps, William E. *The Sexuality of Jesus.* Berea, Ohio: The Pilgrim Press, 1996. Discusses Western interpretations of the biblical teachings of Jesus Christ on sexuality, marriage, and gender.

Rosenblatt, Naomi H., and Joshua Horwitz. *Wrestling with Angels: What Genesis Teaches Us about Our Spiritual Identity, Sexuality, and Personal Relationships.* Des Plaines, Ill.: Bantam Doubleday Dell, 1997. Discusses the biblical treatment of issues including sexuality and gender in the book of Genesis.

Rotenberg, Mordechai. *The Yetzer: A Kabbalistic Perspective on Eroticism and Human Sexuality.* Fort Lee, N.J.: Jason Aronson, Inc., 1997. Examines human sexuality in the contexts of Jewish mysticism and modern psychology.

Seow, Choon Leong, ed. *Homosexuality and Christian Community*. Louisville, Ky.: Westminster John Knox Press, 1996. A collection of essays by faculty members of the Princeton Theological Seminary presents differing views on homosexuality in a Christian context.

Shaw, Teresa M. *The Burden of the Flesh: Fasting and Sexuality in Early Christianity*. Minneapolis, Minn.: Augsburg Fortress Publishers, 2000. Discusses early Christian ideals of sexuality, including virginity, and why they remain meaningful in the modern era.

Spong, John Shelby. *Living in Sin: A Bishop Rethinks Human Sexuality*. Scranton, Pa.: HarperCollins Publishers, 1990. Discusses the traditional teachings of the Episcopal Church on issues including celibacy and homosexuality, and examines their application in the modern era.

Terkel, Susan Neiburg. *Finding Your Way: A Book about Sexual Ethics*. Danbury, Conn.: Franklin Watts, 1995. Discusses religious ideas of sexuality and their application in the modern era in making decisions about sexual behavior.

Thornburg, John, and Alicia Dean, eds. *Finishing the Journey: Questions and Answers from the United Methodists of Conviction*. Dallas, Texas: Northaven United Methodist Church, 2000. The issue of homosexuality in the United Methodist Church is discussed in a collection of 15 essays on various aspects of the issue, including the ordination of gay and lesbian clergy.

Weiser-Hanks, Merry E. *Christianity and Sexuality in the Early Modern World: Regulating Desire, Reforming Practice*. Florence, Ky.: Routledge, 2000. Traces how modern sexual norms evolved from Christian ideas from the 16th through 18th centuries.

Westheimer, Ruth K., and Jonathan Mark. *Heavenly Sex: Sexuality in the Jewish Tradition*. New York: New York University Press, 1995. Discusses sexuality within Judaism and the Jewish culture. Includes a biblical glossary.

SEXUAL HARASSMENT

BOOKS

Achampong, Francis. *Workplace Sexual Harassment Law: Principles, Landmark Developments, and Framework for Effective Risk Management*. Westport, Conn.: Quorum Books, 1990. Provides a comprehensive discussion of workplace sexual harassment law and legal interpretation, written by an attorney for lawyers, students, and business professionals. Presented in four parts, topics covered include the evolution of workplace sexual harassment law, including landmark court cases.

Barickman, R. B., and M. A. Paludi. *Academic and Workplace Sexual Harassment: A Resource Manual.* Ithaca, N.Y.: State University of New York Press, 1992. Presents strategies for the prevention and handling of sexual harassment in workplace and academic settings.

Bingham, Shereen G., ed. *Conceptualizing Sexual Harassment as Discursive Practice.* Westport, Conn.: Praeger, 1994. A discussion of sexual harassment presented through discursive conceptualization, which relies upon the analysis of communication between individuals as a basis for understanding oppressive social conditions, including sexual harassment.

Brandenburg, Judith Berman. *Confronting Sexual Harassment: What Schools and Colleges Can Do.* Williston, Vt.: Teachers College Press, 1997. Focuses on the management and prevention of sexual harassment in schools, with information on the legal duty of educational institutions in the handling of allegations of sexual misconduct.

Brant, Clare, and Yun Lee Too, eds. *Rethinking Sexual Harassment.* London: Pluto Press, 1994. Presents a scholarly examination of sexual harassment, as manifested in a complex variety of forms.

Buss, David M., and Neil M. Malamuth, eds. *Sex, Power, and Conflict: Evolutionary and Feminist Perspectives.* New York: Oxford University Press, 1996. Presents 12 scholarly essays that include some discussions of sexual harassment from a psychological perspective.

Dobritch, Wanda, and Steven Dranoff. *The First Line of Defense: A Guide to Protecting Yourself against Sexual Harassment.* New York: John Wiley & Sons, Inc., 2000. Discusses sexual harassment, with emphasis on measures to reduce the incidence of sexual harassment with the use of hypothetical scenarios in corporate settings.

Dziech, Billie Wright, and Michael W. Hawkins. *Sexual Harassment in Higher Education: Reflections and New Perspectives.* New York: Garland Publishing, 1998. Presents a review of research findings on the issue of sexual harassment in school and university settings.

Gerdes, Louise, ed. *Sexual Harassment.* San Diego, Calif.: Greenhaven Press, 1999. Part of the *Current Controversies* series, this installment discusses the incidence, causes, and prevention of sexual harassment from opposing points of view.

Havelin, Kate. *Sexual Harassment: This Doesn't Feel Right!* Makato, Minn.: Capstone Press, 2000. Presents an overview of sexual harassment, including guidelines on the prevention and handling of incidents of sexual harassment. Written for elementary school students in grades four through six.

Jones, Constance. *Sexual Harassment.* New York: Facts On File, 1996. Part of the series *Library in a Book*, this installment presents a general overview of the issue of sexual harassment and includes a review of laws and legislation on the issue, a chronology of important developments, a guide to further research, and an annotated bibliography.

Kreps, Gary L, ed. *Sexual Harassment: Communication Implications.* Cresskill, N.J.: Hampton Press, 1993. Presents a series of essays by academics in the field of psychology and other social sciences on the nature, causes, and prevention of sexual harassment.

LeMoncheck, Linda, and Mane Hajdin. *Sexual Harassment: A Debate.* Lanham, Md.: Rowman & Littlefield Publishers, 1997. Presented as a debate between the co-authors, the issue of sexual harassment is examined in the context of the broader social issues of gender, sexuality, and power.

Morris, Celia. *Bearing Witness: Sexual Harassment and Beyond—Everywoman's Story.* Boston, Mass.: Little, Brown and Company, 1994. Presents a scholarly analysis of sexual harassment written for a general audience, including first-person accounts of women who were victims of sexual harassment.

O'Donohue, William, ed. *Sexual Harassment: Theory, Research, and Treatment.* Boston: Allyn & Bacon, 1997. Written as a college textbook on sexual harassment, various facets of the issue are presented in 16 chapters, including definitions of sexual harassment, treatment of victims and offenders, prevention, and social policy on the issue.

Office for Civil Rights. *Sexual Harassment: It's Not Academic.* Washington, D.C.: U.S. Department of Education, Office for Civil Rights, 1997. Booklet on recognizing and managing sexual harassment in educational settings, written for school administrators, teachers, students, and parents. Available online. URL: http://www.ed.gov/offices/OCR/ocrshpam.html.

O'Shea, Tracy, and Jane LaLonde. *Sexual Harassment: A Practical Guide to the Law, Your Rights, and Your Options for Taking Action.* Gordonsville, Va.: VHPS, 1998. Presents an overview of the issue and discusses the healing process for victims, written by two victims of sexual harassment.

Paludi, Michele A., and Richard B. Barickman. *Sexual Harassment, Work, and Education: A Resource Manual for Prevention, Second Edition.* Ithaca, N.Y.: Cornell University Press Services, 1998. Presents strategies for the prevention of sexual harassment in the workplace and school settings, and includes information on sexual harassment law.

Sandler, Bernice R., and Robert J. Shoop, eds. *Sexual Harassment on Campus: A Guide for Administrators, Faculty, and Students.* Needham Heights, Mass.: Allyn & Bacon, 1997. Discusses sexual harassment and related topics, including the law on sexual harassment, social policies, managing allegations of sexual harassment, and cross-cultural perspectives on the issue.

Stein, Laura W. *Sexual Harassment in America: A Documentary History.* Westport, Conn.: Greenwood Press, 1999. Presents an overview of the issue of sexual harassment, including significant court rulings and legislation, and discusses the occurrence of sexual harassment in a variety of settings, including workplace, school, and military settings.

Stein, Nan. *Classrooms & Courtrooms: Facing Sexual Harassment in K–12 Schools.* Williston, Vt.: Teachers College Press, 1999. Presents an overview of sexual harassment in schools, including summaries of significant court decisions, first-person accounts of student victims of sexual harassment, and a discussion of bullying as a form of sexual harassment at school.

Stockdale, Margaret S., ed. *Sexual Harassment in the Workplace: Perspectives, Frontiers, and Response Strategies.* Thousand Oaks, Calif.: Sage Publications, 1996. Presents an academic discussion of sexual harassment in university settings, including research findings on the issue, and strategies for the prevention of sexual misconduct in educational settings.

Taylor, Joan Kennedy. *What to Do When You Don't Want to Call the Cops: A Non-adversarial Approach to Sexual Harassment.* New York: New York University Press, 1999. Discusses the law on sexual harassment and its historical evolution, communication barriers between men and women that may contribute to the occurrence of sexual harassment, and prevention strategies.

Webb, Susan L. *Shockwaves: The Global Impact of Sexual Harassment.* New York: MasterMedia Limited, 1994. Presents an overview of sexual harassment, including definitions of sexual harassment from differing cultural perspectives, and discusses the prevalence of sexual harassment in the United States and other countries.

Wetzel, Roberta, and Nina W. Brown. *Student-Generated Sexual Harassment in Secondary Schools.* Westport, Conn.: Bergin & Garvey, 2000. Focuses on sexual harassment in schools and offers a historical overview of the issue, guidelines for developing policies to prevent sexual harassment in school settings, and administrative approaches to victims and offenders.

CHAPTER 8

ORGANIZATIONS AND AGENCIES

The following organizations provide information relevant to the issue of clergy sexual misconduct. Some also provide resources to victims, congregations, and offenders, including referrals for treatment, support groups, and legal assistance. The organizations are presented in three sections:

- information on clergy and sexual misconduct;
- resources for victims and congregations;
- resources for clergy.

These are followed by a section with organizations that provide information and resources on the broader issue of religion and spirituality.

INFORMATION ON CLERGY SEXUAL MISCONDUCT

AdvocateWeb
URL: http://www.advocateweb.
 org
P.O. Box 202961
Austin, TX 78720
Phone: (512) 249-1217
A nonprofit organization that promotes awareness of issues related to the sexual exploitation of helping professionals. Their web site offers access to an extensive database of articles and other information on clergy sexual misconduct in all faiths. In addition, numerous links are provided for victims of clergy sexual misconduct, including referrals for spiritual and psychological counseling, and assistance finding an attorney.

BishopsWatch
URL: http://www.bishopswatch.
 org
1436 U Street, NW
Suite 301

Washington, DC 20009
Phone: (202) 986-6093
An organization of 13 Catholic reform groups formed in response to
the sexual abuse scandal in the U.S.
Catholic Church. Their web site
provides links to media reports and
other information relating to clergy
sexual misconduct, including referrals for victim assistance.

**Center for the Prevention of
Sexual and Domestic Violence
(CPSDV)**
URL: http://www.cpsdv.org
2400 N. 45th Street, # 10
Seattle, WA 98103
Phone: (206) 634-1903
An interfaith organization that pro-
vides such educational resources as
books and videos on sexual abuse
and domestic violence to religious
and secular organizations.

**Crimes Against Children
Research Center (CCRC)**
URL: http://www.unh.edu/ccrc
University of New Hampshire
Horton Social Science Center
20 College Road, #126
Durham, NH 03824
Phone: (603) 862-1888
Provides research and statistics to
the public, policy makers, law en-
forcement personnel, and other
child welfare practitioners on crimes
involving children, including child
sexual abuse.

**Injury and Violence Prevention
Unit**
URL: http://www.health.state.
mn.us/svp/commfaith.html

Minnesota Department of Health
P.O. Box 64882
St. Paul, MN 55164-0882
Phone: (651) 215-8954
Clearinghouse for general informa-
tion of sexual abuse, including
clergy sexual misconduct.

**Interfaith Sexual Trauma
Institute (ISTI)**
URL: http://www.csbsju.edu/
isti/index.html
St. John's Abbey and University
Collegeville, MN 56321
Phone: (320) 363-3994
Institute dedicated to the prevention of sexual abuse, exploitation,
and harassment in religious organizations. ISTI provides a variety of
resources, including publications,
extensive information on the issue
of clergy sexual misconduct, and
links to resources for both victims
and offenders.

**National Clearinghouse on
Child Abuse and Neglect**
URL: http://www.calib.com/
nccanch
300 C Street, SW
Washington, DC 20447
Phone: (703) 385-7565 or
(800) 394-3366
Offers statistics, information on
laws and statutes, and other resources for the prevention and
treatment of child abuse and neglect, including sexual abuse.

**National Sexual Violence
Resource Center (NSVRC)**
URL: http://www.nsvrc.org

123 North Enola Drive
Enola, PA 17025
Phone: (717) 909-0710 or
(877) 739-3895
Clearinghouse for research and resources on sexual violence that works in conjunction with the Pennsylvania Coalition Against Rape, supplying national and state victims' advocacy organizations and community-based programs with information and assistance.

**United States Conference of
Catholic Bishops (USCCB)**
URL: http://www.usccb.org
3211 4th Street, NE
Washington, DC 20017-1194
Phone: (202) 541-3000
Official organization of U.S. Roman Catholic bishops under whose auspices the National Lay Review Board was formed to study and report on clergy sexual misconduct within the U.S. Catholic Church. The USCCB web site provides links to the church's official policy on clergy sexual misconduct and other related information.

Voice of the Faithful (VOTF)
URL: http://www.votf.org
P.O. Box 423
Newton Upper Falls, MA 02464
Phone: (617) 558-5252
Worldwide organization of more than 30,000 practicing Catholics from more than 40 U.S. states and 21 countries that was formed in response to the clergy sexual abuse crisis with the goal of reforming the Catholic Church.

RESOURCES FOR VICTIMS AND CONGREGATIONS

The Awareness Center
URL: http://www.
theawarenesscenter.org
P.O. Box 65273
Baltimore, MD 21209
Clearinghouse for information on clergy sexual misconduct within Judaism, including resources for victims.

**ChildHelp USA National Child
Abuse Hotline**
URL: http://www.childhelpusa.
org
15757 N. 78th Street
Scottsdale, AZ 85260
Phone: (480) 922-8212
Staffed 24 hours, 7 days a week, by counselors who provide assistance in some 140 languages to individuals, including those mandated by law, who are reporting incidents of child abuse and child sexual abuse.

Children of the Night
URL: http://www.
childrenofthenight.org
14530 Sylvan Street
Van Nuys, CA 91411
Phone: (818) 908-4474
Hotline: 1-800-551-1300
A privately funded nonprofit organization that assists minors between the ages of 11 and 17 who suffer from sexual abuse or who engage in street prostitution.

Clergy and Educator Abuse Survivors Empowered! (CEASE)
URL: http://advocateweb.com/
CEASE/Default.htm
Box 251
320 Seventh Avenue
Brooklyn, NY 11215
Phone: (512) 249-1217
Advocacy group for victims of sexual misconduct committed within the Seventh Day Adventist Church. The group also provides educational resources for church leaders on clergy sexual misconduct.

CyberTipline
URL: http://www.cybertipline.com
National Center for Missing or Exploited Children
Charles B. Wang International Children Building
699 Prince Street
Alexandria, VA 22314-3175
Phone: (703) 274-3900
Tipline: 1-800-843-5678
Provides a toll-free line to report any type of sexual exploitation of children on the World Wide Web or in any industry involving child pornography.

Generation Five
URL: http://www.generationfive.org
2 Massasoit Street
San Francisco, CA 94110
Phone: (415) 285-6658
A nonprofit organization of community leaders with the goal of ending child sexual abuse within five generations by working in collaboration with service providers to ensure that affordable support is available to survivors of sexual misconduct, offenders, and affected families.

The Lighthouse Foundation
URL: http://www.thelighthousefoundationinc.org
977 Bennington Street
East Boston, MA 02128
Phone: (617) 567-7575
A support organization providing assistance to victims of clergy sexual abuse.

The Linkup
URL: http://www.thelinkup.org
291 N. Hubbards Lane
Suite B26, #111
Louisville, KY 40207
Phone: (502) 290-4055
A support organization for victims of clergy sexual abuse, congregations, and families of victims, offering a variety of resources, including a set of detailed recommendations for churches on how to prescreen candidates for the ministry.

MaleSurvivor
URL: http://www.malesurvivor.org
5505 Connecticut Ave., NW
Washington, DC 20015-2601
Phone: (800) 738-4181
Provides research, education, advocacy, and support for male victims of childhood and adult sexual abuse.

National Center for Victims of Crime (NCVC)
URL: http://www.ncvc.org
2000 M Street, NW

Suite 480
Washington, DC 20036
Phone: (202) 467-8700 or
   (800) 394-2255
Provides crime victims, victim service providers, criminal justice officials, attorneys, and concerned individuals with information on local services for victims of crime, including assistance with the criminal justice process, counseling, and support groups.

**National Organization for
   Victim Assistance (NOVA)**
URL: http://www.try-nova.org
1730 Park Road, NW
Washington, DC 20010
Phone: (202) 232-6682 or
   (800) 879-6682
Private, nonprofit network of victim and witness assistance programs and practitioners, criminal justice agencies, mental health professionals, researchers, former victims, survivors, and others committed to victim rights and services.

**Rape, Abuse & Incest National
   Network (RAINN)**
URL: http://www.rainn.org
635-B Pennsylvania Ave., SE
Washington, DC 20003
Hotline: (800) 656-4673
Nonprofit organization operates a national hotline for victims of sexual assault, with counselors available 24 hours a day in partnership with rape crisis centers nationwide.

**Survivors Network of those
   Abused by Priests (SNAP)**
URL: http://www.snapnetwork.
   org
P.O. Box 6416
Chicago, IL 60680-6416
Phone: (312) 409-2720
Advocacy group for victims of clergy sexual misconduct by Catholic priests that provides support groups for victims and offers an extensive database of news, legal developments, and other information relating to the sex abuse scandal in the U.S. Catholic Church.

SurvivorsFirst.org
http://www.survivorsfirst.org
P.O. Box 81-172
Wellesley Hills, MA 02481
Phone: (781) 910-5467
Advocacy group for survivors of clergy sexual misconduct whose members include non-victims as well as survivors of clergy sexual abuse. SurvivorsFirst.org is not a support group but, rather, focuses on four main areas relating to clergy sexual misconduct: resources for victims, prevention, public awareness, and fund-raising for victim support groups.

RESOURCES
FOR CLERGY

**American Association of
   Pastoral Counselors (AAPC)**
URL: http://www.aapc.org

Sexual Misconduct and the Clergy

9504A Lee Highway
Fairfax, VA 22031-2303
Phone: (703) 385-6967
Professional association offering a variety of resources to its members and the public, including information on clergy sexual misconduct and treatment referrals for Protestant clergy.

American Professional Society on the Abuse of Children (APSAC)
URL: http://www.apsac.org
13th Street, CHO 3B-3406
Oklahoma City, OK 73104
Phone: (405) 271-8202
A professional membership organization offering publications and training on the assessment, intervention, and treatment of childhood sexual abuse.

Associates in Education and Prevention in Pastoral Practice, Inc. (AEPPP)
URL: http://www.aeppp.org
P.O. Box 63
44 Main Street
North Kingstown, RI 02852
Phone: (401) 295-0698
An interdenominational organization that provides information on how to prevent sexual and domestic violence and promote ethical conduct within religious organizations. Resources provided on the issue of clergy sexual misconduct include treatment and counseling referrals for offending clergy.

The Association for the Treatment of Sexual Abusers (ATSA)
URL: http://www.atsa.com
4900 S.W. Griffith Drive
Suite 274
Beaverton, OR 97005
Phone: (503) 643-1023
A professional membership association for clinicians treating sexual abusers, providing referrals for affiliated sex offender treatment and education programs throughout the United States.

Center for Sex Offender Management (CSOM)
URL: http://www.csom.org
Center for Effective Public Policy
8403 Colesville Road
Suite 720
Silver Spring, MD 20910
Phone: (301) 589-9383
Provides information and resources to individuals and agencies on the management of juvenile and adult sex offenders.

Clergy Recovery Network (CRN)
URL: http://clergyrecovery.com
P.O. Box 313
Joplin, MT 59531
Phone: (406) 292-3322
Nonprofit, nondenominational organization that provides resources on the issue of clergy sexual misconduct aimed at offending clergy, including referrals for mentoring, spiritual and psychological counseling, and support groups. Confiden-

218

tial services are provided online, by telephone, and in person. In addition, links are provided to information on the issue of clergy sexual misconduct.

Justice for Priests and Deacons
URL: http://www.
  justiceforpriests.org
P.O. Box 87
San Diego, CA 92138-7225
Phone: (619) 280-7500
A nonprofit referral organization that advises Catholic priests and deacons accused of sexual misconduct on their rights under Roman Catholic canon law. The organization was founded by a canon lawyer in the wake of the sexual abuse scandal in the Roman Catholic Church.

The National Association for Christian Recovery (NACR)
URL: http://www.nacronline.
  com
P.O. Box 215
Brea, CA 92822-0215
Phone: (714) 529-6227
A clearinghouse for information on recovery from addiction, abuse, and trauma for Christians, including clergy. Their web site provides links to articles and a variety of resources, treatment referrals, and spiritual retreats.

National Center on Institutions and Alternatives (NCIA)
URL: http://www.igc.org/ncia
The Augustus Institute
Public Policy Center
3125 Mt. Vernon Ave.

Alexandria, VA 22305
Phone: (703) 684-0373
Private nonprofit agency providing training, research, and direct services in the area of sexual misconduct, including outpatient treatment for sex offenders through the Augustus Institute.

The Safer Society Foundation, Inc.
URL: http://www.safersociety.
  org
P.O. Box 340
Brandon, VT 05733-0340
Phone: (802) 247-3132
National research, advocacy, and referral center for the prevention and treatment of sexual abuse that offers services including sex offender treatment referrals.

Saint Luke Institute, Inc.
URL: http://www.sli.org
8901 New Hampshire Ave.
Silver Spring, MD 20903
Phone: (301) 445-7970
Resource center for Catholic clergy and religious personnel that provides a variety of resources, including treatment of perpetrators of clergy sexual misconduct and support services for parishes on the prevention of clergy sexual misconduct.

STOP IT NOW!
URL: http://www.stopitnow.org
P.O. Box 495
Haydenville, MA 01039
Phone: (413) 268-3096
Help line: (888) 773-8368
National public health organization on education and research programs,

with a help line for adults at risk for sexually abusing a child. Resources are also provided for friends and family members of sexual abusers, and victims of sexual abuse.

RELIGION AND SEXUALITY

AIDS National Interfaith Network
URL: http://www.thebody.com
1400 I Street, NW
Suite 1220
Washington, DC 20005
Phone: (202) 842-0010
Nonprofit group that provides links to educational, counseling, and other resources for people of faith infected by the HIV virus, and others within religious communities, including clergy.

Center for Sexuality and Religion (CSR)
URL: http://www.ctrsr.org
987 Old Eagle School Road
Suite 719
Wayne, PA 19087-1708
Phone: (610) 995-0341
Provides a forum for the discussion of various aspects of sexuality and religion, including sexual ethics, sexual health, and sexual justice within the institutional framework of religious communities.

Dignity USA
URL: http://www.dignityusa.org
1500 Massachusetts Ave., NW
Suite 11

Washington, DC 20005
Phone: (800) 877-8797
National organization of homosexual, bisexual, and transgender Catholics and their families whose mission is to work toward social reform on issues of sexuality and gender. The group also sponsors the National AIDS Project, which provides various resources to Catholics infected with the HIV virus.

Interfaith Working Group (IWG)
URL: http://www.iwgonline.org
P.O. Box 11706
Philadelphia, PA 19101
Phone: (215) 235-3050
Provides information on a variety of social issues in religious settings, including sexuality, and serves as a forum for the discussion of those issues by members of religious organizations, including clergy.

Sexuality Information and Education Council of the United States (SIECUS)
URL: http://www.siecus.org
130 West 42nd Street
Suite 350
New York, NY 10036-7802
Phone: (212) 819-9770
Provides educational information on sexuality, including the relationship between sexuality and spirituality in religious settings.

Women's Alliance for Theology, Ethics, and Ritual (WATER)
URL: http://www.hers.com/water
8035 13th Street

Silver Spring, MD 20910
Phone: (301) 589-2509
Feminist educational center that promotes the development of women in religious organizations and provides information on ethical issues that affect women in religious settings.

Working Group on Family Ministries and Human Sexuality

URL: http://www.ncccusa.org
Office of Family Ministries in Human Sexuality
National Council of Churches
475 Riverside Drive
Room 848
New York, NY 10115
Phone: (212) 870-2673
An organization representing some 20 religious denominations that promotes awareness of sexual issues in religious settings.

PART III

APPENDICES

APPENDIX A

STATUTES OF
LIMITATION

A statute of limitations is a law that specifies the time period, or period of limitation, during which a suspect may be charged with a crime in criminal court, or a lawsuit may be filed in civil court. For example, if the statute of limitations for rape is 10 years, prosecutors may charge a suspect with the crime of rape at any time during that 10-year period, but not after. Generally, the statute of limitations begins tolling when the specified crime or actionable conduct occurs, but not always. A statute of limitations may contain a tolling doctrine that postpones the time when the period of limitation begins. For example, under a minority tolling doctrine for childhood sexual abuse, the period of limitation would begin when the victim reaches the age of majority, usually 18, not when the crime or injury took place when the victim was a minor. Similarly, if the victim of sexual assault could not report the incident due to repressed memory, an incapacity tolling doctrine would postpone the start of the period of limitation until the victim regained the memory.

Following are a list of statutes of limitation for each state. Laws are continually revised by legislative action as the result of court decisions, public sentiment, or other factors. Accordingly, criminal and civil statutes of limitation, and any applicable tolling doctrines, are subject to change. The offices of a state's attorney general or local prosecutor can generally provide up-to-date information on criminal statutes of limitation. Law libraries and non-subscriber online legal reference services, such as FindLaw, may be useful to verify civil statutes of limitations. Readers are cautioned to consult with an attorney before pursuing any legal action. Local and state bar associations, law schools, and legal aid offices can assist in locating qualified lawyers. It should be noted that the term rape is used in some states, while in other states the same criminal conduct is defined as sexual assault, usually in the first degree.

ALABAMA

Criminal: There is no period of limitation for the offense of rape.
Civil: Claims must be brought within two years of the date of the injury.

ALASKA

Criminal: There is no period of limitation for sexual assault in the first or second degree. The period of limitation for third-degree sexual assault is 10 years.
Civil: Claims may be brought at any time for felony sexual abuse or felony sexual assault of a minor. For acts of non-felonious sexual abuse, claims must be brought within three years of majority, or within three years of discovery that the act caused injury, pursuant to Alaska's minority and disability tolling provisions.

ARIZONA

Criminal: The period of limitation for felony sexual assault is seven years from the commission of the offense.
Civil: Claims must be brought within two years from the date of the injury, pursuant to the general tort statute of limitations. Minority tolling for victims of childhood sexual abuse is two years from reaching the age of majority. Disability tolling is two years from the removal of a mental disability and is available to victims of childhood sexual abuse who suffered from repressed memory, according to the Arizona Supreme Court's decision in *Doe v. Roe* (1998).

ARKANSAS

Criminal: The period of limitation for felony rape is six years from the commission of the offense, but may be extended to 15 years in cases where DNA or other scientific testing used to determine culpability becomes available.
Civil: Under the state's realization statute, claims based on sexual abuse when the victim was a minor, but not discovered until after the victim reaches the age of majority, 18, must be brought within three years from the time of discovery of the sexual abuse by the victim.

Appendix A

CALIFORNIA

Criminal: There is no period of limitation for aggravated rape. The period of limitation for non-aggravated rape is six years from the commission of the offenses. Certain sex offenses carry a period of limitation of 10 years from the commission of the offense, or one year from the date that the identity of the suspect is established by DNA testing, whichever is longer.

Civil: Claims must be filed within eight years of the victim reaching the age of majority, 18, or within three years after the victim discovers that "psychological injury or illness occurring after the age of majority was caused by the sexual abuse" (California Code of Civil Procedure, section 340.1). Beginning in January 2003, victims of childhood sexual abuse who were more than eight years past the age of majority were permitted to bring claims within one year against organizations or individuals who had knowledge of unlawful sexual conduct by an employee, volunteer, representative, or agent, and failed to take reasonable steps to avoid future acts of unlawful sexual conduct.

COLORADO

Criminal: The period of limitation for sexual assault is 10 years from the commission of the offense. If the offense is reported but not prosecuted within 10 years, there is no period of limitation in cases where DNA evidence becomes available that identifies the suspect.

Civil: Claims of childhood sexual abuse must be filed within six years of reaching the age of majority, or six years from when the victim realizes that the sexual abuse occurred and that injury resulted from the sexual abuse. Monetary damages are limited to the costs of medical care and for claims brought more than 15 years after the age of majority, 18.

CONNECTICUT

Criminal: The period of limitation for sexual assault is five years from the commission of the offense. In cases where DNA evidence becomes available that identifies the suspect, the period of limitation is 20 years from the commission of the offense, but only if the offense is reported within five years of its commission. In cases of sexual assault occurring after May 2002, a tolling provision allows prosecution to commence two years from the age of majority of the victim, or five years from the date the offense is reported to law enforcement, whichever is earlier.

Civil: Claims of injury as the result of childhood sexual abuse may be brought within 30 years of the age of majority. The state's age of majority was 21 until October 1, 1972, when it was lowered to 18 years of age.

DELAWARE

Criminal: There is no period of limitation for first-degree rape. For lesser degrees of rape, the period of limitation is five years from the commission of the offense, or 10 years if DNA testing becomes available that identifies the suspect.
Civil: Under the state's statute of limitations for general personal injury, claims must be brought within two years from the date of the injury. If the abuse took place when the victim was a minor, any lawsuit claiming injury from the abuse must be filed within two years of reaching the age of 18.

DISTRICT OF COLUMBIA

Criminal: The period of limitation for sexual abuse of any type is six years from the commission of the offense.
Civil: Under the statute of limitations for personal injury, claims must be within three years "from the time the right to maintain the action accrues" (D.C. Code, section 12-301). If the injury occurs when the victim was a minor, claims must be brought within three years of reaching the age of 18.

FLORIDA

Criminal: The period of limitation for first-degree sexual battery is four years from the commission of the offense.
Civil: For intentional torts based on sexual abuse, including incest, claims must be brought within seven years after the age of majority, 18. Claims may also be brought within four years after the victim leaves the dependency of the abuser, or discovers that the tortious injury was caused by the sexual abuse, whichever occurs later. In addition, under the delayed discovery doctrine, the statute of limitations does not begin to run until such time as the victim knows or should know of the wrongful act that is the basis of the cause of action. In 2000, the Florida Supreme Court held in *Herndon v. Graham* that in cases of repressed memory or traumatic amnesia, the statute of limitations does not begin to run until the victim becomes aware that the sexual abuse occurred.

GEORGIA

Criminal: The period of limitation for forcible rape is 15 years from the commission of the offense.
Civil: Under a special statute of limitations for childhood sexual abuse, claims may be filed within five years of reaching the age of majority, 18.

HAWAII

Criminal: The period of limitation for first-degree sexual assault is six years from the commission of the offense, and three years from the commission of a sexual assault in the second or third degree.
Civil: Under the general statute of limitations, claims must be brought within two years of the date of injury. If the injury results in criminal charges being filed, the statute of limitations is suspended while the criminal case is pending. In addition, under the common law realization-discovery rule, claims may be filed within two years of the discovery of the injury, if the injury was caused by sexual abuse. In 1996, the rule was applied to cases of childhood sexual abuse by the Hawaii Supreme Court in *Dunlea v. Dappen.*

IDAHO

Criminal: There is no period of limitation for rape.
Civil: Under a special statute of limitations for survivors of childhood sexual abuse, claims may be brought within five years of the victim reaching the age of majority, 18, but only in cases where the injury took place after July 1, 1989, when the statute was passed into law.

ILLINOIS

Criminal: The period of limitation for aggravated sexual assault and criminal sexual assault is 10 years from the commission of the offense if reported to law enforcement authorities no later than two years after the offense.
Civil: Under a special statute of limitations for survivors of childhood sexual abuse, amended in 2003, claims for personal injury as the result of childhood sexual abuse must be brought within 10 years from when the victim discovers that the sexual abuse occurred and causes the tortious injury. The period of limitation does not begin to run until the victim is 18 years of age, regardless of when the injury occurred.

INDIANA

Criminal: There is no period of limitation for Class A rape. The period of limitation for Class B rape is five years from the commission of the offense, or one year from the date that DNA evidence is available to identify the suspect, even if the five-year period of limitation has expired.

Civil: Under the general statute of limitations for injuries to the person, claims must be filed within two years of the date of the injury. Claims for injuries that occurred in childhood must be brought within two years of the victim reaching the age of 18.

IOWA

Criminal: The period of limitation is 10 years for sexual abuse in the first, second, or third degree.

Civil: Claims must be brought within four years of the discovery of the injury and the causal relationship between the injury and the sexual abuse, in all cases in which the injury occurred after July 1, 1990. Under the common law discovery rule, claims arising from injuries that occurred prior to July 1, 1990, must be brought within two years of the discovery of the injury and the causal relationship between the injury and sexual abuse.

KANSAS

Criminal: The period of limitation for rape is five years from the commission of the offense.

Civil: Claims must be brought within three years of the victim reaching the age of majority, 18, or three years from the date the victim realizes that the tortious injury was caused by sexual abuse.

KENTUCKY

Criminal: There is no period of limitation for rape.

Civil: Claims for injuries arising from sexual abuse may be brought within five years of the last act of sexual abuse, or within five years after the victim knew of the act of sexual abuse, or within five years after the victim reaches the age of majority, 18.

LOUISIANA

Criminal: There is no period of limitation for aggravated rape. The period of limitation for forcible rape is 10 years from the commission of the offense, and four years from the commission of a simple rape.
Civil: Under the general discovery rule, claims must be brought within one year from date of discovery of the injury.

MAINE

Criminal: There is no period of limitation for childhood sexual abuse. The period of limitation for gross sexual assault is six years from the commission of the offense.
Civil: Claims for childhood sexual abuse may be brought at any time.

MARYLAND

Criminal: There is no period of limitation for the offense of rape.
Civil: Effective October 1, 2003, claims by victims of childhood sexual abuse may be brought within seven years of the victim reaching the age of majority. However, claims barred prior to October 1, 2003, cannot be revived under the revised law.

MASSACHUSETTS

Criminal: The period of limitation for rape is 15 years from the commission of the offense.
Civil: Claims of sexual abuse must be brought within three years from the date of injury, or three years from the victim reaching the age of majority, 18, or three years from when the victim discovered that the tortious injury was caused by the sexual abuse.

MICHIGAN

Criminal: The period of limitation for offenses arising from criminal sexual misconduct is six years after the commission of the offense. If DNA evidence from the offense is determined to be from an unidentified suspect, there is no period of limitation until the identity of the suspect is established, at which time the period of limitation is 10 years from the commission of the offense.

Civil: Claims for childhood sexual abuse may be brought at any time.

MINNESOTA

Criminal: The period of limitation for criminal sexual assault is nine years from the commission of the offense, or three years from when the victim first reports the offense in cases where the victim failed to report the offense within nine years after its commission. In cases where DNA evidence is collected and preserved but the suspect is unidentified, there is no period of limitation.

Civil: Claims of personal injury caused by sexual abuse must be brought within six years of the time the victim knew that the injury was caused by the sexual abuse. In cases where the victim is a minor, the six-year period of limitation begins to run when the victim reaches the age of majority, 18, and expires on the victim's 25th birthday.

MISSISSIPPI

Criminal: There is no period of limitation for rape. The period of limitation for sexual battery is two years from the commission of the offense.

Civil: Claims for childhood sexual abuse may be brought at any time.

MISSOURI

Criminal: There is no period of limitation for forcible rape. The period of limitation for sexual assault is three years from the commission of the offense. In cases involving minors under the age of 18, the period of limitation is 10 years after the victim reaches the age of majority, 18.

Civil: Under a special statute of limitations for childhood sexual abuse, claims must be brought before the victim reaches 30 years of age, or within three years from the date the victim discovers that the injury was caused by sexual abuse.

MONTANA

Criminal: The period of limitation for sexual intercourse without consent is 10 years from the commission of the offense.

Civil: Claims for injury as the result of childhood sexual abuse within three years after the commission of the act of sexual abuse that caused the injury, or three years from when the victim discovers that the injury was caused by the act of childhood sexual abuse. In cases of serial abuse by an individual, the statute begins tolling from the date of the last act of sexual abuse.

NEBRASKA

Criminal: The period of limitation for sexual assault is seven years from the commission of the offense.

Civil: Claims for injury as the result of childhood sexual abuse may be brought at any time.

NEVADA

Criminal: The period of limitation for sexual assault is four years from the commission of the offense. However, if a written report is filed with law enforcement during the four-year period of limitation, there is no period of limitation for the offense.

Civil: Claims of injury caused by childhood sexual abuse must be brought within 10 years of the age of majority, 18, or within 10 years of discovery that the injury was caused by the sexual abuse.

NEW HAMPSHIRE

Criminal: The period of limitation for aggravated felonious sexual assault is six years from the commission of the offense.

Civil: Claims must be brought within three years of the time the plaintiff discovers the injury and its causal relationship to the sexual abuse.

NEW JERSEY

Criminal: There is no period of limitation for sexual assault. The period of limitation for aggravated sexual conduct is five years from the commission of the offense.

Civil: Claims must be brought within two years of the date of the reasonable discovery of the injury and its causal relationship to the act of sexual abuse.

NEW MEXICO

Criminal: There is no period of limitation for criminal sexual penetration in the first degree. The period of limitation for criminal sexual penetration in the second degree is six years from the commission of the offense, and five years from the commission of criminal sexual penetration in the third and fourth degrees.

Civil: Claims for injury due to childhood sexual abuse must be brought prior to the victim reaching the age of 24, or within three years from the date that the victim knew of the childhood sexual abuse and that injury resulted from the abuse.

NEW YORK

Criminal: The period of limitation for rape, first-degree sexual assault, and second-degree sexual assault is five years from the commission of the offense. For certain sexual crimes against minors, the statute of limitation does not begin to run until the victim is 18 years of age, or the offense is reported to a law enforcement agency.

Civil: Claims for an intentional tort must be brought within one year from the date of the actionable conduct. Claims must be brought within three years against an institution that supervised the perpetrator, or in any action based on negligence. In cases where criminal charges are filed based on the actionable conduct, the statute of limitations does not begin to toll until the criminal case is terminated. In cases where the perpetrator is convicted in criminal court, a claim may be brought by the victim within seven to 10 years after the conviction, depending upon the criminal offense.

NORTH CAROLINA

Criminal: There is no period of limitation for rape.

Civil: Claims may be brought within three years of when the victim becomes aware of the sexual abuse and that the injury was caused by the abuse. Under the incompetency tolling provision, claims may be brought within three years of reaching the age of 18, or of the removal of the incompetency.

NORTH DAKOTA

Criminal: The period of limitation for any sexual assault is three years from the commission of the offense.

Civil: Under the common law discovery rule, claims may be brought within two years from when the victim knows that a potential claim exists.

OHIO

Criminal: The period of limitation for sexual battery is 20 years from the commission of the offense.
Civil: Claims must be brought within one year from when the victim recalls or otherwise discovers the sexual abuse.

OKLAHOMA

Criminal: The period of limitation for rape is seven years from the commission of the offense.
Civil: Claims must be brought within two years of the last act, or two years of the victim reaching the age of 18, or two years from the discovery of "objective, verifiable evidence" of sexual abuse.

OREGON

Criminal: The period of limitation for rape in the first, second, or third degree is six years from the commission of the offense.
Civil: Claims must be brought within six years of the victim reaching the age of 18, or within three years of the discovery of the causal connection between the injury and the sexual abuse.

PENNSYLVANIA

Criminal: The period of limitation for rape is five years from the commission of the offense.
Civil: Claims of childhood sexual abuse may be brought within 12 years of the victim reaching the age of majority, 18.

RHODE ISLAND

Criminal: There is no period of limitation for first degree sexual assault. The period of limitation for second degree sexual assault is three years from the commission of the offense.
Civil: Claims for general injury must be brought within three years of the sexual misconduct. Claims of childhood sexual abuse must be brought

within seven years of the last act of sexual abuse, or within seven years of the discovery that the injury was caused by the abuse.

SOUTH CAROLINA

Criminal: There is no period of limitation for criminal sexual conduct.
Civil: Claims for injury caused by childhood sexual abuse may be brought within six years after the victim reaches the age of 21, or within three years from the time the victim realizes that the sexual abuse occurred.

SOUTH DAKOTA

Criminal: The period of limitation for rape is seven years from the commission of the offense.
Civil: Claims for general injury must be brought within three years of the act that caused the injury, or within three years of the discovery that the injury was caused by the act.

TENNESSEE

Criminal: The period of limitation for aggravated rape is 15 years from the commission of the offense, and eight years from the commission of a non-aggravated rape. The period of limitation for sexual battery is two years from the commission of the offense.
Civil: Claims for personal tort actions must be brought within one year of the date of the act that caused the injury. If the victim was under 18 years of age at the time of the injury, claims may be brought within one year of the victim reaching the age of 18.

TEXAS

Criminal: The period of limitation for sexual assault is seven years from the commission of the offense. There is no period of limitation when DNA evidence is collected and the identity of the suspect is not known.
Civil: A claim may be brought within five years of the commission of sexual assault or aggravated sexual assault. If the victim was a minor, the statute of limitations does not begin to run until the victim reaches 18 years of age.

UTAH

Criminal: The period of limitation for rape is four years from the commission of the offense.

Civil: Claims for intentional or negligent sexual abuse suffered as a child may be filed within four years after the victim reaches 18 years of age. If the victim discovers the sexual abuse after reaching the age of 18, a claim for sexual abuse may be brought within four years after the discovery of the sexual abuse.

VERMONT

Criminal: There is no period of limitation for aggravated sexual assault. The period of limitation for sexual assault is six years from the commission of the offense.

Civil: Claims may be brought within six years of the discovery of the act that caused the injury. Claims of injury from childhood sexual abuse may be brought within six years of the abuse that caused the injury, or within six years of the time the victim discovered that the injury was caused by the abuse, whichever period expires later.

VIRGINIA

Criminal: There is no period of limitation for rape.

Civil: Under the general statute of limitation for injuries to the person, claims must be brought within two years after the time of the injury. If the victim is a minor at the time of the injury, the two-year time period begins to toll when the victim reaches 18 years of age. In cases of sexual abuse, the two-year statute of limitations does not begin to run until the injury caused by the abuse is reported to a physician or psychologist. If criminal charges arising from the sexual abuse are pending, the statute of limitations is suspended until the criminal case is resolved.

WASHINGTON

Criminal: The period of limitation for rape is 10 years after the commission of the offense.

Civil: Claims may be brought within three years of the sexual abuse, or three years after the victim reaches 18 years of age, or three years after the discovery of the injury and that the injury was caused by the sexual abuse. In

1999, the Washington Supreme Court ruled in *C.J.C. v. Corporation of the Catholic Bishop of Yakima* that the statute of limitations as extended by minority tolling and the discovery rule is applicable to negligent third parties.

WEST VIRGINIA

Criminal: There is no period of limitation for sexual assault.

Civil: When the victim was sexually abused as a minor, claims may be brought within two years of the victim reaching the age of majority, 18, or within 20 years of the date of the injury and abuse.

WISCONSIN

Criminal: The period of limitation for crimes arising from sexual misconduct is six years from the commission of the offense.

Civil: Claims may be brought within five years after the victim discovers the injury, or within five years from reaching the age of majority, 18.

WYOMING

Criminal: There is no period of limitation for sexual assault.

Civil: Claims arising from childhood sexual abuse may be brought eight years after the victim reaches 18 years of age, or three years after the victim discovers the injury, and that the injury was due to the sexual abuse.

APPENDIX B

MANDATORY REPORTING LAWS

Mandatory reporting laws govern who must report suspected incidents of child abuse, including child sexual abuse. Increasingly, states are including members of the clergy as mandatory reporters. As such, clergy are duty bound to report suspected child sexual abuse to authorities, and the failure to do so places them in violation of the law and subject to applicable criminal or civil sanctions. Some states permit an exception when the mandatory reporter discovers the child abuse during privileged communications, as between an attorney and a client.

The National Clearinghouse of Child Abuse and Neglect (NCCAN) provides current state-by-state information on mandatory reporting laws. Their Internet address is http://nccanch.acf.hhs.gov. The information presented here was largely furnished by the NCCAN, which is a service of the Children's Bureau, Administration for Children and Families, U.S. Department of Health and Human Services.

ALABAMA

Clergy: No.
Mandatory reporters: Health care and mental health professionals, social workers, educators, child care providers, law enforcement personnel, and any other person called upon to provide aid or assistance to any child.
Privileged communications: Attorney-client.

ALASKA

Clergy: No.
Mandatory reporters: Health care and mental health professionals, social workers, educators, child care providers, law enforcement personnel, employees of domestic violence programs and drug and alcohol treatment

239

facilities, child protective services providers, commercial and private photographic processors.
Privileged communications: None specified by statute.

ARIZONA

Clergy: Yes, including Christian Science practitioners.
Other mandatory reporters: Health care and mental health professionals, social workers, educators, child care providers, law enforcement personnel, parents, anyone responsible for the care or treatment of a child, and domestic violence advocates.
Privileged communications: Clergy-penitent, attorney-client.

ARKANSAS

Clergy: Yes, including Christian Science practitioners.
Other mandatory reporters: Health care and mental health professionals, social workers, educators, child care providers, law enforcement personnel, prosecutors, judges, domestic violence shelter employees and volunteers, foster parents, and court-appointed special advocates.
Privileged communications: Clergy-penitent, attorney-client.

CALIFORNIA

Clergy: Yes.
Other mandatory reporters: Health care and mental health professionals, social workers, educators, child care providers, law enforcement personnel, firefighters, animal control officers, commercial film and photographic print processors, court-appointed special advocates.
Privileged communications: Clergy-penitent.

COLORADO

Clergy: Yes, including Christian Science practitioners.
Other mandatory reporters: Health care and mental health professionals, social workers, educators, child care providers, law enforcement personnel, veterinarians, firefighters, victim advocates, commercial film and photographic processors, dieticians, Department of Human Services employees.
Privileged communications: Clergy-penitent.

CONNECTICUT

Clergy: Yes.

Other mandatory reporters: Health care and mental health professionals, social workers, educators, child care providers, law enforcement personnel, substance abuse counselors, sexual assault and battered women counselors, child advocates.

Privileged communications: None specified by statute.

DELAWARE

Clergy: Yes, as included in "any other persons."

Other mandatory reporters: Health care and mental health professionals, social workers, educators, child care providers, law enforcement personnel, and "any other persons."

Privileged communications: Clergy-penitent, attorney-client.

DISTRICT OF COLUMBIA

Clergy: No.

Mandatory reporters: Health care and mental health professionals, social workers, educators, child care providers, and law enforcement personnel.

Privileged communications: None specified by statute.

FLORIDA

Clergy: Religious healers.

Other mandatory reporters: Health care and mental health professionals, social workers, educators, child care providers, law enforcement personnel, and judges.

Privileged communications: Clergy-penitent, attorney-client.

GEORGIA

Clergy: No.

Mandatory reporters: Health care and mental health professionals, social workers, educators, child care providers, law enforcement personnel, and producers of visual or printed matter.

Privileged communications: None specified by statute.

HAWAII

Clergy: No.
Mandatory reporters: Health care and mental health professionals, social workers, educators, child care providers, law enforcement personnel, and employees of recreational or sports activities.
Privileged communications: None specified by statute.

IDAHO

Clergy: Yes, as included in "any other persons."
Other mandatory reporters: Health care and mental health professionals, social workers, educators, child care providers, law enforcement personnel, and "any other persons."
Privileged communications: Clergy-penitent, attorney-client.

ILLINOIS

Clergy: Yes, including Christian Science practitioners.
Other mandatory reporters: Health care and mental health professionals, social workers, educators, child care providers, law enforcement personnel, homemakers, substance abuse treatment personnel, and commercial film photographic print processors.
Privileged communications: Clergy-penitent.

INDIANA

Clergy: Yes, as included in "any individual."
Other mandatory reporters: Health care and mental health professionals, social workers, educators, child care providers, law enforcement personnel, and "any individual."
Privileged communications: None specified by statute.

IOWA

Clergy: No.
Mandatory reporters: Health care and mental health professionals, social workers, educators, child care providers, law enforcement personnel, commercial film and photographic print processors, employees of substance abuse programs, and coaches.
Privileged communications: None specified in statute.

KANSAS

Clergy: No.
Mandatory reporters: Health care and mental health professionals, social workers, educators, child care providers, law enforcement personnel, firefighters, and juvenile intake and assessment workers.
Privileged communications: None specified in statute.

KENTUCKY

Clergy: Yes, as included in "any person."
Other mandatory reporters: Health care and mental health professionals, social workers, educators, child care providers, law enforcement personnel, and "any person."
Privileged communications: Clergy-penitent, attorney-client.

LOUISIANA

Clergy: No.
Mandatory reporters: Health care and mental health professionals, social workers, educators, child care providers, law enforcement personnel, mediators, and commercial film or photographic print processors.
Privileged communications: Clergy-penitent.

MAINE

Clergy: Yes.
Other mandatory reporters: Health care and mental health professionals, social workers, educators, child care providers, law enforcement personnel, fire inspectors, guardians ad litem appointed by the court to safeguard a minor legal right and court-appointed special advocates, homemakers, commercial film processors, and humane society agents.
Privileged communications: Clergy-penitent.

MARYLAND

Clergy: Yes, as included in "any other persons."
Other mandatory reporters: Health care and mental health professionals, social workers, educators, child care providers, law enforcement personnel, and "any other persons."
Privileged communications: Clergy-penitent, attorney-client.

MASSACHUSETTS

Clergy: Yes, including Christian Science practitioners.
Other mandatory reporters: Health care and mental health professionals, social workers, educators, child care providers, law enforcement personnel, drug and alcoholism counselors, probation and parole officers, clerks and magistrates of district courts, and firefighters.
Privileged communications: Clergy-penitent.

MICHIGAN

Clergy: Yes.
Other mandatory reporters: Health care and mental health professionals, social workers, educators, child care providers, and law enforcement personnel.
Privileged communications: Clergy-penitent, attorney-client.

MINNESOTA

Clergy: No.
Mandatory reporters: Health care and mental health professionals, social workers, educators, child care providers, and law enforcement personnel.
Privileged communications: Clergy-penitent.

MISSISSIPPI

Clergy: Yes.
Other mandatory reporters: Health care and mental health professionals, social workers, educators, child care providers, law enforcement personnel, and attorneys.
Privileged communications: None specified in statute.

MISSOURI

Clergy: Yes, including Christian Science practitioners.
Other mandatory reporters: Health care and mental health professionals, social workers, educators, child care providers, law enforcement personnel, probation and parole officers, commercial film processors, and Internet service providers.
Privileged communications: Clergy-penitent, attorney-client.

MONTANA

Clergy: Yes, including Christian Science practitioners and religious healers.
Other mandatory reporters: Health care and mental health professionals, social workers, educators, child care providers, law enforcement personnel, and guardians ad litem.
Privileged communications: Clergy-penitent.

NEBRASKA

Clergy: Yes, as included in "all persons."
Other mandatory reporters: Health care professionals, social workers, educators, child care providers, and "all persons."
Privileged communications: None specified in statute.

NEVADA

Clergy: Yes, including Christian Science practitioners and religious healers.
Other mandatory reporters: Health care and mental health professionals, social workers, educators, child care providers, law enforcement personnel, alcohol and drug abuse counselors, attorneys, and youth shelter workers.
Privileged communications: Clergy-penitent, attorney-client.

NEW HAMPSHIRE

Clergy: Yes, including Christian Science practitioners.
Other mandatory reporters: Health care and mental health professionals, social workers, educators, child care providers, and law enforcement personnel.
Privileged communications: Clergy-penitent, attorney-client.

NEW JERSEY

Clergy: Yes, as included in "any person."
Other mandatory reporters: "Any person."
Privileged communications: None specified in statute.

NEW MEXICO

Clergy: Yes.
Other mandatory reporters: Health care and mental health professionals, social workers, educators, child care providers, law enforcement personnel, and judges.
Privileged communications: Clergy-penitent.

NEW YORK

Clergy: Christian Science practitioners.
Other mandatory reporters: Health care and mental health professionals, social workers, educators, child care providers, law enforcement personnel, district attorneys, alcoholism and substance abuse counselors.
Privileged communications: None specified in statute.

NORTH CAROLINA

Clergy: Yes, as included in "any person or institution."
Other mandatory reporters: "Any person or institution."
Privileged communications: Attorney-client. The clergy-penitent privilege is denied by statute.

NORTH DAKOTA

Clergy: Yes, including religious healers.
Other mandatory reporters: Health care and mental health professionals, social workers, educators, child care providers, law enforcement personnel, and addiction counselors.
Privileged communications: Clergy-penitent, attorney-client.

Appendix B

OHIO

Clergy: Religious healers.
Other mandatory reporters: Health care and mental health professionals, social workers, educators, child care providers, law enforcement personnel, attorneys, and agents of humane societies.
Privileged communications: Attorney-client, physician-patient.

OKLAHOMA

Clergy: Yes, as included in "any other person."
Other mandatory reporters: Health care professionals, educators, child care providers, commercial film and photographic print processors, and "any other person."
Privileged communications: None specified by statute.

OREGON

Clergy: Yes.
Other mandatory reporters: Health care and mental health professionals, social workers, educators, child care providers, law enforcement personnel, attorneys, firefighters, court-appointed special advocates.
Privileged communications: Clergy-penitent, attorney-client, mental health professional–patient.

PENNSYLVANIA

Clergy: Yes, including Christian Science practitioners.
Other mandatory reporters: Health care and mental health professionals, social workers, educators, child care providers, law enforcement personnel, and funeral directors.
Privileged communications: Clergy-penitent.

RHODE ISLAND

Clergy: Yes, as included in "any person."
Other mandatory reporters: "Any person," any physician or duly certified registered nurse practitioner.
Privileged communications: Attorney-client. The clergy-penitent privilege is denied by statute.

SOUTH CAROLINA

Clergy: Christian Science practitioners and religious healers.
Other mandatory reporters: Health care and mental health professionals, social workers, educators, child care providers, law enforcement personnel, judges, funeral home directors and employees, film processors, substance abuse treatment center staff, and computer technicians.
Privileged communications: Clergy-penitent, attorney-client.

SOUTH DAKOTA

Clergy: Religious healers.
Other mandatory reporters: Health care and mental health professionals, social workers, educators, child care providers, law enforcement personnel, chemical dependency counselors, parole or court service officers, and employees of domestic abuse shelters.
Privileged communications: None specified by statute.

TENNESSEE

Clergy: Yes, as included in "any other person."
Other mandatory reporters: Health care and mental health professionals, social workers, educators, child care providers, law enforcement personnel, judges, neighbors, relatives, friends, and "any other person."
Privileged communications: None specified by statute.

TEXAS

Clergy: Yes, as included in "any person."
Other mandatory reporters: Health care professionals, educators, child care providers, juvenile probation or correctional officers, employees of clinics that provide reproductive services, and "any person."
Privileged communications: The clergy-penitent privilege is denied by statute.

UTAH

Clergy: Yes, as included in "any person."
Other mandatory reporters: Any person licensed under the Medical Practice Act or the Nurse Practice Act, and "any person."
Privileged communications: Clergy-penitent.

VERMONT

Clergy: Yes.
Other mandatory reporters: Health care and mental health professionals, social workers, educators, child care providers, law enforcement personnel, camp administrators and counselors, and probation officers.
Privileged communications: Clergy-penitent.

VIRGINIA

Clergy: Christian Science practitioners.
Other mandatory reporters: Health care and mental health professionals, social workers, educators, child care providers, law enforcement personnel, mediators, probation officers, and court-appointed special advocates.
Privileged communications: None specified by statute.

WASHINGTON

Clergy: No.
Mandatory reporters: Health care and mental health professionals, social workers, educators, child care providers, law enforcement personnel, responsible living skills program staff members, and any adult with whom a child resides.
Privileged communications: None specified by statute.

WEST VIRGINIA

Clergy: Yes, including Christian Science practitioners and religious healers.
Other mandatory reporters: Health care and mental health professionals, social workers, educators, child care providers, law enforcement personnel, and judges and family-law masters or magistrates.
Privileged communications: Attorney-client. The clergy-penitent privilege is denied by statute.

WISCONSIN

Clergy: No.
Mandatory reporters: Health care and mental health professionals, social workers, educators, child care providers, law enforcement personnel, al-

cohol and drug abuse counselors, mediators, financial and employment planners, court-appointed special advocates.

Privileged communications: None specified by statute.

WYOMING

Clergy: Yes, as included in "any person."

Other mandatory reporters: "Any person."

Privileged communications: Clergy-penitent, attorney-client, physician-patient.

APPENDIX C

EXCERPTS FROM CENTER FOR SEX OFFENDER MANAGEMENT PUBLICATIONS, 2000 AND 2001

The term *sex offender* commonly means an individual convicted of illegal sexual behavior, such as a rapist or child molester. Because clergy sexual misconduct encompasses a range of behaviors, from sexually inappropriate comments to sexual assault, not all clergy who engage in sexual misconduct are sex offenders. However, clergy who engage in criminal behavior of a sexual nature, including serial sexual abuse of minors, clearly fit the definition of a sex offender.

The Center for Sex Offender Management (CSOM), a division of the Office of Justice Programs, U.S. Department of Justice, was created in 1996 to promote public safety through the effective management of sex offenders in the community. CSOM provides technical support on sex offender management to agencies and professionals in corrections, research, treatment, and other disciplines. In addition, CSOM serves as a clearinghouse for information on sex offender management and treatment. Among CSOM publications available on their website (http://www.csom.org) are *Myths and Facts about Sex Offenders* and *Recidivism of Sex Offenders*, which contain the following excerpts.

EXCERPTS FROM MYTHS AND FACTS ABOUT SEX OFFENDERS, 2001

There are many misconceptions about sexual offenses, sexual offense victims, and sex offenders in our society. Much has been learned about these behaviors and populations in the past decade and this information is being used to develop more effective criminal justice interventions throughout the country. This document serves to inform citizens, policy makers, and

251

practitioners about sex offenders and their victims, addressing the facts that underlie common assumptions both true and false in this rapidly evolving field.

Myth: Most sexual assaults are committed by strangers.

Fact: Most sexual assaults are committed by someone known to the victim or the victim's family, regardless of whether the victim is a child or an adult.

Statistics for adult victims indicate that the majority of women who have been raped know their assailant. A 1998 National Violence Against Women Survey revealed that among those women who reported being raped, 76 percent were victimized by a current or former husband, live-in partner, or date. Also, a Bureau of Justice Statistics study found that nearly 9 out of 10 rape or sexual assault victimizations involved a single offender with whom the victim had a prior relationship as a family member, intimate, or acquaintance.

Statistics for minor victims indicate that approximately 60 percent of boys and 80 percent of girls who are sexually victimized are abused by someone known to the child or the child's family. Relatives, friends, baby-sitters, persons in positions of authority over the child, or persons who supervise children are more likely than strangers to commit a sexual assault.

Myth: The majority of sexual offenders are caught, convicted, and in prison.

Fact: Only a fraction of those who commit sexual assault are apprehended and convicted for their crimes. Most convicted sex offenders eventually are released to the community under probation or parole supervision.

Many women who are sexually assaulted by intimates, friends, or acquaintances do not report these crimes to police. Instead, victims are most likely to report being sexually assaulted when the assailant is a stranger, the victim is physically injured during the assault, or a weapon is involved in the commission of the crime.

A 1992 study estimated that only 12 percent of rapes were reported. The National Crime Victimization Surveys conducted in 1994, 1995, and 1998 indicate that only 32 percent of sexual assaults against persons 12 or older were reported to law enforcement. The low rate of reporting leads to the conclusion that the approximate 265,000 convicted sex offenders under the authority of corrections agencies in the United States represent less than 10 percent of all sex offenders living in communities nationwide.

While sex offenders constitute a large and increasing population of prison inmates, most are eventually released to the community. Some 60 percent of those 265,000 convicted sex offenders noted above were supervised in the community, whether directly following sentencing or after a term of incarceration in jail or prison. Short of incarceration, supervision allows the criminal justice system the best means to maintain control over offenders, monitor their residence, and require them to work and participate in treatment. As a result, there is a growing interest in providing community supervision for this population as an effective means of reducing the threat of future victimization.

Myth: Most sex offenders reoffend.

Fact: Reconviction data suggest that this is not the case. Further, reoffense rates vary among different types of sex offenders and are related to specific characteristics of the offender and the offense.

Persons who commit sex offenses are not a homogeneous group, but instead fall into several different categories. As a result, research has identified significant differences in reoffense patterns from one category to another. Looking at reconviction rates alone, one large-scale analysis reported the following differences:

- Child molesters had a 13 percent reconviction rate for sexual offenses and a 37 percent reconviction rate for new, nonsex offenses over a five year period.
- Rapists had a 19 percent reconviction rate for sexual offenses and a 46 percent reconviction rate for new, nonsexual offenses over a five year period.

Another study found reconviction rates for child molesters to be 20 percent and for rapists to be approximately 23 percent.

Individual characteristics of the crimes further distinguish recidivism rates. For instance, victim gender and relation to the offender have been found to impact recidivism rates. In a 1995 study, researchers found that offenders who had extrafamilial female victims had a recidivism rate of 18 percent and those who had extrafamilial male victims recidivated at a rate of 35 percent. This same study found a recidivism rate for incest offenders to be approximately 9 percent.

It is noteworthy that recidivism rates for sex offenders are lower than for the general criminal population. For example, one study of 108,580 nonsex criminals released from prisons in 11 states in 1983 found that nearly 63 percent were rearrested for a nonsexual felony or serious misdemeanor within three years of their release from incarceration; 47 percent were reconvicted; and 41 percent were ultimately returned to prison or jail.

It is important to note that not all sex crimes are solved or result in arrest and only a fraction of sex offenses are reported to police. The reliance on measures of recidivism as reflected through official criminal justice system data (i.e., rearrest or reconviction rates) obviously omits offenses that are not cleared through an arrest (and thereby cannot be attributed to any individual offender) or those that are never reported to the police. For a variety of reasons, many victims of sexual assault are reluctant to invoke the criminal justice process and do not report their victimization to the police.

For these reasons, relying on rearrest and reconviction data underestimates actual reoffense numbers.

Myth: Sexual offense rates are higher than ever and continue to climb.

Fact: Despite the increase in publicity about sexual crimes, the actual rate of reported sexual assault has decreased slightly in recent years.

The rate of reported rape among women decreased by 10 percent from 1990 to 1995 (80 per 100,000 compared to 72 per 100,000). In 1995, 97,460 forcible rapes were reported to the police nationwide, representing the lowest number of reported rapes since 1989.

More recently, when examining slightly different measures, it appears that rates have continued to drop. The arrest rate for all sexual offenses (including forcible rape and excluding prostitution) dropped 16 percent between 1993 and 1998. In 1998, 82,653 arrests were logged for all sexual offenses, compared to 97,955 arrests in 1993.

Myth: All sex offenders are male.

Fact: The vast majority of sex offenders are male. However, females also commit sexual crimes.

In 1994, less than 1 percent of all incarcerated rape and sexual assault offenders were female (fewer than 800 women). By 1997, however, 6,292 females had been arrested for forcible rape or other sex offenses, constituting approximately 8 percent of all rape and sexual assault arrests for that year. Additionally, studies indicate that females commit approximately 20 percent of sex offenses against children. Males commit the majority of sex offenses but females commit some, particularly against children.

Myth: Sex offenders commit sexual crimes because they are under the influence of alcohol.

Fact: It is unlikely that an individual who otherwise would not commit a sexual assault would do so as a direct result of excessive drinking.

Annual crime victim reports indicate that approximately 30 percent of all reported rapes and sexual assaults involve alcohol use by the offender. Alcohol use, therefore, may increase the likelihood that someone already predisposed to commit a sexual assault will act upon those impulses. However, excessive alcohol use is not a primary precipitant to sexual assaults.

Myth: Children who are sexually assaulted will sexually assault others when they grow up.

Fact: Most sex offenders were not sexually assaulted as children and most children who are sexually assaulted do not sexually assault others.

Early childhood sexual victimization does not automatically lead to sexually aggressive behavior. While sex offenders have higher rates of sexual abuse in their histories than expected in the general population, the majority were not abused. Among adult sex offenders, approximately 30 percent have been sexually abused. Some types of offenders, such as those who sexually offend against young boys, have still higher rates of child sexual abuse in their histories. While past sexual victimization can increase the likelihood of sexually aggressive behavior, most children who were sexually victimized never perpetrate against others.

Myth: Youths do not commit sex offenses.

Fact: Adolescents are responsible for a significant number of rape and child molestation cases each year.

Sexual assaults committed by youths are a growing concern in this country. Currently, it is estimated that adolescents (ages 13 to 17) account for up to one-fifth of all rapes and one-half of all cases of child molestation committed each year. In 1995, youths were involved in 15 percent of all forcible rapes cleared by arrest—approximately 18 adolescents per 100,000 were arrested for forcible rape. In the same year, approximately 16,100 adolescents were arrested for sexual offenses, excluding rape and prostitution.

The majority of these incidents of sexual abuse involve adolescent male perpetrators. However, prepubescent youths also engage in sexually abusive behaviors.

Myth: Juvenile sex offenders typically are victims of child sexual abuse and grow up to be adult sex offenders.

Fact: Multiple factors, not just sexual victimization as a child, are associated with the development of sexually offending behavior in youths.

Recent studies show that rates of physical and sexual abuse vary widely for adolescent sex offenders; 20–50 percent of these youths experienced physical abuse and approximately 40–80 percent experienced sexual abuse. While many adolescents who commit sexual offenses have histories of being abused, the majority of these youths do not become adult sex offenders. Research suggests that the age of onset and number of incidents of abuse, the period of time elapsing between the abuse and its first report, perceptions of how the family responded to the disclosure of abuse, and exposure to domestic violence all are relevant to why some sexually abused youths go on to sexually perpetrate while others do not.

Myth: Treatment for sex offenders is ineffective.

Fact: Treatment programs can contribute to community safety because those who attend and cooperate with program conditions are less likely to re-offend than those who reject intervention.

The majority of sex offender treatment programs in the United States and Canada now use a combination of cognitive-behavioral treatment and relapse prevention (designed to help sex offenders maintain behavioral changes by anticipating and coping with the problem of relapse). Offense specific treatment modalities generally involve group and/or individual therapy focused on victimization awareness and empathy training, cognitive restructuring, learning about the sexual abuse cycle, relapse prevention planning, anger management and assertiveness training, social and inter-personal skills development, and changing deviant sexual arousal patterns.

Different types of offenders typically respond to different treatment methods with varying rates of success. Treatment effectiveness is often related to multiple factors, including:

- The type of sexual offender (e.g., incest offender or rapist)
- The treatment model being used (e.g., cognitive-behavioral, relapse prevention, psycho-educational, psycho-dynamic, or pharmacological)
- The treatment modalities being used
- Related interventions involved in probation and parole community supervision

Several studies present optimistic conclusions about the effectiveness of treatment programs that are empirically based, offense-specific, and comprehensive. The only meta-analysis of treatment outcome studies to date has found a small, yet significant treatment effect—an 8 percent reduction in the recidivism rate for offenders who participated in treatment. Research also demonstrates that sex offenders who fail to complete treatment programs are at increased risk for both sexual and general recidivism.

Myth: The cost of treating and managing sex offenders in the community is too high—they belong behind bars.

Fact: One year of intensive supervision and treatment in the community can range in cost between $5,000 and $15,000 per offender, depending on treatment modality. The average cost for incarcerating an offender is significantly higher, approximately $22,000 per year, excluding treatment costs.

As noted previously, effective sex offender specific treatment interventions can reduce sexual offense recidivism by 8 percent. Given the tremendous impact of these offenses on their victims, any reduction in the reoffense rates of sex offenders is significant.

Without the option of community supervision and treatment, the vast majority of incarcerated sex offenders would otherwise serve their maximum sentences and return to the community without the internal (treatment) and external (supervision) controls to effectively manage their sexually abusive behavior. Managing those offenders who are amenable to treatment and can be supervised intensively in the community following an appropriate term of incarceration can serve to prevent future victimization while saving taxpayers substantial imprisonment costs.

Source: Center for Sex Offender Management (CSOM), *Myths and Facts about Sex Offenders*, August 2000, Office of Justice Programs, U.S. Department of Justice.

Appendix C

EXCERPTS FROM
RECIDIVISM OF SEX OFFENDERS, 2000

The following sections present findings from various studies of the recidivism of sex offenders within offense categories of rapists and child molesters. The studies included in this paper do not represent a comprehensive overview of the research on sex offender recidivism. The studies included represent a sampling of available research on these populations and are drawn to highlight key points. Overall recidivism findings are presented, along with results concerning the factors and characteristics associated with recidivism.

RAPISTS

There has been considerable research on the recidivism of rapists across various institutional and community-based settings and with varying periods of follow-up. A follow-up study of sex offenders released from a maximum-security psychiatric institution in California found that 10 of the 57 rapists (19 percent) studied were reconvicted of a rape within five years, most of which occurred during the first year of the follow-up period. These same authors reported that among 68 sex offenders not found to be mentally disordered who were paroled in 1973, 19 (28 percent) were reconvicted for a sex offense within five years.

In a study of 231 sex offenders placed on probation in Philadelphia between 1966 and 1969, 11 percent were rearrested for a sex offense and 57 percent were rearrested for any offense. In a more recent study of 54 rapists who were released from prison before 1983, after four years 28 percent had a reconviction for a sex offense, and 43 percent had a conviction for a violent offense.

The significant variation in recidivism across studies of rapists is likely due to differences in the types of offenders involved (e.g., institutionalized offenders, mentally disordered offenders, or probationers) or in the length of the follow-up period. Throughout these studies, the proportion of offenders who had a prior sex offense was similar to the proportion that had a subsequent sex offense. In addition, the rates of reoffending decreased with the seriousness of the offense. That is, the occurrence of officially recorded recidivism for a nonviolent nonsexual offense was the most likely and the incidence of violent sex offenses was the least likely.

CHILD MOLESTERS

Studies of the recidivism of child molesters reveal specific patterns of reoffending across victim types and offender characteristics. A study involving mentally disordered sex offenders compared same-sex and opposite-sex child molesters and incest offenders. Results of this five-year follow-up study found that same-sex child molesters had the highest rate of previous sex offenses (53 percent), as well as the highest reconviction rate for sex crimes (30 percent). In comparison, 43 percent of opposite-sex child molesters had prior sex offenses and a reconviction rate for sex crimes of 25 percent, and incest offenders had prior convictions at a rate of 11 percent and a reconviction rate of 6 percent. Interestingly, the recidivism rate for same-sex child molesters for other crimes against persons was also quite high, with 26 percent having reconvictions for these offenses. Similarly, a number of other studies have found that child molesters have relatively high rates of nonsexual offenses.

Several studies have involved follow-up of extra-familial child molesters. One such study included both official and unofficial measures of recidivism (reconviction, new charge, or unofficial record). Using both types of measures, researchers found that 43 percent of these offenders (convicted of sex offenses involving victims under the age of 16 years) sexually reoffended within a four-year follow-up period. Those who had a subsequent sex offense differed from those who did not by their use of force in the offense, the number of previous sexual assault victims, and their score on a sexual index that included a phallometric assessment (also referred to as plethysmography: a device used to measure sexual arousal, or erectile response, to both appropriate and deviant sexual stimulus material). In contrast to other studies of child molesters, this study found no difference in recidivism between opposite-sex and same-sex offenders.

In a more recent study, extrafamilial child molesters were followed for an average of six years. During that time, 31 percent had a reconviction for a second sexual offense. Those who committed subsequent sex offenses were more likely to have been married, have a personality disorder, and have a more serious sex offense history than those who did not recidivate sexually. In addition, recidivists were more likely to have deviant phallometrically measured sexual preferences.

In a study utilizing a 24-year follow-up period, victim differences (e.g., gender of the victim) were not found to be associated with the recidivism (defined as those charged with a subsequent sexual offense) of child molesters. This study of 111 extrafamilial child molesters found that the number of prior sex offenses and sexual preoccupation with children were related to sex offense recidivism. However, the authors of this study noted that the finding of no victim differences may have been due to the fact that the offenders in this study had an average of three prior sex offenses before their prison release. Thus, this sample may have had a higher base rate of reoffense than child molesters from the general prison population.

Characteristics of recidivists include:

• multiple victims
• diverse victims

Appendix C

- stranger victims
- juvenile sexual offenses
- multiple paraphilias
- history of abuse and neglect
- long-term separations from parents
- negative relationships with their mothers
- diagnosed antisocial personality disorder
- unemployment
- substance abuse problems
- chaotic, antisocial lifestyles

Researchers concluded that sex offenders are at most risk of reoffending when they become sexually preoccupied, have access to victims, fail to acknowledge their recidivism risk, and show sharp mood increases, particularly anger.

Source: Center for Sex Offender Management (CSOM), *Recidivism of Sex Offenders*, May 2001, Office of Justice Programs, U.S. Department of Justice.

APPENDIX D

STATISTICS ON SEX OFFENDERS

In November 2003, the Bureau of Justice Statistics published the report *Recidivism of Sex Offenders Released from Prison in 1994.* The report presented findings on some 9,691 males convicted of rape, statutory rape, child molestation, or sexual assault who were released from 15 state prisons in the United States in 1994 and tracked until 1997. The tables presented are from the report, which is available online at http://www.ojp.usdoj.gov/bjs/pub/pdf/rsorp94.pdf.

PERCENT OF U.S. SEX OFFENDERS RELEASED IN 1994 AND ARRESTED AND CONVICTED FOR A NEW SEX CRIME WITHIN THREE YEARS

Sex Offenders	All	Rapists	Statutory Rapists	Child Molesters	Sexual Assaulters
Percent arrested for a new sex crime in three years	5.3%	5.0%	5.0%	5.1%	5.5%
Percent convicted of a new sex crime in three years	3.5%	3.2%	3.6%	3.5%	3.7%
Total released out of 272,111 from 15 states in study	9,691	3,115	443	4,295	6,576

Source: Lanagan, Patrick A., et al. *Recidivism of Sex Offenders Released from Prison in 1994.* Report, Bureau of Justice Statistics, Office of Justice Programs, U.S. Department of Justice, November 2003, p. 24.

CHARACTERISTICS OF VICTIMS OF RAPE OR SEXUAL ASSAULT, 1997

Victim Characteristic	Percent of Victims of Rape or Sexual Assault		
	All	Victim Age	
		18 Years or Older	Under 18 Years
Total	100%	100%	100%
Gender			
Male	8.8%	2.8%	11.1%
Female	91.2	97.2	88.9
Race			
White	73.2%	66.0%	76.4%
Black	22.8	30.2	19.4
Other	4.0	3.8	4.2
Hispanic origin			
Hispanic	11.3%	9.9%	12.1%
Non-Hispanic	88.7	90.1	87.9
Age			
12 or under	36.4%	. . .	51.6%
13–17	34.1	. . .	48.4
18–24	10.8	36.7%	. . .
25–34	11.2	37.9	. . .
35–34	7.0	23.8	. . .
55 or over	0.5	1.6	. . .
Victim was the prisoner's			
Spouse	1.1%	3.8%	0%
Ex-spouse	0.6	2.0	0
Parent/step-parent	0.6	0.4	0.6
Own child	11.5	1.4	15.7
Stepchild	11.2	0.4	15.8
Sibling/stepsibling	1.3	0.4	1.7
Other relative	9.4	2.1	12.7
Boy/girlfriend	5.5	8.2	4.4
Ex-boy/girlfriend	1.1	2.0	0.8
Friend/ex-friend	22.7	24.8	22.0
Acquaintance/other	19.4	20.1	19.6
Stranger	15.6	34.4	6.7
Total estimated number	73,116	20,958	50,027

Note: Data are from the BJS Survey of Inmates in State Correctional Facilities, 1997. This table is based on 73,116 prisoners who reported having one victim in the crime for which they were sentenced to prison. (They accounted for approximately 84 percent of an incarcerated male sex offenders in 1997). Data identifying victim's sex were reported for 99.8 percent of the 73,116 males incarcerated for sex crimes; victim's race was reported for 98.9 percent; Hispanic origin for 98.2 percent; victim's age for 97.1 percent; victim's relationship to prisoner for 98.3 percent. Detail may not sum to total due to missing data for age of victim.

Source: Lanagan, Patrick A., et al. *Recidivism of Sex Offenders Released from Prison in 1994.* Report, Bureau of Justice Statistics, Office of Justice Programs, U.S. Department of Justice, November 2003, p. 36.

INDEX

Locators in **boldface** indicate main topics. Locators followed by *c* indicate chronology entries. Locators followed by *b* indicate biographical entries. Locators followed by *g* indicate glossary entries.

A

AAPC. *See* American Association of Pastoral Counselors
abbot 141*g*
abet 141*g*
Abraham 7
abstinence 141*g*
abuse 141*g*
accomplice 141*g*
accountability 141*g*
acquittal 141*g*
Adam 7, 9, 106*c*
Adeodatus I (pope) 8
adult 141*g*
adultery 7
Advocate Web 213
AEPPP (Associates in Education & Prevention in Pastoral Practice, Inc.) 218
affiant 141*g*
affidavit 141*g*
Agapitus (pope) 8, 10
Aids National Interfaith Network 220

Alabama
    mandatory reporting laws 239
    statute of limitations 226
Alaska
    mandatory reporting laws 239–240
    statute of limitations 226
Alexander VI (pope) 13
allegation 141*g*
allegations of clergy sexual abuse
    from 1950 to 2002 4–5
    Charter for the Protection of Children and Young People on 83–84
    Code of Ethics for Rabbis on 94–95
    Episcopal Church *Guidelines* on 88–89

Essential Norms on 85–86
    Five Principles and 81
    Greek Orthodox Archdiocese *Statement of Policy* on 92–93
    Presbyterian Church *Sexual Misconduct Policy* on 98–100
    Roman Catholic *Canon Law* on 79
    vindications from 26–28
American Association of Pastoral Counselors (AAPC) 217–218
American Professional Society on the Abuse of Children (APSAC) 218
Anastasius I (pope) 8
Anastasius II (pope) 8

262

Index

265

Index

267

Index

Index

Index